Dimensions of faith

YESTERDAY AND TODAY

James A. Mohler, S.J.

LOYOLA UNIVERSITY PRESS
Chicago   60657

Library of Congress Catalog Card Number: 69-13120
SBN 8294-0100-8

Preface

The Church today seems to be facing a crisis of faith. On the
one side are the De-Hellenizers and the De-Romanizers, who
would tend to diminish the importance of some of the long-standing Greek and Roman traditions of the Church. On the other, are
the Traditionalists, adamantly refusing to adapt to the changing
times. Then there are the exaggerated personalists who minimize
the importance of institutionalism, and, finally, the radical theologians who, asserting man's coming of age, deny that he has any
need of faith in a transcendent God. Most of these, except the
Traditionalists, are placing the emphasis on man, the here and
now, the personal, the importance of adaptation and change. In
all of these the problem of faith is of the essence, whether it is
personal faith, opposed to ecclesial, existential vs. Hellenistic,
or even the denial of any need for faith at all.

It is our purpose here to go back and study some of the major
dimensions of faith from the Old Testament to modern personal
faith. We hope to show that through the ages have run certain
common faith themes, illustrating man's relationship with God.
For example, the modern "I-Thou" rapport has firm roots in
early Hebrew and Christian faith. Moreover, the history of faith
is a history of man's reliance on God and lack of confidence in
himself. In the first chapters we will examine some major dimensions of faith from the Bible to Vatican I; then, we will study
personal faith which has made such an impact on the world today.

Abbreviations

BGPTM	Beiträge zur Geschicte der Philosophie und Theologie des Mittelalters
BT	Bible Today
CC	Cross Currents
CW	Catholic World
D	Martin Luther, Selections From His Writings, J. Dillenberger, ed., Garden City, Doubleday & Company, 1961
DB	Dictionary of the Bible, J. McKenzie, Milwaukee, Bruce Publishing Company, 1965
DS	Enchiridion Symbolorum, Denzinger Schönmetzer, Barcelona, Herder, 1963
DSp	Dictionnaire de spiritualité
DTC	Dictionnaire de théologie catholique
DTF	Divus Thomas, Freiburg
ER	Études et Recherches
Greg	Gregorianum
HJ	Hethrop Journal
IPQ	International Philosophical Quarterly
JBL	Journal of Biblical Literature
JTS	Journal of Theological Studies
LCC	Library of Christian Classics
LTK	Lexikon für Theologie und Kirche
LXX	Septuagint
NRT	Nouvelle revue théologique
NTRG	New Testament Reading Guide

NTS	New Testament Studies
P	Luther's Works, J. Pelikan and H. Lehmann, eds., Philadelphia, Muhlenberg & Fortress
PL, PG	Migne, Patrologia Latina & Graeca
RHE	Revue d'histoire ecclésiastique
TCT	The Church Teaches, J. Clarkson, et al, eds., St. Louis, B. Herder, 1962
TD	Theology Digest
TS	Theological Studies

Thomas Aquinas

3S	Commentary on the Third Book of the Sentences
DV	De Veritate
SCG	Summa Contra Gentiles
CT	Compendium Theologiae
In Hebr, In Jn, etc.	Commentaries on Scripture
De Vir	De Virtutibus
Qdl	Quaestiones Quodlibetales
In Boeth. De Trin	Commentary on Boethius' De Trinitate
ST	Summa Theologiae

ACKNOWLEDGMENTS

The Bruce Publishing Company for permission to reprint Chapters One and Two from Speaking of God, edited by D. Dirscherl. Copyright © 1967 by Bruce Publishing Company.

T. & T. Clark, Edinburgh, for permission to reprint excerpts from Church Dogmatics by Karl Barth.

Cross Currents for permission to reprint excerpts from "Pauline and Johannine Theology: a Contrast" by P. Benoit.

Doubleday & Company, Inc., for permission to reprint excerpts from Martin Luther, Selections from His Writings, edited by J. Dillenberger. Copyright © 1961 by John Dillenberger. Reprinted by permission of Doubleday & Company, Inc.

Farrar, Straus & Giroux, Inc., for permission to reprint excerpts from Creative Fidelity by G. Marcel.

Harper & Row, Inc., for permission to reprint excerpts from Act and Being, Christ the Center, Communion of Saints, and Life Together by D. Bonhoeffer; Being and Having by G. Marcel; Christian Faith by F. Schleiermacher; Kerygma and Myth by R. Bultmann; and Works of Love by S. Kierkegaard.

Herder and Herder, Inc., for permission to reprint excerpts from New Testament Introduction by A. Wikenhauser. Copyright 1963; Personal Faith by C. Cirne-Lima. Copyright 1965.

John Knox Press for permission to reprint excerpts from Anselm: Fides Quaerens Intellectum by Karl Barth.

The Macmillan Company for permission to reprint excerpts from the Cost of Discipleship by D. Bonhoeffer; and Essays, Philosophical and Theological by R. Bultmann.

Cover photograph
Santa Monica State Beach,
California
by Algimantas Kezys, S.J.

Table of Contents

Augustine's Religious Experience; Faith and Reason; Thinking with Assent; Affective Faith; Light of Faith; Eschatology of Faith; Confessions: Story of Faith; The Law of Works and the Law of Faith; Summary of Augustine's Theology of Faith; Augustine's Influence in the Middle Ages

xiii

xv

DIMENSIONS OF FAITH

CHAPTER I

Israel and Yahweh

FAITH IN THE OLD TESTAMENT

Although a type of faith in the gods can be found in most early nations, it is not until the Old Testament that we find faith as a special relationship of one people, the Israelites, with their one God, Yahweh. The great men of Israel's history personify her faith relationship with Yahweh (Hebr 11:17-39): for example, Abraham, Isaac, Jacob, Joseph, Moses, David, Elijah, Hosea, Isaiah, Jeremiah, Josiah, Ezekiel, Nehemiah, Esdras, Judas Maccabeus; and the great realities or key events in the Old Testament are all essentially faith relationships between the one true God and his chosen people: the election, the promise, covenant, kingdom, exile, and return. It is God's choosing of Israel, and Israel's reliance on him and sometimes a lack of this reliance that dominate Old Testament history.

Abraham and the Promise

Abraham had a special relationship with the one true God. His mystical experiences, his faith in the promise, and his reliance on God

1

in spite of his severe test, mark him as the father of all believers. Abraham relied fully on Yahweh because he was true to his promises. As Paul was to point out, Abraham was justified by his great faith and not by the Law. And it is by this great faith that the fatherhood of Abraham extends even to the Gentiles (Gal 3:6-9).

Moses and the Covenant

It is in the divinely inspired Exodus and in the covenant that we see a special faith relationship between Yahweh and Israel. Yahweh revealed himself to Moses as the one who would save the Israelites, leading them out of Egypt and into the land of promise. He made a covenant with his people, gave them his Law, and dwelt among them in a special manner. Revealing himself to Moses on Mt. Sinai, Yahweh chose Israel as his own people (Ex 19:5).

It is in the covenant that we find an explicitly stated faith agree-ment between Israel and Yahweh. God promised his merciful protec-tion, his hesed to Israel. But Israel had to have faith in him, rely on him, and believe that he would manifest his loving kindness. The covenant was a common agreement in the bedouin world of the time and often was sealed in blood.

But the covenant was not just a mutual agreement between the two parties, Yahweh and Israel. No, it was a freely given gift from God to his chosen people. Yahweh was under no duress or obligation to extend his largess to them. Rather he took the initiative as one who makes out his will freely and generously. The covenant, nevertheless, had a certain mutuality. Yahweh will give his hesed, but Israel must humbly obey and believe (Deut 26:17-19). The Ten Commandments are a charter of this covenant and are to be obeyed as part of the contract (Deut 4:13). Moses sealed the covenant with the blood of oxen (Ex 24:1-8); the Israelites felt a new vigor with Yahweh as their strength under the covenant. He was their true God and his power was much greater than that of the gods of surrounding nations. Yahweh would protect his people and lead them into the promised land.

The Kingdom

With the establishment of the kingdom we find the faith-cove-nant with Yahweh taking on a concrete visible form (2 Sam 7:16, 23:5). The king seemed to personify the faith of his people in Yahweh. In a sense the king represented the corporate personal-ity of his people. When the king was unfaithful, the whole nation was punished. When the king was loyal to Yahweh, all the people were blessed.

The king was the messiah, the anointed one, and so he had a special relationship with Yahweh. This can be seen illustrated in God's promise to David (Ps 88 (89):19-37). The kingdom reached perfect form under David, the first of the great kings of Israel, when the Israelites, wanderers no longer, were united under their king. This is in a special way the Lord's kingdom, this is the basis of the hope of the future that a descendant of David will establish an eternal reign of justice and mercy (Amos 9:11; Hosea 3:5; Jeremiah 30:9; Ezekiel 34:23-24).

Prophets

The great prophets arose in the kingdom of Israel as special emissaries between God and his people. Some prophets were advisers to the kings and sought to reform them when they were unfaithful to the covenant. Elijah, Amos, Hosea, Isaiah, Jeremiah, Ezekiel were inspired by God to prepare the way for the future messianic kingdom.

Isaiah in the 8th century B.C. was perhaps the greatest of the prophets. It is in Isaiah that we find the best example of Hebrew theology of faith. The Israelites had lived the great faith experiences of the promise, the covenant, the conquest, and the kingdom. But they had forgotten the mutual nature of the promise and the covenant. God's loving hesed was contingent on Israel's faithfulness. Pagan neighbors began to influence Israel (1K 12:28-33); materialism and luxury abounded (Amos 8:4-6, 6:4-6); because Israel had played the harlot, the unfaithful bride of Yahweh (Hosea 1 & 2), she soon felt the punishments of her unfaithfulness. Yahweh withdrew his protection and Assyria reasserted her claims on Syria and Palestine. Tiglathpileser (475-727), Shalmaneser (727-722), and Sargon II (722-705) destroyed Israel, and Sinnacherib (705-681) invaded Judah (701-688). King Ahaz (736-716) pledged Judah as a vassal of Assyria, with consequent religious and economic decline (2K 16:1-20). Under Hezekiah (716-687) religious reform was inaugurated (2K 18:1-8). Moreover, he joined up with Egypt against Assyria.

This is the turmoil into which Isaiah came to proclaim his message (742-687). From an aristocratic family, well educated and possessing great literary skills, Isaiah was a counselor at the royal court. As many of the prophets, Isaiah too had an ardent group of followers. A highly spiritual man with a great faith and humility,

3

he received his mission to preach to the wayward about the year 742 (Is 6:1-13).

Isaiah roundly condemned the false worship of the people of Judah (1:9-31). He spoke against the ruling classes (1:21-31; 2:6-22; 5: 1-7). In the midst of Ahaz' alliance with Assyria, we have Isaiah's Immanuel prophecy (7:10-17). Only through faith and reliance on Yahweh will Judah be saved (7:9); do not rely upon human plans and alliances, but only upon God (8:10-12), for God alone has the power to punish the Assyrians (10:12). Rely upon Yahweh and not upon material things nor upon human aid. This complete reliance on Yahweh seems to typify the faith of Isaiah and the faith of the Hebrew people, in general.

In Jeremiah we find the faith relationship with Yahweh taking on a more individual nature. Yahweh is not only the God of the group, but also of the individual (Jer 11:18-12:6; 15:10-21). Although the covenant is still between Yahweh and the whole nation, nevertheless, Jeremiah places a new emphasis on the inner rapport between the individual person and God.

THEMES IN OLD TESTAMENT FAITH

Yahweh[1]

Unique among the Gods, Yahweh revealed himself as one having little in common with the gods of the Canaanites and the Egyptians. First, he is the one God, distinguishing him from the many gods of the neighboring peoples. The true God, the God of the Amen, he is faithful to his promises, not at all like the false gods of the Canaanites. Yahweh is faithful to his covenant (Deut 7:9); his word is reliable (Ps 111 (110):7); his love is constant and unswerving (Gen 32:11; 24:27; Ex 34:6-7). Yahweh's fidelity is, in a sense, his most important attribute, for it is the very basis of Israel's faith in him.

Yahweh is a moral God. There is no immorality in his life as was sometimes found in the lives of pagan deities. Nor did he demand immoral sacrifices such as the offering of the first born child to Marduk. Yahweh taught his people his code of morality on which they were to model their lives and which was to be a visible measure of their faithfulness to him (Ex 20-24).

Yahweh revealed himself to his people, and the whole Old Testament is the history of this revelation. Taking the initiative, he enters into history to save his chosen ones (Ex 3:6; 13:4). Yahweh is not to be represented by graven images (Deut 4:15-

4

19) such as the bulls of the Canaanites. In fact, his Holy Name was not even to be uttered, especially in later times. Substitutes for his name were "The Face of Yahweh" (Ex 20:24), "The Glory of Yahweh" (1K 8:11), "The Name of Yahweh" (Ex 20:24). Yet often in the Old Testament we find Yahweh described in an anthropomorphic manner, perhaps to make him seem more realistic to his people. Thus Yahweh is angry (1K 11:9), jealous (Deut 6:15); he hates (Prov 6:16), he walks in the garden (Gen 3:8), and he eats with Abraham (Gen 18:1-8).

Yahweh is a spiritual God (Wis 1:7; 12:1). He is transcendent and his greatness emphasizes man's weakness by comparison so that man is fearful in his presence (Gen 18:27; Ex 3:6; Is 6:4-5; Job 42:2-3). He is a mysterious and powerful God, majestic and frightening. Man, by contrast, feels his own nothingness, experiences a reverential awe (Is 6).

Israelites

Of all the peoples on the face of the earth, Yahweh chose the Israelites. He took the initiative, extending his graciousness to them (Ex 19:5). Why did Yahweh pick the Israelites? Because he loved them. Albert Gelin[2] develops the theme that the Hebrews were attractive to Yahweh because they needed him (Zeph 3:19-20). Constantly subjected to more powerful neighbors, they were the poor, the needy, the anawim, the most destitute of peoples. We find biblical poverty exemplified in many of the Old Testament leaders: Moses, Samuel, Jeremiah, Anna, Judith, the Psalmist. But are the poor necessarily faithful to Yahweh by the very fact that they are needy? No, it is only when they see in their poverty, misery, and suffering an external sign of their complete dependence on God that it becomes truly poverty of spirit and opens the way to humility, obedience and faith.

In a sense, the anawim of the Old Testament, and of the New Testament too, epitomize man's reliance on God. The anaw is the little man, humble and poor. His suffering can bring him closer to God for he relies less and less upon himself and upon material things and comes to rely more upon God. The anawim were a religious class made up of these little ones, the poor, the pious, the humble. Their lot was diametrically opposed to the rich, the sinful, and the proud (Sir 13:19-25). The poor are rejected, yet the evil seem to have good fortune (Jer 12: 1-3; Ps 72:4-5; 12-13; 18-19). Throwing themselves on the mercy of God, they clung to him and sought conversation with

5

him (Ps 72:28). In the Psalms we find Yahweh promising help to his people, who relied on him for his promised aid (Ps 33, 36, 24, 9). This is the story of Old Testament faith.

The Israelites, besides their deep sense of need and reliance on God, had a keen realization of their own corporate personality.[3] As most primitive peoples, they had a fierce tribal loyalty; the individual was to the group what a member was to the living body (Judges 11:2; 2Sam 5:1; 19:13). What one of the tribe did, the whole group was responsible for. If one of the tribe was injured, all felt the need of vengeance. According to this principle, the great faith figures of the Old Testament--Abraham, Isaac, Jacob, Joseph, Moses, and David--represented the faith relationship of their whole people with Yahweh. Later we find in Paul his teachings on the sin of Adam and the grace of Christ bearing heavily on the Hebrew tradition of corporate personality (Rom 5:12-21). Abraham is the father of all believers (Gal 3:6-9), so that all who believe are his sons and belong to his corporate personality even though not related by blood.

In later Old Testament times, the tribal and national unity of the Israelites was broken and the faith relationship with Yahweh became more of a personal matter, as we have seen. However, there always remained, even in New Testament times, a strong feeling of oneness with the early Hebrews.

Israel's Faith in Yahweh

In order to understand the psychology, and the theology too, of Israelite faith, we should examine for a moment basic Hebrew epistemology. Far from the Greek theories of knowledge which separated man into faculties of will and intellect, practical and speculative, the Hebrew mode of knowledge involved the whole man. It was an experiential contract between the complete person and the thing to be known or believed, a personal contact with reality. Hebrew knowledge, and faith also, for faith is a kind of knowledge, concerned the whole man and not just his intellect and will. Moreover, Hebrew knowledge was orientated to action. The true and faithful Hebrew acted according to his conviction. His faith was seen in action.

Hebrew knowledge included knowing, as we would use the term today, but also loving and embracing. For example, yada (he knew) designated the marital act: he knew his wife and she bore him a son. He knew her, loved her, embraced her, gave himself to her. This was truly a personal knowledge, not merely conceptual.

6

Yahweh often complained that his people did not know him. They certainly knew that he existed, they knew certain facts about him: his theophanies, his promise, his covenant, his salutary help, his commandments, his punishments. But they did not really know and love him personally, yada. They did not acknowledge him, accept him, love and obey him. In a word, they were not his friends.

Yada is the personal knowledge of friendship, yadid. Friends should be distinguished from mere acquaintances, for friendship includes love, concern, commitment. To know and love God as a personal friend is the chief duty of man (Deut 4:39; 29:2-6; Is 43:10; Hos 6:6; Ps 46:10). Yada is described as an experiential knowledge such as in intercourse (Ex 1:8; Deut 9:2; 24; 1 Sam 10:11). It can express either a good or a bad experience (Is 42: 25; Jer 16:21; 44:28). In the LXX yada is translated by ginōskein, or eidenai, and in the passive participle by gnōstos, meaning a friend or confidant (Ps 31:11; 55:13; 88:8; 18). Yada is perception accompanied by emotion, by movement of the will. It recognizes the acts of God, that Yahweh is God (Deut 4:39; 8:5; 29:5; Is 53: 10). It is, moreover, a moral choice, including obedience. Thus not knowing God implies disobedience and immorality.[4]

"Amen," the Hebrew concept of faith, is parallel to that of personal knowledge. It is an experiential contact between the whole person, or the whole corporate personality, and Yahweh, the true God. Thus Hebrew faith is the total dependence of the whole man on Yahweh. Including fear, trust, strength, it recognizes that God is God, man is man, and man is totally dependent upon God. It is the exact opposite of complete self-reliance or self-deification on the part of man.

Derivatives of mn, although less frequent than other words signifying trust or faith in the Old Testament, bring out the special quality of Hebrew faith. The qal participial form can express the reliance of a child upon its mother (Prov 8:30). In the niphal or passive form it means to be trustworthy, firm, reliable. Something or someone is that which it or he is supposed to be. Thus a tent peg holds firmly in the desert winds (Is 22:23). A man's words are reliable and true (Gen 42:20).

The niphal form of mn can be used either of God or of man. Thus God is faithful and true to his covenant (Deut 7:9). His word is a sure promise (1K 8:26), which stands firm forever (Ps 111: 7). Emuna with hesed means that God is constantly expressing his love (Gen 32:11; 24:23; Ex 34:6-7). When the niphal is used of man it implies an interior obedience, a complete reliance and

7

dependence on Yahweh (Ps 78:8; 1Sam 2:35). The prophet is true
when he speaks the truth and his words lead to action (1K 27:16; 17:24;
1Sam 3:19).

The hiphil or causative form says "Amen" to an idea and all of its
consequences. It recognizes one as a loyal vassal, a friend or a ser-
vant (1 Sam 27:12; Mic 7:5; Job 4:18). A personal reciprocal relationship which is binding on both parties is established and recognized.
By his belief a man professes that his friends or servants are true
and can be depended upon. We see this in Israel's relationship with
Yahweh. She relies upon him because he is true to his promise, he
is a true friend.

So when the Israelite believes in God, a personal relationship, a
loyal friendship with God is established (Gen 12:1-3; 15:6). Yahweh
took the initiative, entering into history to help his people; Israel,
believing in God, relives these redemptive experiences (Ex 4:31).
Both God and man are true to their part of the faith-relationship. Man
is obedient (Deut 9:23; Ps 119:66), he is trustful of God's promises
and power (Gen 15:6; Ps 106:12; Num 20:12), he accepts God as God
and lives according to the full relationship binding him to God (Ex 14:
31; Num 14:11; Deut 1:32). He knows God (Is 43:10), loves (Hos 4:1),
and fears him (Ex 14:31).

Yahweh gave to his people certain visible signs by which they could
show their faith covenant with him. He gave them the rite of circumcision (Gen 17:1-27), the Law (Ex 20-24), the Sabbath (Ex 31:12-17),
and special feasts such as the Passover as a reminder of his faithfulness
to his promises (Ex 12:1-28).

Although faith was the key relationship between Israel and Yahweh,
many times throughout their history the Israelites were scolded by their
prophets and chastised by Yahweh for their unfaithfulness, for falling
into sinful habits and idolatry, for self-deification, for relying on themselves rather than on Yahweh, for breaking their personal friendship
with him. Yet in spite of their faults, he still loved them (Josh 24:2 &
14; Judges 10:6; Is 17:8; 40:19-20; 44:9-20; Jer 2:27; 10:1-16; 16:20;
Hos 1 & 2).

CONCLUSION

Throughout the Old Testament emuna is used of both God and man.
Yahweh is the true God. He is faithful to his promises and, therefore,
worthy of belief; he is truly God. On the human side emuna declares
that man is truly man, intrinsically dependent on Yahweh, necessarily
reliant upon him. Deification of self or of human or material means,
therefore, is not compatible with faith in Yahweh.

8

Old Testament faith is directed primarily to the personal God, Yahweh. Yet it also includes intellectual elements, namely, who Yahweh is, what marvelous deeds he has done and will continue to do for his people. The nation Israel with all her children comes to know and believe in Yahweh, and her personal knowledge of friendship increases as her relationship with him grows with the passage of time. Yahweh begins this faith relationship and helps it increase with the years. The Israelites, in turn, have faith in their Yahweh because he is true and faithful. Moreover, this divine faithfulness will also serve as the unshakable basis of belief in Jesus Christ in the New Testament.[5]

Notes

1 See A. Gelin, Key Concepts of the Old Testament (Glenrock: Paulist Press, 1963), pp. 22 ff.

2 The Poor of Yahweh (Collegeville: Liturgical Press, 1964).

3 See J. DeFraine, Adam and the Family of Man (Staten Island: Alba House, 1965).

4 See R. Bultmann, "Gnosis" in Bible Key Words, from Kittel's Worterbuch (New York: Harper & Row Publishers, 1958), pp. 15-18.

5 For Martin Buber's comparison of Hebrew faith with Christian faith see Chapter VII, section 3.

CHAPTER II

Faith in Jesus Christ

FAITH IN THE NEW TESTAMENT

The New Testament writers followed the LXX in their use of pistis in place of the Hebrew emuna. In classical Greek pisteuein can mean to trust, to show confidence, to accept as true. Pistis means assurance, confidence, belief, trust, guarantee, reliance. In general, New Testament pistis parallels Old Testament emuna with some differences which we will bring out as we go along.

As one might expect, many Hebrew faith themes are carried over into the New Testament theology of faith. For example, in the gospels it is the whole man who believes. Thus faith is a personal relationship between the whole person and the person of Jesus Christ. New Testament faith is a reliance on Christ, opposed to self-sufficient reliance on the world.

1 FAITH IN THE NEW TESTAMENT, IN GENERAL

We see the spirit of the Old Testament anawim in Jesus' sermon on the beatitudes, in his deep concern for the anawim of his time, and in his own death on the cross by which he identified himself with the most rejected. The anawim need his help and manifest a great faith in his wonderful powers.

We find a sense of corporate personality in the New Testament, especially in Paul's theology of original sin and the mystical body of Christ. As through one man sin and death came into the world, so through one man, Jesus Christ, grace and eternal life came to mankind. Through his faith in Jesus, one becomes a member of his corporate personality, his mystical body.

New Testament faith differs in some ways from that of the Old Testament. Its central object is Jesus Christ in lieu of Yahweh, the God of the Hebrews. New Testament faith does not give as much emphasis to the return to the prophets, nor a renewing of salvific acts, nor a trust in God's fidelity to the covenant. However, we do find the preaching of the messianic prophecies. Moreover, the eucharist is certainly a renewal of the greatest of all salvific acts. And New Testament faith is a firm trust in the new covenant in place of the old. New Testament faith centers itself on God's eschatological action through Christ. We who have died with Christ, will live with him forever. In a sense New Testament faith seems less historical than that of the Old Testament, but more eschatological.

Pistis in the New Testament means the act by which man separating himself from the world, turns towards God and Christ. Rely on Christ, for he is true. Because he cannot deceive us, we accept him and what he says. The use of pisteuein eis, the personal, affective acceptance of Christ and his kerygma, is peculiar to the New Testament. It is a conversion to Christ and to what he has done. Along with this faith are the allied virtues of hope, fear, obedience, confession, and assent.

Faith in the Synoptics[1]

Jesus demands faith of his followers (Mt 9:28; Mk 4:36; Lk 8:25). He praises faith (Mt 8:10; Lk 7:9), and teaches that faith has saved (Mt 9:28, Mk 5:34, Lk 8:48). All things are possible for the man who believes. What is the content of faith in the Synoptics? It is an acceptance of Jesus as true; that is, he is what he says he is. As in the Old Testament, so in the Synoptics faith is an acceptance of the person and his claims, inspiring trust and confidence.

Faith in the Acts of the Apostles

Faith as described in the Acts is what makes a man one of the believers, that is, one of those who accept the preaching of the Apostles

11

and join the Christian community. To become a Christian is to believe (A 4:4; 13:12, 14:1, 15:7). This belief in the word of the Apostles is faith in the Lord (A 5:14; 9:42), faith in Jesus Christ (A 11:17).

What is the content of the faith of the early Christians? It is contained in the preaching of the Apostles, for example, the kerygma of Peter on Pentecost Sunday (A 2:22-40): "Jesus of Nazareth was a man attested to you by God with mighty works and wonders and signs . . . This Jesus . . . you crucified and killed by the hands of lawless men . . . This Jesus God raised up and of that we are all witnesses . . . Therefore, exalted at the right hand of God, and having received from the Father the promise of the Holy Spirit, he has poured out this which you see and hear . . . Let all the house of Israel, therefore, know assuredly that God has made him both Lord and Christ, this Jesus whom you crucified . . . Repent and be baptized."[2]

The early Christians believed that Jesus was truly Lord and Christ because God had raised him up and the Apostles were witnesses to it. One can easily see here the centrality of the resurrection to the faith of the early Church.

Faith and Miracles

The faith-miracle relationship in the New Testament parallels that of the amen-hesed agreement of the old era. In the Old Testament Yahweh gave miraculous protection, security, covenant love to those who were faithful to him, who relied on him rather than on themselves or on material things. These were especially the anawim.

In the New Testament we frequently find faith rewarded by miracles, healings, exorcisms. The anawim at the time of Jesus were the sick, the blind, the lame, outcasts, lepers, possessed, sinners. In these people we often find a lack of self-reliance and a faith in God typical of the anawim. To these Jesus gives his hesed, his loving mercy. By their faith his power is released. For example, in the story of the woman with the issue of blood (Mk 5:25-34), Jesus felt power go out of him when the believing woman touched his garment: "Daughter, your faith has made you well. Go in peace and be healed of your disease" (Mk 5:34). This is a frequent response of Jesus and indicates the close relationship between faith and miracles.

Where there was a lack of faith, Jesus could not perform miracles. In a sense, his power almost depended on faith. For example, when he visited his own country (Mk 6:5), "he could do no mighty work there, except that he laid his hands upon a few sick people and healed them. And he marveled because of their unbelief."

sin, orientates everything to himself instead of opening himself to God and to others. It is this "sin" that must be destroyed in us. And, let to itself, Law is incapable of the task. But by permitting "Transgression," Law makes sin unfold itself and helps man through his painful experience to seek his Savior. This is the way St. Paul understands the role of law, a role that is indispensible, ultimately beneficent and salutary.[5]

Paul often contrasted the external law with the inner law of the Spirit. "The law of the Spirit of life in Christ Jesus has set me free from the law of sin and death" (Rom 8:2). The Law of the Spirit is not just another code; it is rather a law produced in us by the Holy Spirit, a new, inner source of spiritual energy. It is the new Law which gives that justification which the old Law wished to give, but could not (Rom 8:4). It is the Law of love. "For the whole Law is fulfilled in one word, 'You shall love your neighbor as yourself'" (Gal 5:14; Rom 13:8-10). With this dynamic love, the spiritual man flees from what is carnal.

But is there no longer a need of an external law? Yes, it is needed for the unjust (1Tim 1:9). As soon as the inner movement of the Spirit is no longer felt, the Law is there to constrain him and to warn him that he is no longer being led by the Spirit. But what about the just? Do they have need of this Law? Yes, they do, for even the just possess the Spirit only imperfectly on earth (Rom 8:23; 2C 1:22) where man is never completely free from the influence of the flesh. In this unstable condition the Law will guide him in distinguishing works of flesh from fruits of the Spirit. Although law is indispensable for sinners and helpful to the just, grace is the chief element in spiritualization and alone able to justify.

External law remains secondary and an expression of the primary interior law of love. Works are commanded only because of their necessary relationship to the inner grace of the Holy Spirit, reflecting the inner dynamism of faith working through charity (Gal 6:7). Thus man does not obey the Law or transgress the Law for itself, but as an outward observance of the inner law, as a minimum standard of the inner dynamism of the Spirit. The norm of new Christian Law is an imitation of the Father (Eph 4:32; 5:2; 24:26). Love one another, as Christ has loved us, his Church.

For the Christian the Person of Christ is the whole law, not only with regard to its principal element, the Spirit of Christ imparted to him, but even with regard to its secondary element, which is reducible to the imitation of Christ.[6]

Freed by the inner law, the Christian is no longer a slave of the external law because he is motivated by the inner dynamism of love, flowering into good works, not the self-reliant works of the Law, but works of love, reflecting an internal faith and dependence on God (Rom 13:8-10; Gal 5:6; 14; James 2:14-20).

Paul knew the Law. As a Pharisee he was an expert in it. He knew its strong points and its weaknesses. He knew how easy it was to become lost in details in the observance of the written and oral Torah and thus lose sight of the motivating principle of love which must stand behind all external law. The Law had been necessary as a tutor to guide men till the coming of Christ, and although Paul had kept the Law strictly, it was through faith in Jesus Christ that he was justified.

Faith and Law

Paul's most urgent theme in Galatians and Romans is the antithesis between faith and the Law, brought on by the Judaizers and their unreasonable demands that the Gentile Christians undergo circumcision according to the Law. In Galatians (3 & 4) Paul teaches that it is faith, not the Law, which saves man. The earlier experiences of the Galatians themselves in their conversion to Christ showed them that the Spirit was renewed through faith (3:1-5). Scripture teaches that the real descendants of Abraham are men of faith as Abraham was (3:6-9). A persistent theme in Galatians is that man is justified by faith and not by the works of the Law (2:16; 3:24-25; 5:1; 6:12-15), for faith has superseded the Law (3:23-25), introducing the new era of Christian freedom contrasting with the old slavery of the Law (3:26-4:20).

The allegory of Sarah and Hagar illustrates well the freedom of the children of faith versus the slavery of the children of the Law (4:21-31). Those who rely upon the works of the Law instead of having faith in God's promise are to be excluded from the inheritance.

Now we, brethren, like Isaac, are children of the promise.
But as at that time he who was born according to the flesh
persecuted him who was born according to the Spirit, so
it is now. But what does scripture say? 'Cast out the
slave and her son; for the son of the slave shall not in-
herit with the son of the free woman.' So brethren, we
are not children of the slave, but of the free woman.
(4:28-31)

So faith in Jesus Christ frees the Christian from the slavery of
the Law and gives him the right to his lawful inheritance.

The Inheritance

It is through pistis, faith or trust, that man receives the inheritance of Abraham. Greer M. Taylor has recently brought
out an interesting parallel between the use of pistis in Galatians
and the fidei commissum of Roman law.[7] It is through pistis
that man receives justification, righteousness, the promise of
Abraham, the heirship, the adoption as son of God, the Spirit,
and life itself. Paul uses pistis frequently in juridical contexts
often describing a legal transaction similar to the fidei commissum (Gal 2:16-3:26; Rom 3:22-5:2). The Christian receives
through Christ what the Law claimed to offer, namely, justification or righteousness.
In Chapters 2 and 3 of Galatians Paul speaks of diathēkē, or
testament, as a juridical transaction by which benefits are transmitted by one person to others. It is a legal device for the distribution of benefits including justification (dikaiosunē), but also
other benefits which the law does not even claim to offer. Christ
is the sole agent of this distribution. And the benefits come as a
free distribution, without being earned, to beneficiaries of all
nations, Jews and Gentiles, all on the same terms.
God has made this testament, this diathēkē, with man. There
are two named donees of the benefits to be transmitted by the
diathēkē, Abraham and a single lineal descendant, Jesus Christ
(3:16), who have exclusive legal right to, and exclusive power
to transmit these benefits. Thus the claim of the Law to transmit
them is false (3:15-18).
The enjoyment of the benefits to be transmitted by the diathēkē
is to be shared by numerous persons of all nations. Jews are included, but with no special status (3:8-9; 14), since all receive
these benefits through the exclusive donee, Christ (3:14; 22).

17

The enjoyment of the benefits is made dependent upon and so delayed until, the occurrence of certain events designated in the diathēkē itself, namely, the coming of the second named donee, who, though the Son of God, comes as the child of a woman and subject to the Law (3:19; 4:4) and his crucifixion by the Law (3:13). Meanwhile, the other intended beneficiaries are subject to tutors and so are in very much the same status as slaves (3:19-20).

When these terms and conditions have been fulfilled, the beneficiary is freed from the legal penalties he has incurred in the past, and is freed from the tutelage of the Law and from his obligation to obey it for the future (2:18-19; 3:13; 4:4-9). He becomes a new and different person, his old person having been done away with (2:20; 3:27-29). He becomes dikaios, justified (2:16; 3:8), an heir of Abraham (3:29), the adopted son of God (3:26; 4:5-7).

What part does pistis, trust, play in the diathēkē of Abraham and Christ? It is involved in the terms and conditions of the testament. It was first seen in Abraham's receipt of the promise (3:6). And it is integrally involved in the very purpose of the diathēkē, namely, that the Gentiles should be made dikaioi through pistis (4:8). It is intrinsic to the reason for Christ's designation as the sole successive named donee that the benefits should come to the Gentiles through pistis and so through him (3:14). The benefits transmitted through pistis are absolutely incompatible with the system of rewards and punishments provided by the Law. This conclusively disproves the Law's claim to be the source of dikaiosunē, righteousness. To assert this claim is to deny that diakaiosunē comes by the diathēkē which is based on pistis (3:11-12; 18). The intended beneficiaries of the diathēkē are those who derive their status as seed of Abraham from pistis (3:7). It is ek pisteōs Iēsou Christou that the benefits are conferred on the beneficiaries (3:22-23).

Pistis plays an important part in the realization of the benefits of the diathēkē. Man's exoneration from the penalties and obligations of the Law takes place through the crucifixion and so through the coming of pistis (3:22-25). The beneficiary has his new personality by the pistis of the Son of God (2:20) in whom he is made one, through pistis, with the other beneficiaries (3:27-29). It is by pistis Iēsou Christou that one is made dikaios (2:16). And it is by pistis that we are in Christ sons of God, for it is through pistis that our adoption is brought about (3:26).

Taylor goes on to point out the parallels between pistis Christou of Galatians and the fidei commissum of Roman testamentary law. The parallels are, indeed, striking. Taylor prefers to translate

18

pistis, as used in Galatians, in a legal sense. Thus it is "trust" rather than "faith." Some places it is the fidei commissum on which the diathēkē is based. This can be attributed to Christ. In other contexts, pistis can be "trustfulness," appropriate to a beneficiary. In this way it is used of Abraham and the Christian. Paul probably was familiar with Roman law and may well have used fidei commissum to illustrate the Christian's relation of trust to the diathēkē. According to Taylor, the diathēkē of Galatians is not the new covenant of Second Corinthians, but it is the old covenant going back to Abraham (3:17). Thus the Gentile Christian through pistis can be a true heir of Abraham.

Whether or not we agree with G. Taylor's trust-interpretation of pistis Christou in Galatians, we cannot deny Paul's basic theme, namely, that pistis, faith or trust in Christ, succeeds the tutelage of the Law. It is through pistis that man is justified and receives his heritage as the adopted son of God and brother of Christ.

Dynamic Faith

Pistis for Paul is not merely the act of becoming faithful, but the dynamic state of being faithful, with all the acts that this living faith involves. By our faith we become children of God (Gal 3:26; 29; 5:1; 3:8). The just man lives by faith (Rom 1:17; Gal 2:20; 3:11); he stands firmly by faith (Rom 11:20; 2C 1:24). Paul's faith is a living faith, not just the acceptance of the kerygma as a fact, or as a group of facts. Rather it is an obedience to the kerygma. Consequently, faith is not merely a single act, which takes place only once, nor is it a mystical experience to which one can look back and repeat if necessary or which can maintain its élan throughout life. "Rather it determines one's living in its manifold historical reality. And there is no moment in which the man of faith is released from the obedience of constantly living out of the grace of God."[8] Therefore, whatever does not proceed from faith is a sin (Rom 14:23). Paul's whole life was according to his faith in Jesus Christ (Gal 2:20).

Faith realizes itself in the living, concrete acts of the man of faith. There are grades of faith ranging from the lack of it (1Thes 3:10) to increasing faith (Phil 1:25; 2C 10:15); when one strays from the path of faith, he should correct himself (Gal 6:1; 1C 1:10; 2C 13:11). As faith is individualized according to the measure which God has assigned to each one (Rom 12:3), so also divine grace is individualized in various gifts (Rom 12:6), for example, Paul's grace of Apostleship to the Gentiles (Rom 1:5;

19

12:3; 15:15; 1C 3:10; Gal 2:9). There are other gifts such as the glossolalia, prophecy (Rom 12:6ff; 1C 12:4ff; 28ff), and manifestations of brotherly love given in proportion to our faith (Rom 12:6; 8f).

One of these gifts of living faith is knowledge (gnōsis). To the Philippians Paul wrote: "And it is my prayer that your love may abound more and more, with knowledge and all discernment" (Phil 1:9). He is glad when a congregation is rich in understanding and knowledge (1C 1:5; 2C 8:7; Rom 15:14), for this develops the knowing that is contained in faith into ever clearer and more comprehensible knowledge. Knowledge as a special aspect of faith is a gift of the Spirit, yet the believer should develop it (Phil 1:9f; Rom 12:2). It includes knowledge of the will of God, of the mysteries of the history of salvation, or of the eschatological occurrence (Rom 11:25; 1C 2:7; 15:51). By the power of the Spirit this knowledge can soar into wisdom (1C 2:6). Far from the self-satisfying gnōsis of Gnosticism, this is rather an existential knowledge in which faith unfolds itself, an understanding of self under divine grace (1C 8). It is not genuine knowledge if it gets puffed up and damages the love in which faith ought to be working. The partial self-knowledge through faith will only be succeeded by clear vision in the consummation (1C 13:10-12; 2C 5:7).

Living in Christ

The individual believer, living not out of self, but out of the divine deed of salvation, is determined by Christ.[9] The believer can be in Christ, or Christ in the believer (Rom 8:10; 2C 13:5; Gal 2:20); either can express one living according to the Law of Christ (Gal 6:2). As there are degrees of faith so there are degrees of existence in Christ (1C 3:1; Rom 16:10; 1C 4:10).

Paul's intense faith brings him to a firm personal commitment to Christ. He is a loyal friend of Christ. He has a personal knowledge (yada) of Christ through faith, believing with his whole heart (Rom 10:9-11). Paul frequently speaks of faith in and of Jesus Christ (Gal 2:16, 19-20; 3:22; Rom 3:22, 26; Phil 3:9; Eph 3:12; 1:15; Col 1:4). "In Christ," an early form of "Christian," should characterize all the Christian's attitudes and actions (2C 2:17; 12:19; Phil 2:1; 4:2; Rom 16:22; 16:8), even to imprisonment in Christ (Phil 1:13), and death in Christ (1C 15:18; 1Thes 4:16; Rom 14:7-9).

20

Through his faith in Christ the Christian receives the communication of adopted filiation and becomes a brother of Christ. This brotherhood expresses perhaps more than any other word the close relationship between the believer and Christ (Gal 3:26; Eph 1:15; Col 1:4; 1Tim 1:13), for the man of faith is united mystically with Christ and joined with his fellow Christians in a common brotherhood with Christ (Rom 15:7; 1C 1:9). Through faith and grace we are united to Christ as members of his body. No longer is there Jew or Gentile, male or female, slave or free, but all are one in Christ (Gal 3:28-29). When one member suffers, all suffer; when one rejoices, all rejoice (1C 12:12-31).

Faith in Christ is to put on Christ (Gal 3:27), to partake of Christ, to belong to him (Rom 7:4, 19-20; Eph 2:5-8). It is to be joined with Christ crucified and risen. The believer is crucified with Christ to the world (Rom 6:7; Gal 2:19f; 5:24; 6:14; Phil 3:10). Christ's sufferings overflow into the Apostle (2C 1:5; 4:10). The faithful suffer with Christ in order to be glorified with him (Rom 8:17); as brothers they enter equally into his sufferings and joy (Gal 2:20-21; 4:19; Rom 6:5-8). Paul is rooted in Christ through faith (Col 2:6-7): "And that Christ may dwell in your hearts through faith; that you, being rooted and grounded in love, may have power to comprehend with all the saints what is the length and height and depth, and to know the love of Christ which surpasses knowledge, that you may be filled with the fullness of God" (Eph 3:17-19). The believer through his faith puts on Christ, Christ enters into his heart, and he becomes one with Christ.

Kerygma of Faith

For Paul faith is a personal brotherly commitment to Christ. But were there not certain things about Christ that he believed? Basically the content of Paul's faith was identical with the kerygma, namely, that Jesus is the Messiah, and that God has raised him up (Rom 10:9). We believe that Jesus was delivered for our sins and raised up for our righteousness (Rom 4:25f).

As Father McKenzie writes,[10] the content of Paul's faith is summed up best in what may have been an early Christian profession of faith: Jesus was revealed in the flesh, proved righteous in the Spirit, was seen by the angels, preached among nations, believed in the world, and assumed in glory (1Tim 3:16). Jesus is the Messiah, Lord, Son of God. Through his death we are delivered from our sins, and through his resurrection he gives new life to those who believe in him and are baptized. Paul not only believes in Jesus, but in all his claims as well. Through his faith he becomes one with Christ and with his kerygma.

Virtues Related to Faith

Obedience: Paul understands faith primarily as obedience (Rom 1:5; 15:18). Thus unbelievers are those who disobey God (Rom 11:30-32; 15:31; Gal 5:7). Faith is obedience in acknowledging the gospel of Christ (2C 9:13). True obedience to God, free of boasting (1C 4:7; Rom 11:18; 1C 1:29), is a work or an accomplishment in which the will does not surrender, but asserts itself.

> Faith is the radical renunciation of accomplishment, the obedient submission to the God-determined way of salvation, the taking over of the cross of Christ. It is the free deed of obedience in which the new self constitutes itself in place of the old.[11]

Confession: "If you confess with your lips that Jesus is Lord and believe in your heart that God raised him up from the dead, you will be saved" (Rom 10:9). The confession of faith in Paul can be expressed by the words: "believe that" (hoti), (Rom 10:9; 1Thes 4:14; Rom 6:8); "believe in" (eis), (Gal 2:16; Rom 10:14; Phil 1:29); "believe toward" (pros), (Phlm 5). Faith, the acceptance of the word of faith (Rom 10:8; Gal 3:2; 5), is derived from what is heard (Rom 10:17) and so contains a knowing. Thus Paul at times speaks as if knowledge were the basis of faith (Rom 6:8f). "But since this knowledge can be appropriated only in obedient, comprehending faith, and hence contains an understanding of one's self, knowledge may also appear as arising out of faith" (Rom 5:3; 2C 1:7; 5:6).[12] In Paul, "we know" and "you know" often refer to a statement taken out of the kerygma (1Thes 5:2; Rom 6:3; 2C 5:1; 8:9). Ultimately faith and knowledge are identical as a new understanding of one's self (Rom 1:5; 2C 4:6).

Faith is not just an objective knowledge, for the kerygma is a personal address, an act of divine grace, whose acceptance in faith is obedience, acknowledgment, confession. Faith is what it is only with reference to divine grace actively present in the word. In the confession of faith, the believer turns away from himself, confessing that what he is and has is through and from God.

Hope: Insofar as faith is a turning away from self, it is also hope, for the faithful look to the future in which they will live (Gal 3:11; Rom 1:17; 6:8; 10:10). Man's righteousness through faith is an eschatological now, which is both here and ahead of the believer (Rom 5:1; Gal 5:5). He is saved now, but hopes for what he does not yet see (Rom 8:24).

> This hope is the freedom for the future and the openness toward it which the man of faith has because he has turned over his anxiety about himself and his future to God in obedience. For the sin of unbelief is this: the unbeliever insists upon living out of his own resources, and so is anxious about his own future in the illusion of being able to dispose over it.[13]

He who is concerned for himself lives in fear of the future. The faithful man does not have this fear because in his faith he has let anxiety about self go. Following the lead of Abraham, he hopes where there is no ground for human hope (Rom 4:18; 5:5), waiting in patience and rejoicing in suffering (Rom 8:25; 5:3; 12:12). Faith, hope, and charity are bound up closely together (1C 13:13; 1Thes 1:3).

Fear: This fear is not the anxiety of the unbeliever, but is God-centered, placing the believer's attention on God's grace (1C 2:1-5).

> The man of faith, who in view of God's grace is freed from fear, must not forget that the grace that emancipates him is the grace of a Judge. When the man of faith looks to himself, his faith must ever contain fear, as the knowledge of his own insignificance and his constant dependence on God's grace.[14]

Hope and fear are parallel in Paul (2C 5:11; 3:12). Fear helps destroy false security and directs the believer's attention away from self and towards God's grace, which alone is his support (Rom 11:20). Thus the believer has a new sense of responsibility for he is now free from the Law and what he does now matters.

> Therefore, my beloved, as you have always obeyed, so now, not only as in my presence but much more in my absence, work out your own salvation with fear and trembling; for

God is at work in you, both to will and to work for his
good pleasure. (Phil 2:12-13)

The man of faith should be constantly on guard lest he fall
into temptation (Gal 6:1) from Satan (2C 2:11; 1Thes 3:5; 1C
7:5). He should examine himself to see if he is truly faithful
(2C 13:5; 1C 11:28; Gal 6:4; 1C 10:12). Urging his followers to
stand firm in their faith (1C 16:13; 15:58), Paul prayed earnestly
for their perseverance (1Thes 3:13; 5:23).

Hope and fear are correlative in Paul's faith: fear of our own
weakness and hope of the future grace of God. "The man of faith
utterly surrenders to God's care and power, waiving all care
and power of his own and all security that might be at his own
disposal"[15] (Phil 3:21-14). Although no longer a slave under the
tutelage of the Law, he is not yet in full participation of the
beatitude for which he longs.

Confidence: Confidence is closely allied to the hope of faith
(2C 3:4). Because of obedience, faith is confidence, trust, for
confidence in God is a complete surrender to God in the obedience of faith. This trust accepts the cross and is firmly founded
on God's great deed of salvation, because, for the man of faith,
trusting in self (2C 1:9) or in the flesh (Phil 3:3f) gives place to
trusting in God (2C 1:9). Boasting of self is replaced by boasting
of the Lord. Out of such trust a certain boldness grows (Phil
1:20), similar to the boldness of hope (2C 3:12) and opposed to
cowardice (2C 4:1, 16).

This trust gives Paul support in his apostolic consciousness
and ministry (2C 3:4; 10:2; Phil 1:6, 25; 2:24). And the trust
that Paul places in his congregation comes out of faith also (Gal
5:10; 2C 1:15; 2:3).

Poverty: It was as one of the anawim that Paul pictured himself as a true believer and follower of Christ. Jesus' portrayal
of the least ones (Mt 25:44-45) seems to fit well Paul's description of himself as hungry, thirsty, cold, naked, in prison, on
journeys (2C 11:23-27; 1C 4:11). He is a loyal disciple of Jesus
even to the cross, the climax of the Master's life of poverty (Rom
6:6; Gal 2:19f; 5:24; 6:14; Phil 3:10). As a poor man of faith, one
of the little ones, Paul shows his complete independence of creatures and his total dependence on God. Although Paul does not
call his fellow Christians poor, the term was used of the early
Jewish Christians.[16]

Faith, the response to the proclaimed word, is an eschatological occurrence, a newly opened way of salvation. Thus faith comes and is revealed (Gal 3:23, 25). The concrete realization of the possibility of faith is itself an eschatological event, for it is God who accomplishes man's willing and doing, his concrete, historical existing, in faith. If faith is an eschatological gift of God (Phil 1:29), is it not brought about by God outside of man's decision, outside the pale of free obedience?

> Faith is God-wrought to the extent that provenient grace
> first made the human decision possible, with the result
> that he who has made the decision can only understand it
> as God's gift. But that does not take its decision-char-
> acter away from it.[17]

Paul's faith decision is truly eschatological. It begins eternal life for him here and now in these last days and will be fulfilled soon in the vision of glory (Rom 5:1; Gal 5:5). Did Paul believe that he was in the last days, and that the time was short? (Rom 8:23; 2C; 1C 1:22; 5:5; 7:17-31). Authors do not agree. However, there seems to have been a close parallel between Christian millenarianism and Jewish messianism in the early days of the Church. The Jews expected the Messiah to deliver them from the oppressive Roman rule, while the Christians, Jews and Gentiles alike, no less fervently awaited the second coming of Christ. At his return he will lead the just to heaven where faith will be fulfilled in vision (2C 5:7).

The eschatology of faith is clearly taught in the Epistle to the Hebrews. Although not written by the Apostle, this letter was placed with the Pauline epistles especially in later canons of the New Testament. The author reflects Paul's theology in trying to bolster up the weakening faith of his readers, probably recent Jewish converts to Christianity. They are hankering for the old ways of the Law. In Chapter 11 he gives them what was to become the classical Christian definition of faith, namely, the assurance of the things to be hoped for and the conviction of things unseen (Heb 11:1). He reminded them of the patriarchs and prophets of old who had had faith in God in time of tribulation and of how God had rewarded them. So now in these troubled times, have faith in Jesus Christ, our priest and leader in place of Moses on this pilgrimage to the promised land of beatitude. Faith is the very substance (hypostasis) and assurance of the future rewards. In a sense, the believer already possesses them in anticipation. This brings out the "now" and the "then" of Pauline eschatology. Moreover, faith is the proof or conviction (elenchos) of the unseen mysteries of revelation which will be seen in the future vision.

Conclusion

Paul's Pharisaic training qualified him to preach the antithesis of faith and law. Faith has supplanted the Law so that man is justified by faith, not by the works of the Law. The Christian, led by the Spirit, is freed in Christ from the Law of Moses as law. The interior Law of the Spirit, the Law of love, has delivered man from the Law of sin and death.

The Law had pointed out transgressions, and by permitting transgressions, had allowed sin to unfold itself, helping man to seek his Savior. The interior Law of love is the new motivating force. However, the external law although secondary is still needed, for man is imperfect and needs an exterior rule to remind him of the interior. Although faith has supplanted the works of the Law, Paul does not reject all works, but rather promotes the works of faith through charity which flows from the inner dynamism of the Law of the Spirit.

Perhaps reflecting Roman law, pistis can be considered as a mutual trust through which the Christian, Jew or Gentile, receives the inheritance of the testament of Abraham and Christ. Pistis succeeds the tutelage of the Law.

Paul's faith is a dynamic and a living event. It is a personal knowledge and commitment to Christ with all the personal feeling of the Hebrew yada. Paul puts on Christ; he lives, dies, and rises in Christ. He is a loving brother of Christ through his filial adoption by the Father, as all Christians are brothers of Christ and so brothers in Christ through faith. Paul not only believed in Christ, but also in his claims, in his kerygma, namely, that he is Christ and Lord and that God has raised him up.

Some virtues related to Pauline faith are obedience to the word, confession of Christ and his kerygma, fear of unfaithfulness, hope and confidence in Christ, poverty with the poor Christ.

Paul's faith, finally, is eschatological. It is not only a personal commitment to Christ here and now in these last days, but it is an anticipation and an assurance of the eternal union in heaven.

3 UNITED IN CHRIST - FAITH IN JOHN

John, the youngest of the Apostles, son of Zebedee, brother of
James, was called by Jesus in the early days of his ministry. John
was one of the three Apostles closest to Jesus, especially on outstanding occasions such as the transfiguration or the agony in the
Garden of Gethsemane. John, tradition tells us, sat next to Jesus
at the Last Supper. It was John, alone of the Apostles, who was
to follow his Master to Calvary, where Jesus gave his mother to
John for his special care. After Pentecost, John lived at Jerusalem
where we find him participating in the first council of the early
church. Later he went to Ephesus. Banished to the Isle of Patmos
in the Domitian persecution, he wrote his book of Revelation there.
His gospel was composed at Ephesus around the years 90-100.
Tradition says he was buried in Ephesus.

Hearing of the Word

John wrote his gospel "that you may believe that Jesus is the
Christ, the Son of God, and that believing, you may have life in
his name" (20:31). God sent his only Son "that whosoever believes
in him may not perish but have eternal life" (3:16, 36). To those
who believed in him he promised the power to become children of
God (1:12). In John's gospel we find Jesus frequently demanding
faith in himself (6:29; 12:36; also 1J 3:23), and promising a reward
to believers (6:35, 40, 47; 7:37, 38a; 11:25f; 12:44-46; 14:12; 1J
5:1, 10, 13). There are other phrases in John which can signify
belief, for example: "to come to Jesus" (5:40; 6:37, 44f, 65), "to
follow him" (8:12), "to enter through him" (10:9), "to drink the
water which he gives" (4:13f). Belief can also mean to accept
Jesus (1:12; 5:43) and to love him (8:12; 14:15, 21ff; 16:27).
John uses pisteuein as an acceptance of the Christian message,
for example, "believe that" (pisteuein hoti) (6:69; 10:38; 11:27,
42; 17:8; 20:31; 1J 5:1, 5). Sometimes it is "believe in" (pisteuein
eis), or "believe in his name" (1:12; 2:23; 3:18; 1J 5:13). Pisteuein
can alternate with "believe that" (11:40, 42; 16:30f) and with
"believe in" (3:18; 4:39, 41), or it can be used with the dative
(5:38, 46; 8:45f). If Jesus is believed, so also are his words, for
his words are identical with himself (5:47), as are his works also
(10:38). His words (12:48; 17:8) and his testimony (3:11, 32f) are
to be accepted.

That explains why "Believe him" (dative) and "believe in him" are identical for John. It is not as if one first had to believe him, trust him, in order that one might believe in him. But that one ought to believe him and so trusting him is in fact believing in him. One can do neither without doing both. Thus it becomes clear that in the proclaimed word the Proclaimer himself is present, acting.[18]

So, accepting the word is accepting Christ; rejecting it is rejecting Christ.

Lightfoot maintains[19] that it might be possible for a man to believe him, that is, give him a favorable hearing (2:22; 4:50), and still not give him the complete devotion and obedience implied in believing in him. By believing in him one becomes one of his disciples and possesses eternal life (6:29, 40).

Faith and the World

In contrast to the faith and law theme of Paul, we have the teachings of John on faith and the world. In John we find a recurrent dualism. Jesus is the light coming into the darkness of the world, which does not know him. To those who receive him and believe in him, he will give life, and they will become sons of God (1:9-13; 3:15; 5:24; 1J 3:14; 11:26).

There are a number of proposed explanations of John's dualism. Bauer, Windisch and Bultmann say it is a derivative of Eastern Gnosis. Although it is true that John and Gnosis share dualism, Wikenhauser clarifies:

> Both John (and also Paul) and the Gnosis share a fundamental dualism which is clearly expressed in the antitheses of light and darkness, truth and falsehood, above and below, freedom and slavery. But it is only in the Gnosis that we find a metaphysical dualism. In the case of John we can speak only of an ethical or historical dualism. He does not say that man belongs to the heavenly world because his hidden "self" has the nature of light. According to John, man must freely decide for the heavenly world or its opposite (dualism of decision).[20]

C. H. Dodd[21] points to a late Hellenistic influence in John's theology; the Dead Sea Scrolls and the Damascus Document also show a striking similarity to John's dualism. Whether or not he was influenced by

28

the Gnostics or the Essenes, eastern dualism can be seen clearly reflected in his theology of faith.

Teaching faith as the true way of life, John attacks the world's false understanding of life. The world longs for life and thinks it has it (5:39), but it is in death (5:25). The world thinks that it sees, but it is blind (9:39). It supposes that it knows God, but the true God is unknown to it (5:37, 7:28). The true light, the true bread of life, the true tree of life, all are unknown to it (1:9; 1J 2:8; J6:32; 15:1). "But the world is not simply in error, it is a liar. It does not believe Jesus, precisely because he tells the truth. The world does not want to come to light" (3:19).[22]

Jesus demands faith of the world, that it revamp its false security, its false presumptuous independence of the Creator.

> Faith is a turning away from the world, the act of de-secularization, the surrender of all seeming security and every pretense, the willingness to live by the strength of the invisible and uncontrollable. It means accepting completely different standards as to what is to be called death and what life. It means accepting the life that Jesus gives and is (5:19ff; 12:25f): a life that to the world's point of view cannot even be proved to exist.[23]

Faith must overcome the offense or the scandal that true life is found through Jesus of Nazareth, that God is encountering the world in him, the Word become flesh. As a victory over this offense, faith is a victory over the world (1J 5:4).

The man of faith does not get fed up with the world and then turn away to God. "Faith is not a flight from the world, nor an asceticism, but desecularization in the sense of a smashing of all human standards and evaluation."[24] "It is in this sense that the believer is no longer 'of the world' (15:19; 17:14, 16); since the world is no longer his determining origin, he no longer belongs to it."[25] The world does not recognize the believers, just as it did not recognize him (1J 3:1). It hates them as it hated him (15:18-20; 1J 3:13). Jesus' persecution and death are paralleled in theirs (12:24-26; 16:1-4). Must the believers, then, retreat from the world? "I do not pray that thou shouldst take them out of the world, but that thou shouldst keep them from the evil one" (17:15). As the Father sent his Son into the world, so Jesus sends his own into the world (17:18).

John's world is not the Gnostic world, equating material and evil. Rather it is a historical power constituted by man who has rebelled against God. John teaches a dualism of decision. Thus faith is the decision which removes man from the world of darkness and places him in the world of light. Although still in the world, the man of faith is no longer of the world (17:11, 14, 16). With death behind him (8:51; 11:25f), he already possesses Life (3:36; 6:47; 1J 5:12). Darkness is driven away by Light (1J 2:8). As Jesus is a foreigner to the world, so are his followers, for he gave his unworldly glory to them (17:10, 22). What is his glory? Knowledge, the stuff of eternal life, knowing God and his Son (17:3), the Truth (8:32). This knowledge, comprehending that God is the unique reality, frees the believer from the world's sham. As Jesus overcame the world (16:33), so faith is a victory over the world (1J 5:4). As the ruler of the world is defeated and powerless to harm Jesus (12:31; 14:30), neither can he harm the believers, for they have overcome the evil one (1J 2:13f). Freedom from the world is freedom from sin (8:31-36; 1J 3:9) and freedom from the evil one (1J 5:18). Thus freed from sin and death, the man of faith possesses the Light that is Life.

Faith and Love

Love follows closely on John's dualism, for the man of faith no longer loves the world, but loves his brother Christ, and his brothers in Christ. John places faith and love in the same commandment of God: "And this is his commandment, that we should believe in the name of his Son, Jesus Christ, and love one another, just as he has commanded us" (1J 3:23). Do not love the world (1J 2:15), keep free from worldly desires (1J 2:16), pleasing Jesus (1J 3:22) and walking in the light (1J 1:6f). What is this "walking in the light"? It is loving one's brother (1J 2:9-11), for this is Jesus' commandment (15:12; 1J 3:23; 4:21). Out of the love that we have received arises the obligation to love: "A new commandment I give you: that you love one another; even as I have loved you, that you also love one another" (13:34; 1J 4:11, 19).

The unity of faith and love is shown in the parable of the vine (15:1-11). Be loyal in faith and abide in my love (15:10) and share in my joy. The close link between faith and charity is the major theme in the First Epistle of John. It is in love that faith makes good its freedom from the world. The commandment of love is new because it comes to realization in the new, the eschatological existence (1J 2:8). Whoever hates his brother is in darkness (1J

2:9, 11); he is a murderer as Cain (1J 3:12, 15). Whoever merci-
lessly shuts the door on a brother in need does not have God's
love abiding in him (1J 3:17). Whoever claims to love God while
he hates his brother is a liar (1J 4:20). By the very loving of his
brothers, the man of faith is aware of his new eschatological
existence. "We know that we have passed out of death into life
because we love the brethren" (1J 3:14; J 13:35).

God loved man and proved his love by giving his only Son. Yet
man loves himself and the world more than God. The loves opposed to true faith are the love of darkness (3:16-21), the love of
the glory of men (12:43), love of one's own life (12:25), and love
of the world (1J 2:15).

Loving faith and reliance on God should be man's response to
God's love. The unfaithful man relies on himself, loves himself,
the world, the lust of the flesh, the lust of the eyes, the pride of
life (1J 2:15-16). He does not love the glory of God (12:43; 1:14),
the light (3:19; 8:15; 12:35), Christ (8:42-47), God (5:40-44).

> In Christ God offers himself to men out of love. Christ is
> the concrete manifestation of God's love in the world. To
> believe in Christ means to accept him as God's offer of
> himself. In other words, it means to comply with the ad-
> vance of God's love. Those who love themselves inordinate-
> ly, who desire a glory independent of the borrowed glory
> they can have from God in Christ, or who love the evil which
> they have apart from God, can only reject the offer of God's
> love and refuse to believe. Only those who love God's glory
> and who, therefore, love Christ, the manifestation and of-
> fer of that glory, will accept the advances of God's love.
> These are the men who have the "love of God" within them.[26]

So the true man of faith is a man of love. He believes in Christ,
his beloved.

Believing and Knowing

Genuine faith is a knowing faith. Jesus promises knowledge of
the truth to believers if they loyally abide in his word (8:31f).
This is not merely a faith in signs (2:23f; 7:31; 10:42; 11:45; 12:
11), or a faith evoked by a discourse (8:30), which may be the
beginning of faith but has yet to prove itself as the real thing.
Hearing of the word must be followed by keeping it, so genuine
faith can be called a keeping of the word (8:51; 14:23; 15:20; 17:6),

or an abiding in the word (8:31), an abiding in the Revealer (15: 4-7; 1J 2:6, 27f; 3:6, 24), an abiding in God (1J 4:13, 15f), an abiding in the light (1J 2:10), or an abiding in love (15:9f; 1J 4:16).

Faith and knowledge do not differ in their substance. That the Father sent Jesus is equally what is believed (11:42; 17:8, 21) and what is known (17:3). That Jesus came from the Father is believed (16:27-30); it is known that his teaching derives from the Father (7:17). Jesus Christ is believed (11:27; 20:31) and known (6:69). The unity of the disciples will bring the world both to the belief (17:21) and to the knowledge (17:23) that the Father sent Jesus (17:8).

Sometimes John does not distinguish between believing (pis- teuein) and knowing (ginōskein): "We have believed and come to know that you are the Holy One of God" (6:69; also 8:31, 10:38). Other times it seems as if believing were the first turning, whereas knowing seems to be the knowledge growing out of it, towards which faith is moving. However, sometimes the order is reversed, with believing growing out of knowing (16:30; 17: 8; 1J 4:16).

When belief means the first turning not yet developed into a full faith, then knowing can be distinguished from believing (8: 30-32). "Even though you do not believe me, believe the works, that you may begin to know and understand that the Father is in me and I am in the Father" (10:38; also 6:69). But believing in the full sense and knowing are the same and can be used inter- changeably (17:8; 16:30): "And so we know and believe the love God has for us" (1J 4:16). John's knowledge, then, is not a Gnostic gnosis which follows simple faith and ascends beyond it into mystic vision. For John knowing is a part of faith. Believing, in the full sense, is knowing until believing will be succeeded by the direct vision of beatitude.

In what sense can knowledge be considered a higher stage of faith, that is, faith in the full sense? Lightfoot[27] explains: first, faith is never used of the Lord's relation to the Father. Rather it only expresses the relationship of the disciples to the Father and to the Lord. Knowledge, however, does signify the relationship between the Father and the Son (10:14-15): "I am the good shepherd; I know my own and my own know me. As the Father knows me and I know the Father; and I lay down my life for the sheep." For the disciples it is belief and partial knowledge here below and it will be full knowledge then in glory.

Secondly, John strictly avoids the substantives of belief and knowledge, rather using their proper verbs, emphasizing that faith is a life of energy and growth, in which, although the end is implicit in the beginning, there is always more in front of the believer than he has been granted, or has been able as yet to make his own. And in this process, which is throughout a matter of believing, knowledge itself can never dare to cease to learn. From time to time, it also dies to live (10:38). Both faith and knowledge are processes which cannot be more than partial and preliminary in human experience, and in the light of Christian revelation nothing is too good to be true. The foundation of the truth has been laid once for all, but the truth itself, although present, is always on the advance.[28]

Faith constantly seeks a further knowledge and understanding of the unseen First Truth, for man cannot rest satisfied until he sees the Unseen.

What did John mean by "knowing"? C. H. Dodd has made a study of various concepts of saving knowledge prevalent at the time of John.[29] For the Hermetists, saving knowledge was a discipline of cosmological, anthropological, and theological speculation, culminating in a mystical vision, a type of deification. The gnōsis of the Gnostics was a quasi-scientific knowledge of that realm of being which transcends all human experience, communicated in terms of mythology, a knowledge which the soul can put to practical use when it leaves the body. Philo's gnōsis is attained through the understanding of the divine revelation given in Holy Scripture. It is both an awareness of pure being and a communion with God through faith and love.

The Greek and Hebrew modes of knowing are of more interest to us. Greek knowing, analogous to seeing, externalizes the object of knowledge, contemplates it (theōria) from a distance, and endeavors to ascertain its essential qualities in order to grasp its reality (alētheia).

Known and knower, therefore, stand over against one another, and direct communication between the two would be felt as introducing an element of kinēsis or genesis, and so disturbing the pure apprehension of the to on. This determines the Greek ideal of the Bios theōrētikos.

The Hebrew, on the other hand, conceives of knowledge as consisting in an experience of the object in its relation to the subject. Yada implies an immediate awareness of

something as affecting oneself. It is the object in action
and its effects, rather than the thing in itself, that is
known. And in knowing, there is also an activity of the
subject in relation to the object. To know anything is to
concern oneself about it, to take account of it, the will
as well as the intelligence being involved.[30]

Accordingly, for the Greek, to know God means to con-
template the ultimate reality (to ontōs on) in its changeless essence. For the Hebrew to know God is to acknowledge Him in His works and to respond to His claims.
While for the Greek knowledge of God is the most highly
abstract form of pure contemplation, for the Hebrew it
is essentially intercourse with God. It is to experience
His dealing with men in time, and to hear and obey His
commands.[31]

Does John follow the Greek sense of knowing or the Hebrew
sense in his gospel? It would seem to be more the Hebrew experiential knowing. Knowledge of God, in John, is knowledge of
Christ. Jesus through the incarnation has a double role. He is,
as Logos, the divine object of man's knowledge and the subject
of God's knowledge of man. But, as man, Jesus is the object of
God's knowledge of man and the subject of man's knowledge of
God.

God knows man. He knows those who are his for he has chosen
them (10:14; 13:18), and he leads them himself (6:44). Man knows
God, for this is eternal life (17:3), and he will know more of God
(8:28, 32; 10:38). From this moment on ignorance of God is for
Christ's disciples a thing of the past, for seeing and knowing Christ,
they know God (14:7). [32]

Knowledge of God in John either takes on the form of knowledge
of Christ or it is dependent on knowledge of Christ. Only between
the Father and the Son does full mutual knowledge exist indepen-
dently (10:14-15). Thus Christ has intimate knowledge of God (7:
28-29; 8:54-55). As the mediator between God and man, Christ
knows God and is known by him, and the knowledge that Christ
has from his vision of the Father (6:46) Christ mediates to men
(14:9; 12:45).

The content of man's knowledge of God, as expressed by John,
is enlarged to include the unity of men in and with Christ in God
(14:20), and an awareness of the relation of mutual indwelling of
God and man. "For John this experience is made possible through

34

the recognition of Christ as the Revelation of God, of Christ as inseparably one with God. And it finds its completion in an experience of our own unity with Christ in God."[33]

Truth is the object of John's gnōsis. The object is what he appears to be; he is real, genuine, and his words are true. In the LXX alētheia replaces the Hebrew emet, meaning firm, steadfast, faithful, trustworthy. Alētheia is used with charis (hesed we emet), e.g., "Grace and truth came through Jesus Christ" (1:14, 17).

In the Fourth Gospel alētheia means the eternal reality revealed to men--either the reality itself, or the revelation of it.[34]

> On one side at least, the knowledge of God which is eternal life is an apprehension of ultimate reality--that reality which stands above the world of Phenomena, and is eternal, while they change and pass away. This eternal reality is manifested in Christ, who, as Logos, is Bearer not only of the divine charis, but also of the divine alētheia, and through whom this alētheia is revealed to men. To put the matter even more strongly, he is not only the Revealer of alētheia, He is himself hē alētheia (14:10). The extent to which this identification of ultimate reality with a concrete Person known to history transforms the effective meaning of the term will appear hereafter. The form of expression, at any rate, indicates that the relation of men to Christ through which they "Know the Truth," is more intimate than that of disciples to a teacher. To "Know the Truth" they must also be united with him who is the Truth. Thus even when the concept of knowledge of God is most fully intellectualized, it remains true that it involves a personal union with Christ, which goes beyond mere intellectual apprehension.[35]

Christ, First Truth, the eternal Reality is, then, the object of the personal knowledge of the man of faith.

Believing and Seeing

Seeing is a knowing that is peculiar to faith. As John combines seeing and knowing or uses them as alternatives (14:7, 9, 17; 1J 3:6), he also joins or parallels seeing and believing (6:40; 12:44f). This seeing is not merely a physical sense-sight, but rather a faith-sight whereby one recognizes the Son of God in the Incarnate

One. This may coincide with sensory perception of Jesus (1:4; 6:40; 12:45; 14:9). But the two may also be separated (lJ 4:14).

Seeing for John is faith-perception, recognizing in Jesus the Truth and the Life which only he transmits. "He who has once seen me, has seen the Father" (14:8f). "The Word became flesh . . . we have beheld his glory" (1:14).

John clearly distinguishes between sense-sight and faith-sight. For example: "But I said to you that you have seen me and yet do not believe" (6:36); "Not that any one who has seen the Father except him who is from God; he has seen the Father. Truly, truly, I say to you, he who believes, has eternal life" (6:46-47); "Have you believed because you have seen me? Blessed are those who have not seen and yet believe" (20:29). Faith-vision is not a physical vision. When simple vision is accompanied by faith, it leads to vision in a deeper sense, a life-giving vision, eternal life, knowledge of God. Thomas saw Christ physically, believed, and then saw him in the true sense. More blessed are those who do not see him physically, yet believe. "If you have faith, you will see the glory of God" (11:40; 1:14).

> Faith, then, is a form of vision. When Christ was on earth, to have faith was "to see his glory"--to apprehend and acknowledge the diety through the veil of humanity. Now that Christ is no longer visible to the bodily eye, faith remains the capacity for seeing his glory. This is vital to the evangelist's whole conception of the Incarnation. Eternal life is the knowledge or vision of God. But no man has seen God at any time, as the mystics do vainly talk. He who has seen Christ, has seen the Father. To see the Father in Christ, to see his glory, was and always is the part of faith. And this is just as possible and just as necessary for us as for those who saw him in the flesh. Thus pistis is that form of knowledge, or vision, appropriated to those who find God in an historic Person of the past, a Person who, nevertheless, through it remains the object of saving knowledge, the Truth and the Life.[36]

Personal Union with Christ

Faith is a personal knowledge and union with Christ, the Truth. John describes the unity of the believer in Christ and in the Father (15:4, 5; 14:20): "The glory which thou hast given me I have given to them that they may be one even as we are one, I

in them, and thou in me, that they may be perfectly one" (17:22f).
The Father and Son will actually dwell in the loving believer (14:23).

Some passages in John illustrate the personal union of the believer with Christ and the Father: "I am the good shepherd; I know
my own and my own know me, as the Father knows me and I know
the Father; and I lay down my life for the sheep" (10:14-15). The
Son and the Father are in each other in mutual union. "Believe
me that I am in the Father and the Father in me; or else believe
me for the sake of the works themselves" (14:11; 17:21, 23).
There is a mutual indwelling of the Son and men; "In that day you
will know that I am in the Father, and you in me, and I in you"
(14:20; 17:21, 23, 26). The believers are one with the Father
and the Son (17:21).

In Chapter Ten (10:30) when Jesus declares that he and the
Father are one, the Jews are scandalized (10:31-33). Jesus
answers, "If I am not doing the works of my Father, do not believe me. But if I do them, even though you do not believe me,
believe the works, that you may know and understand that the
Father is in me and I am in the Father" (10:37-38; 14:8-11). The
dynamic union of the Father and the Son, expressed in the works
of Jesus (5:17, 19; 8:28-29; 9:4), reveals their unity in mutual
works and life (6:57; 5:26) and in the union of love (5:20; 3:35,
14, 31). Christ's disciples, if they obey him, will be united with
the Father and the Son, who will come and abide in them (14:
21, 23).

Clearly faith brings one into union with Christ and the Father.
This is a personal union of love, perhaps best expressed by the
Hebrew yada.

> At every point the unity of the Father and Son is repro-
> duced in the unity of Christ and the believers. As the
> love of the Father for the Son, returned by him in obedi-
> ence, establishes a community of life between the Father
> and the Son, which exhibits itself in that he speaks the
> Father's word and does his works, so the disciples are
> loved by Christ and return his love in obedience. In do-
> ing so, they share his life, which manifests itself in
> doing his works. It is really he who does them (just as
> the works of Christ are done by the Father). And by doing
> them, the Father is glorified in the Son. This is what is
> meant by the expression "I in you and you in me."[37]

This unity with Christ is further illustrated by John in the parable of the vine and the branches, where the unifying life flows through the common stem into the branches and issues forth in fruit (15: 1-12; also Paul, Rom 11:16-24).

Through loving faith, not only is union with Christ attained, but also a union of love among the disciples: "This is my commandment, that you love one another as I have loved you" (15: 12).

> It is made clear that what is meant is the unity of the disciples in love, which is perfectly mutual between the Father and the Son, manifesting itself, once again, in obedience to the word or command of Christ (which is the word of the Father given to him), which issues in action.

> The triangle of relations is complete: the Father, the Son, and the disciples dwell in one another by virtue of a love which is the very life and the activity of God. In the Father, it is the love that gave the Son for the world. In the Son, it is the love that brings forth perfect obedience to the Father's will and lays down his life for his disciples. In the disciples, it is the love that leads them to obey his command and to love one another. And by their obedience the Father is glorified in the Son.[38]

Christ's prayer for unity epitomizes the unity of faith: "That they may be one" (17:11). "That they may all be one; even as thou, Father, art in me, and I in thee, that they also may be in us . . . That they may be one even as we are one, I in them and thou in me, that they may become perfectly one, so that the world may know that thou hast sent me and hast loved them even as thou hast loved me" (17:21-23). This close union of the believers with Christ and the Father is neither pantheism nor ecstasy. Rather it is the close personal relationship of yada, an intimate friendship with the living God (15:12), based upon mutual love.

> It is by becoming first the objects of this love, and then, in turn, the subjects of the same love, directed towards Christ and towards one another, that we become one by mutual indwelling both with the Father and the Son and with one another in him. But all this at every stage is in

terms of living action, doing the works of God, bearing fruit to his glory.[39]

True, self-giving love of the agapē best expresses this union with Christ. Through our faith in Christ, we enter into a personal community of life with the eternal God, which has the character of agapē, which is essentially supernatural and not of this world. And yet this love plants its feet firmly in this world, not only because real agapē cannot but express itself in practical conduct, but also because the crucial act of agapē was performed in the world at the last supper and on Calvary. This love is in the world, but not of it. The unity of Christ with the believers, then, is a unity of love, which is so dynamic that it cannot remain dormant, but must burst forth in loving action.

The man of loving faith must be a man of action. As the branches connected with the vine must produce good fruit, so the man of faith must continue the works done by the Father through Jesus. "Truly, truly, I say to you, he who believes in me will also do the works that I do. And greater works than these will he do, because I go to the Father" (14:12). The union between the Father, the Son, and the faithful flows out into these works of God's love.

Paul and John

In comparing the theologies of faith of Paul and John we might, following Father Benoit,[40] look briefly at the diverse characters of the two men. John is a contemplative, taken up with the realities of knowledge, light, and truth. His gospel, a product of many years of reflection and redaction, mirrors his contemplative spirit.

> Paul, on the other hand, is a fighter, a man of action, dynamic, creative, founder of churches. He cannot remain in one spot for long, but rushes about establishing the church of Christ. Paul is particularly preoccupied with the new creation which is the work of Christ. For Paul, as for John, it is a question of opening oneself to the light, but his predominant concern is building a new world in place of the old one which is in the process of collapsing.[41]

Their religious experiences: Paul's conversion was occasioned by his startling vision of the Risen Christ on the road to Damascus. Urged on by devotion to his new Master, Paul moved from the old Judaic world into a new world, where all things became possible because the power of the resurrection was already at work in it. He dedicated his fiery

personality to the work of the Risen Christ. John's initial experience
was less striking, yet not less profound. Captivated as a youth by
the light of Christ, he remained steadfast right up till Calvary and
beyond. John is less flamboyant than Paul, less aggressive, perhaps
more contemplative and mystical.

The faith of Paul and John:

> For both theologians faith is a commitment of one's whole
> being, heart as well as spirit. Without such a commitment,
> faith would be neither authentic nor Christian. Yet in John's
> gospel faith appears to be more contemplative in nature,
> while for Paul it is more creative. John closely likens it to
> a vision. "He saw and believed" (John 20:8). This dialectic
> of seeing and believing clearly illustrates how Johannine
> faith utilizes the category of light (1:50; 2:23; 3:11-12; 4:
> 48; 7:3-5; 9:37-39; 11:40; 12:44-45; 14:19-20).[42]

Paul's faith is also an acceptance of the Word (Rom 10:14-17) and
an adherence to a doctrine (Rom 6:17; Col. 2:6-7). But it is also
a radical incorporation in Christ (Gal 2:20; Eph 2:8-9). Moreover,
it is a stage of the divine plan of salvation replacing the Law and
introducing a new era, the era of man recreated in Christ (Gal
3:23-28).[43] For both Paul and John faith is a firm personal commitment to Christ, freeing the believer from the Law and the
world, and thus giving the liberty and independence to follow
Christ, united with him and with the other believers in a bond of
love.

4 CONCLUSION

New Testament faith is a personal commitment to Jesus Christ,
the Word of God, the Revelation of the Father. We find a faithful
dependence on Christ on the part of the poor, the rejected, the
sick, and the sinners of the gospels, whom he helps with his
wonderful words and deeds. The new covenant fulfills the old so
that faith in Jesus is rewarded by the gracious mercy of the Father through his divine Son. New Testament faith places less
emphasis on the historical salvific acts of God and more on his
eschatological action through Jesus.
Pistis is the act whereby man separates himself from dependence on the world and turns toward God in Christ. We rely on
Christ because he is true. Our faith is a personal experiential

relationship with our brother Christ, whose inheritance we share; moreover, it unites us in loving union with our fellow brothers in Christ.

For both Paul and John faith is a total personal commitment to Christ. However, they stressed different antitheses: Paul, faith and the Law; John, faith and the world. But both insisted that faith is a full reliance on and dedication to Christ. John taught a personal faith-knowledge and vision, and close union with Christ, the Truth. Paul lives with Christ and is crucified with him in order to share his victory. Both Paul and John taught the unity of the believers as brothers of Christ and brothers in Christ, living in a common bond of love. For both Paul and John faith begins the new eschaton of eternal life. The old life of the Law and the world is left behind and the new life begins the loving union with the unseen Christ, which will be fulfilled in the vision of beatitude.

Through both testaments flows the theme of man's need to rely on God. Man is man, and it is an essential part of him to be of and to God. But this "Yes" to God does not necessitate a "No" to man as some of the radical theologians would imply. Scriptures teach an emphatic "Yes" to man through brotherly love, based on man's "Yes" to God, namely, his faithful love of him. Perhaps a thorough study of biblical faith as a total reliance of man upon God and an understanding that this dependence, far from being a weakness, is rather a source of strength, may help to relieve the desperate, hand-wringing flight from God of today's radical theologians.

Finally, biblical faith, as passed on in the traditions of the Church, is at the very foundations of Christian theology, whether as interpreted by the Fathers, Scholastics, or the Reformers.

Notes

1 See J. McKenzie, "Faith," Dictionary of the Bible (Milwaukee: Bruce Publishing Company, 1965), pp. 268f.

2 New Testament quotes from Revised Standard Version (Camden, New Jersey: Thomas Nelson & Sons, 1965).

3 Around the time of Paul the necessity of circumcising proselytes was disputed. Hellenistic Jews of the diaspora would admit Gentiles as full proselytes after the baptism of regeneration by living water. Palestinian Jews, however, would not admit them without circumcision. It would seem that some of the Palestinian

zealots may have been the Judaizers preaching circumcision to the Galatians.

4 See S. Lyonnet, "St. Paul: Liberty and Law, " TD, XI (Spring, 1963), 12-18. Much of this section on Law relies on this article.

5 Ibid., p. 15.

6 Ibid., p. 18.

7 "The Function of pistis christou in Galatians, " JBL, LXXXV (March, 1966), 58-76. Much of this section on "The Inheritance" relies on Dr. Taylor's article.

8 R. Bultmann, Theology of the New Testament (New York: Charles Scribner's Sons, 1965), I, 324. The theme of the rest of this section relies on Bultmann.

9 Ibid., p. 327f.

10 "Faith, " DB (Milwaukee: Bruce Publishing Company, 1965), p. 269.

11 Bultmann, Theology of the New Testament, p. 316. This section on the virtues related to faith relies on section 35, "The Structure of Faith, " pp. 314-24.

12 Ibid., p. 318.

13 Ibid., p. 320.

14 Ibid., p. 321.

15 Ibid., p. 322.

16 Ibid., p. 39.

17 Ibid., p. 330.

18 Bultmann, Theology of the New Testament, II, 70-71.

19 St. John's Gospel, A Commentary (Oxford: Clarendon Press, 1956), pp. 25-26.

20 A. Wikenhauser, New Testament Introduction (New York: Herder and Herder, Inc., 1963), p. 313.

21 Interpretation of the Fourth Gospel (New York: Cambridge University Press, 1953), p. 130.

22 Bultmann, Theology of the New Testament, II, 75.

23 Ibid.

24 Ibid., p. 76.

25 Ibid.

26 T. Barrosse, "The Relationship of Love to Faith in St. John, " TS, XVIII (December, 1957), 559.

27 St. John's Gospel, A Commentary, p. 25.

28 Ibid.

29 Dodd, Interpretation of the Fourth Gospel, pp. 151ff.

30 Ibid., p. 152.

31 Ibid., p. 152.

32 Ibid., p. 165.

33 Ibid., p. 169.

34 Ibid., p. 177.

35 Ibid., p. 178.

36 Ibid., p. 186.

37 Ibid., pp. 195, 196.

38 Ibid.

39 Ibid., p. 197.

40 "Pauline and Johannine Theology: a Contrast," CC, XIII (Summer, 1965), 339-53.

41 Ibid., p. 353.

42 Ibid., p. 351.

43 Ibid.

CHAPTER III

Thinking with assent

FAITH AND REASON IN AUGUSTINE[1]

The place of Augustine in the development of Western theology is undisputed. In fact, he has been called the first and last of the great Latin Doctors of antiquity. An area of current interest is Augustine's contribution to Western theology of faith. In Augustine's theology we find a point of union between East and West, for it was Augustine who took Neo-Platonism, sprung from Alexandria, and incorporated it into Western Christian thought. Both Origen, father of Eastern theology, and Plotinus, father of Neo-Platonism, had studied in Alexandria under the great Ammonius Saccas in the third century. Perhaps in the affective, Neo-Platonic thought of Augustine we may find a source of union with the affective Eastern asceticism.

Augustine's Religious Experience

When we study Augustine's theology of faith, we see that it reflects his own religious experience, his search for the truth, and his conversion. Augustine, brilliant young student and educator, earnestly sought the truth through Manichaeism. Yet he was soon disillusioned by the ignorance of Faustus, whom he had admired from afar. Moreover, he soon tired of the scepticism of the Academics. It was in Neo-Platonism that Augustine was to find a line of thought that appealed to him as true. As Clement of Alexandria, Augustine, too, felt that there was some of God's truth in pagan authors.

It was the Neo-Platonists who inspired Augustine to begin his ascent to the Truth with the help of both a loving faith and reason.[2]

> After many centuries and much contention, a philosophy has finally been evolved which, in my opinion, is entirely true. It is not limited to this world, -- it reveals another, the intelligible world.[3]

Neo-Platonism gave Augustine his solution to the problem of evil, releasing him from the materialism of Manichaeism, and showing him that evil is really a privation of the good. Moreover, Neo-Platonism helped him to see the wisdom of the gospel approach to spirituality. Deeply impressed by the conversion of the Neo-Platonist, Victorinus, Augustine made his own voluntary, loving assent to Christ in 386 following the intellectual preparation of Neo-Platonism.[4]

Faith and Reason

The problem of faith and reason interested Augustine. He had sought the truth through reason, yet it was through reason enlightened by faith that he was to find it. Never separating faith and reason as has been done in more modern times, Augustine rather tried to penetrate by his understanding the Christian faith and to see the world and human life in the light of Christian wisdom.[5] Reason helps to bring a man to faith, and once a man has faith, reason aids him to penetrate the truths of faith. Based on his own experience, Augustine would say that reason helped him towards an understanding of what he believed, just as it had aided him on his way to faith.[6]

Augustine does not split man into the natural and supernatural, but treats him as he really is, that is, with a supernatural end. Augustine is always interested in man in his concrete relationship with God here and now. Perhaps we could describe the Christian philosophy of Augustine as man's rational contemplation of Christian revelation, faith seeking understanding.

Faith and reason aid each other in pursuit of Christian wisdom. Reason plays an important part in faith, for it is only a reasoning, thinking creature, such as man, who can believe. Understand in order to believe, believe in order to understand. Augustine explains the cooperation of faith and reason in man's conversion in one of his sermons.

> From one aspect he is right when he says, "May I understand in order to believe." And I am right when I say with the Prophet, "Believe in order that you may understand." We both speak the truth and agree. Therefore, understand in order that you may believe; believe in order that you may understand. Briefly I explain how we can accept each other's opinion without controversy. Understand my word in order that you may believe. Believe God's word in order that you may understand.[7]

Understand my word that you should believe. This is the reasonable affirmation of the authority upon which faith is based. Certainly the authoritative words and example of Ambrose and Victorinus led Augustine to belief, but not without God's guidance. Faith is reasonable, for no one believes any thing unless first he thinks it should be believed.[8]

Which comes first, faith or reason? As we have seen, Augustine did not clearly separate the two. Each aids the other on the road to beatitude.

> Therefore, it is reasonable that in great things which cannot be grasped, faith precedes reason. Of course, the reason, however small, which persuades this, antecedes faith.[9]

Reason somehow precedes faith, for only a rational man can believe. Man's intellect must be capable of accepting the reasonable authority on which faith is based.

> For unless a man understands something, he cannot believe God. Nevertheless, by the very faith by which he believes, he is restored that he may understand more.[10]

Reason and faith work together, faith perfecting reason, leading it to further understanding. By our faith, our eyes are opened so that reason purified by faith, can seek the truth.

Faith builds on reason, elevates it so that man may attain the heights of understanding and vision. In faith the divine object is unseen, yet the believer desires to see him, faith seeking understanding. Christ promised that those who believed in him would see.

> What does he promise to believers, brothers? You will
> know the truth. What? Had they not known it when the
> Lord spoke? If they did not know, how did they believe?
> We believe in order to know, we do not know in order to
> believe. What we will know, "Eye hath not seen . . ."
> (Is 64:4; 1C 2:9). What is faith, except to believe what
> you do not see. Truth is to see what you have believed.[11]

Faith is the necessary prelude to a partial understanding of re-vealed truths here below and the full vision of eternity.

Should we just accept revelation on faith alone without in any way seeking to understand what we believe? Augustine answers:

> Then you must revise your rule, not indeed to the extent
> of throwing your faith over board, but to allow you to
> bring the light of reason to bear on what you already
> hold firmly by faith.[12]

Faith seeking understanding is a good epitome of Augustine's theology of faith. Faith, under the guidance of Christ, has a tension for understanding which will be complete only in the future vision.[13]

Is the faith of Augustine a prelude to understanding in the Manichaean sense, where the simple faith of the hearers was looked down upon as inferior to the superior gnōsis of the elect? Augustine's faith is a necessary prerequisite to under-standing, but it continues to work along with reason. Augustine's gnōsis is a cooperative effort of God and man. God further en-lightens the believer so that he can partially understand the re-vealed truths and eventually be united with Truth himself in the everlasting vision.

Thinking with Assent

Augustine, reflecting the rapport between faith and reason, describes the act of faith as "thinking with assent."

To believe is nothing more than to think with assent.
Not every one who thinks, believes, since many think
in order not to believe. But everyone who believes,
thinks. Believing, he thinks; and thinking, he be -
lieves.[14]

What is this "thinking" of Augustine? In his Trinity he describes
"thinking" as a restless turning over of things of the mind.[15]
Augustine's assent of faith, resembling that of Clement of Alexandria,[16] was not just an intellectual assent, but involved the
whole man in a judgment of the truth and goodness of the object.
So the affective power plays an important part in Augustine's
faith.

In Augustine's act of belief, the thinking precedes the assent.
This mirrors Augustine's own experience, for he thought long
and hard before he finally assented to Christ. However, the
thinking does not cease with the assent, but continues along with
it, using reason perfected by faith in order to search for the
understanding of the things believed. Both the intellectual and the
affective powers of man cooperate in Augustine's faith-quest for
the true and the good God.

Affective Faith

Augustine's whole theory of morality emphasized the affective
line, reflecting the gospels and the Neo-Platonists.[17] Love played
an important part in his conversion: "Late have I loved Thee."[18]
From his own life, Augustine knew that man can either turn away
from God to the love of creatures, or he can turn toward the good
God in loving faith. Through faith man seeks the beatifying vision
of Truth, but he seeks it willingly and rejoices in him in charity.[19]
In order for faith to be a virtue, it must somehow act in the order
of love.[20]

Following the Neo-Platonic line, Augustine taught the primacy
of the will in human knowledge. What is known cannot be divorced
from what is loved, since all cognition is somehow dependent
upon interest. Nothing is really fully known without the consent
of the will. Complete cognition lies with affection. Hence the
recognition of Christ through faith is primarily a movement of
the will. It is true that man's reason takes in and knows reality,
both eternal and temporal. But since reason is primarily passive
and neutral, it must be directed to recognize what it does recognize by the will. In Augustine it is the will which is corrupt and

48

needs cleansing by faith in order to command the recognition of Christ.[21]

God must be primarily in the will, not the intellect, for the intellect is under the will. In faith man conforms his will to God's. Without faith man does not recognize God because he does not love him. Men use the divine light for science, but do not recognize the light.[22] Blinded by their perverted wills, and refusing to submit to the inward illuminator, the Platonists turned outwards to nature in search of God. It was love and desire that they lacked, namely, the love and desire that turns diffused awareness into true cognition.[23]

Augustine saw clearly the function of love in his own conversion. Although his intellect had ample knowledge of the gospels, yet it was his will that was moved through the gift of faith. The noetic function of reason is dependent on the operation and direction of the practical and valuative reason, for theoretical reason and sensitive nature have predisposing affections.[24] In contrast with Aristotle for whom appetite follows intellect,[25] Augustine taught that in knowledge as well as in faith, love precedes.[26] So man's awareness of God cannot pass to knowledge without desire.[27] However, since man's will is perverse, he turns from the divine light to creatures illuminated by the light. There follows an immoderate love of the senses, pride, and self-love.

Christ enlightens man, healing his sick will. Curing man's blindness, he awakens him so that he can recognize God. Freeing man from inordinate love of material things and from self-love, Christ moves his will through faith so that man can love the Good of which he was aware without acknowledging it. Thus humbled and purified by faith, man consents to the Truth and the Good.[28]

If one wants to understand correctly the sense of faith seeking understanding in Augustine, he should see how charity, or love, plays an important part in each aspect of inquiring faith. Man's reason seeking understanding, seeking greater purity and union with God, is voluntarily subordinated to him and in charity rejoices in him.[29]

Augustine taught a three-fold belief, namely: to believe God, (credere Deo), to believe God (credere Deum), and to believe in God (credere in Deum). The first is to believe that God speaks the truth, the second is to believe that he is God. The third is to love him.[30] It is in the third part of the three-fold credere that the living, loving faith of the believer is found.

Commenting on John 6:29, "This is the work of God, that you believe in him whom he has sent," Augustine writes that not every one who believes God believes in him. For example, the demons believed him, but did not believe in him. "What is to believe in him? Believing, to love, believing, to prize him highly; believing, to go to him and be incorporated in his members."[31] This is the faith acting through love described by the Apostle (Gal 5:6). The difference between the faith of the unholy people and that of the elect is love.[32] Augustine in one of his sermons exhorts his hearers to charity rather than to faith, for if they have charity and love, they will have faith.[33] For Augustine to believe in Christ is the belief of supernatural love, charity.

Light of Faith

Augustine taught an illumination theory of knowledge, rooted in Christian tradition and reflecting Plato and Plotinus. It is the divine light in whom and by whom and through whom all those things which are luminous to the intellect become luminous.[34] For Plotinus the One, God, was the transcendent light, illuminating the minds of men. Augustine's theory of divine illumination is a theory of intuition of direct, immediate contact and participation in the divine light.[35]

Why did Augustine demand divine illumination? Because the human mind is changeable and temporal and needs help to see the unchangeable and eternal truths.[36] Only Changeless Truth himself can illuminate us so that we can see. The divine light enables us to see the relationship of temporal things to the eternal truths. By it we can see the true meaning of creation, the world sustained, sanctified, and recreated by the Word Incarnate, in whose image it was made.[37]

Augustine compared the divine illumination of the soul to the light of the sun in the visible world. The sun, created facsimile of the divine light, shines on the visible world, enabling the eye to see. In a similar manner, God enlightens the mind, the eye of the soul, with an incorporeal light.[38]

Can man make use of this divine light outside of faith? Yes, he must in order to perceive the eternal truths. So the Platonists used the divine light, but they did not recognize it as divine light. Truly there is a vast gulf between being enlightened by God, and acknowledging the light. God is used by many, but only recognized by the few who go within themselves to discover the source of the light, the author and exemplar of the world, the Word Incarnate. It is only by faith that we can recognize the divine light and seek the beatifying union with the source of the light.

Augustine taught the purifying effects of the divine light, reflecting the gospels and Plotinus.[39] The sick mind, the eye of the soul loving the darkness, is healed by the light of faith which cleanses it of earthly desires.[40] As in Plotinus, so in Augustine the purification line is the reverse of the illumination line, culminating in union with the One, the Good, the source of the light. In Augustine illumination and purification seem to be simultaneous for man is purified by the divine light. As the light is intensified, man is drawn into union with the source of the light. Union can be temporary as in mystical experiences or eternal in the next life. The purification, illumination, union line of Plato, Plotinus, and Augustine led the way for future developments in mystical theology.[41]

It is the healing light of faith that begins man's road to union and vision.

> Faith precedes reason, it cleanses the heart that it may
> bear the light of greater reason. Therefore, it is reason-
> ably said by the Prophet, "Unless you believe, you will
> not understand" (Is 7:9). In discerning these two, he
> meant that we believe so that we may be able to under-
> stand that which we believe.[42]

Belief is a necessary prelude to the partial understanding on earth and the full vision of eternity. With his mind purified by faith, man is free to go on to vision and union with divine Truth.

> Unless we walk by faith, we shall not be able to reach
> that vision which passes not, but abides, that vision which
> comes from our being fastened to truth by a purified mind.[43]

Eschatology of Faith

Faith begins our ascent to the Truth which culminates in beatifying union. Augustine, following the lead of Scriptures, taught an eschatological faith. Quoting the Epistle to the Hebrews, he wrote of faith as the assurance of the things to be hoped for and the conviction of things not yet seen.[44] Augustine clearly taught the rapport between faith and vision. Faith is as the foundation of a house, or the root of a tree. The beautiful tree

of beatitude grows from the humble root of faith.[45] Although
the foundation of a house and the root of a tree are not pleasing
to the eye, yet they have a necessary rapport with their more
attractive fulfillment. So humble faith is the foundation, the
beginning of eternal life. It is the root which will flower into
beatitude.

Confessions: Story of Faith

Augustine's Confessions give us a good meditative account of
his own faith history and conversion. When he wrote, "Understand
in order to believe; believe in order to understand," he may well
have been thinking of himself and how he had studied Plotinus and
read the gospels and listened to Ambrose, Alpius, and Nebridius.
"Understand in order to believe." After his conversion, he sought
understanding through faith. "Believe in order to understand."
Augustine himself experienced the way of purgation, illumination, and union. With God's help he was cleansed from sin and from
earthly desires. By the grace of God, he experienced a conversion, with the purifying light drawing him towards union with the
source of the light, the one, true, and good God.
The I-Thou theme of the Confessions illustrates Augustine's
striving for union. "You have made us for yourself, and our
heart is restless until it rests in you."[46] Since his faith represented security of mind and heart for which he had struggled so
long, he now felt the need to communicate his experience to
others seeking the same beatitude.[47]

The Law of Works and the Law of Faith

Although in his earlier works he had emphasized the part of
man in the act of faith, in his later anti-Pelagian writings
Augustine stressed man's total dependence on God for the gift
of faith rather than on his own efforts. In his On the Spirit and
the Letter (412) Augustine is strongly Pauline in opposing the
law of faith to the law of boastful works. Man is justified "not
by the law of works, but by the law of faith; not by the letter,
but by the spirit; not by merits of deeds, but by free grace"
(c.22). Man's righteousness is entirely from God, for if it is
by the works of law, Christ died in vain. By our faith in Jesus
Christ we obtain our salvation, both as it is begun within us
and insofar as its fulfillment is awaited in hope (c.51). Let the
fearful soul flee to the mercy of God, whose grace through the

Holy Spirit causes the soul to delight in his teaching more than in that which opposes (c.51). Man's will to believe is entirely from God who aids him both internally and externally.

In his Predestination of the Saints (428-429) Augustine answered the Semi-Pelagians, insisting that even the beginning of faith is of God, for "what have you that you have not received" (I Cor 4:7). Man is not justified by his own good works but by faith, for "faith itself is given first, from which may be obtained other things, which are especially characterized as works in which man may live righteously" (c.12). Although Cornelius gave alms and prayed before he believed in Christ, he could not have done this without some faith, for the Lord not only builds the spiritual edifice, but also digs the foundation (c.12).

Surely all deserve condemnation; therefore, the gift of faith to any one is from God's bountiful mercy and should be received with gratitude. Why God predestines some and not others is his own secret. This we know: the elect are not chosen because they have believed, but in order that they might believe. "You have not chosen me, but I have chosen you" (Jn 15:16). Before the beginning of the world, God predestined those whom he would elect: "Thus God elected believers, but he chose them that they might be so, not because they were already so" (c.34).

Summary of Augustine's Theology of Faith

Augustine's whole life had been a search for the Truth, first as a student of Manichaeism, then as an Academic and as a Neo-Platonist. But it was only through faith that he was to find Christ, God's begotten Truth, the cause and exemplar of all true things.

Augustine taught the close rapport between faith and reason: "Understand in order to believe, believe in order to understand." Faith leads the way to an understanding of the things that we believe. Yet somehow reason precedes faith, for one must understand something in order to believe. Faith is "thinking with assent" in which reason strives to see the unseen Truth, while at the same time giving firm assent.

Since the assent of faith is a willing one, unless a man's sick will is healed, he cannot turn from the love of creatures to the love of the Creator. It is the affective belief in God, inspired by charity that separates the believers from the unholy people.

Augustine's faith is a divine illumination reflecting the gospels and Neo-Platonism. Christ, God's Truth Incarnate, illumines the soul in the light of faith, purifying the heart that it may bear the light of greater reason, drawing the believer into union with the source of the light. By the divine light one can not only see the eternal truths, but also recognize the light as from God, and perceive in the world the reflections of the divine ideas according to which it was made. Far from separating man from the world, faith aids him to see its true image and end, divine Truth.

Finally, faith is all from God, not in any way due to man's good works. Even its beginning is from God who from all eternity has predestined the faithful, not because they have believed, but in order that they might believe.

Augustine's Influence in the Middle Ages

Medieval tracts on faith reflected Augustine strongly even after the trend towards Aristotle in the twelfth and thirteenth centuries. God as First Truth, revealing and revealed, and his Divine Son as Begotten Truth were frequent themes in medieval theology. Augustine's rapport between faith and reason, aiding each other in pursuit of the Truth, is echoed in Anselm's "faith seeking understanding."

Augustine's classical description of belief as "thinking with assent" is found in most medieval treatises on faith. Moreover, his Neo-Platonic illumination was popular especially in the early Middle Ages, developing into the light of faith as taught by William of Auxerre and Thomas Aquinas. Augustine's three-fold belief was discussed by most medieval theologians, who, as their mentor, had called loving belief in God faith in the fullest sense. Earlier theologians placed more emphasis on the affective nature of faith contrasting with Aquinas' more intellectual faith, reflecting Aristotle.

Ascetical theology in medieval times and later reflects the purification, illumination, and union of Augustine. This agrees with his basic eschatology in which faith has a rapport with vision and is the beginning of eternal life.

Even though Aquinas' theology of faith tends to emphasize the intellect as specified by First Truth, nevertheless, all of Augustine's teachings mentioned above can be found in Thomas' tract on faith, but with a mixture of Aristotelian epistemology.

Augustine's theology of faith can be a help to the ecumenical movement of today, for the faith of the Reformers is based strongly on Augustine, especially on his anti-Pelagian works.

54

As at Trent, so today Augustine must be at the foundation of serious discussion on faith, justification, and grace.

Notes

1 This chapter and the next first appeared in Speaking of God (Milwaukee: Bruce Publishing Company, 1967).
2 Against the Academics, 1.3, a.20, n.43, (PL 32, 957).
3 Ibid., 1.3, c.19, n.42, (PL 32, 956).
4 F. Copleston, A History of Philosophy, Vol. II, Medieval Philosophy, Pt. 1, Augustine to Bonaventure (Garden City, New York: Image Books, Doubleday & Company, Inc., 1962), pp. 56-57.
5 Ibid., p. 63.
6 Concerning the True Religion, c.24, n.45, (PL 34, 141).
7 Sermon 43, c.7, (PL 38, 258).
8 Predestination of the Saints, c.2, n.5, (PL 44, 963).
9 Epistle 120, c.1, n.3, (PL 33, 453-54).
10 On Psalm 118, c.18, n.3, (PL 37, 1552).
11 On John, tr. 40, n.9, (PL 35, 1690).
12 Epistle 120, c.1, n.2, (PL 33, 452).
13 On Free Choice, 1.2, c.2, (PL 32, 1243).
14 Predestination of the Saints, c.2, n.5, (PL 44, 963).
15 Trinity, 1/15, c.16, n.25, (PL 42, 1079). In his Confes-sions, (1.10, c.11, (PL 32, 787), he describes cogitatio as a bringing together (cogere) of things hidden in the memory.
16 Stromata, 7, 10, (PG 9, 481). See H. Wolfson, The Philosophy of the Church Fathers (Cambridge, Massachusetts: Harvard University Press, 1956), p. 129.
17 Copleston, A History of Philosophy, pp. 74, 94.
18 Confessions, 1.10, c. 27, n.38, (PL 32, 795).
19 On John, tr.26, n.44, (PL 35, 1607); tr. 29, n.6, (PL 35, 1631). Predestination of the Saints, c.5, (PL 44, 968).
20 Morals of the Catholic Church, 1.1, c.5, (PL 32, 1322).
21 See R. Cushman, "Faith and Reason in the Thought of Augustine," Church History, XIX (New York: AMS Press, Inc., 1950), p. 274.
22 Ibid., p. 285.
23 Trinity, 1.9, c.12, n.18, (PL 42, 970-71).
24 On John, tr.26, n.4, (PL 35, 608).
25 The Soul, 431a, 11; Metaphysics, 1072a, 30. See Cushman, "Faith and Reason in Augustine," p. 287.

26 Cushman, "Faith and Reason in Augustine," p. 288.

27 Trinity, 1.9, c.12, n.18, (PL 42, 970-71).

28 Trinity, 1.4, c.18, n.24, (PL 42, 904-05). See Cushman, "Faith and Reason in Augustine," p. 289.

29 See R. Holte, Beatitude et Sagesse, Saint Augustin et le probleme de la fin de l'homme dans la philosophie ancienne (Paris: Etudes Augustiniennes, 1962), p. 385.

30 Sermon on the Creed, (PL 40, 1190, 91). On Psalm 77, n.8, (PL 36, 988). On John, tr. 29, n.6, (PL 35, 1631).

31 On John, tr.29, c.7, n.6, (PL 35, 1631).

32 Sermon 158, c.6, (PL 38, 865).

33 Sermon 90, c.8, (PL 38, 564).

34 Soliloquies, 1.1, c.8, n.15, (PL 32, 878). City of God, 1.11, c.10. See also Copleston, History of Philosophy, p. 77.

35 See C. Schuetzinger, German Controversy on St. Augustine's Illumination Theory (New York: Pageant Press, Inc., 1960), p. 79. See also E. Gilson, Christian Philosophy of Saint Augustine (New York: Random House, Inc., 1960), pp. 79, 92. Also see R. Holte, Beatitude et Sagesse, pp. 313ff.

36 On Psalm 119, n.4, 5, (PL 37, 1600). Sermon 23, c.1, (PL 38, 155). See Copleston, History of Philosophy, p. 78.

37 City of God, 1.8, c.6, (PL 41, 231). Trinity, 1.12, c.14, n.22, (PL 32, 1009). See Cushman, "Faith and Reason in Augustine," pp. 277, 278.

38 Trinity, 1.12, c.15, (PL 42, 1011).

39 For example, John's Prologue; Luke 11:34-36; Plotinus, Enneads, 1.1, c.2, n.4-6.

40 Soliloquies, 1.1, c.14, n.25, (PL 32, 882). City of God, 1.11, c.2.

41 See J. Pieper, Scholasticism, tr. by R. and C. Winston (London: Faber and Faber, 1960), p. 51.

42 Epistle 120, c.1, n.3, (PL 33, 453).

43 Christian Doctrine, c.2, n.12, (PL 34, 43).

44 Enchiridion on Faith, Hope, and Charity, c.1, n.18, (PL 40, 235).

45 On John, tr. 40, c.8, n.8, (PL 35, 1690).

46 Confessions, 1.1, c.1, n.1, (PL 32, 661).

47 See A. Brunhumer, "The Heart of Augustine's Confessions," Thought, XXXVII (Spring, 1962), 126.

CHAPTER IV

The beginning of eternal life

THE DYNAMIC FAITH OF THOMAS AQUINAS

The theology of faith today emphasizes the personal, seeking refuge from the abstract, dialectical faith of the Scholastics. Faith today is a personal, existential, phenomenological re-lationship, the "I-Thou" rapprochement between man and God, right now, in man's own particular existential circumstances. Is the faith of Thomas Aquinas foreign to the "I-Thou" of Buber, the ultimate concern of Tillich, or the personal faith of Cirne-Lima? Really, the overly intellectual, dialectical, dessicated faith often attributed to Catholic tradition is not that of Thomas.[1]

When we examine the teachings of Thomas Aquinas, we find that, far from being abstract and sterile, he describes a living, existing faith in which man has a personal relationship with God, First Truth, here and now. It is the beginning of eternal life. The dynamism which begins in faith now will be perfected and completed in vision then.

Can Thomas' faith be called existential in any way at all? Certainly he wrote of a living, existing faith in which the hoped for things pre-exist in man here and now. However, to equate existence in Thomas' faith with the dasein of the existentialist might cause problems. Although Thomas speaks of an existing faith, he does not teach specifically of the faith of this or that concrete individual here and now. Although the faith of Thomas is an existing, living faith, it does abstract from individual existential circumstances, thus attaining a universal faith, applicable to all men in various times and circumstances. Existential faith, on the other hand, seems to stress the uniqueness of each man's faith-relationship with God.

Modern existential faith differs from that of Thomas Aquinas in another way, namely, in concentrating on the existential, personal, and subjective, it sometimes neglects the eschatological, the tension for vision, which is so essential to Thomas' faith. Faith for Thomas is not only a living, existing, personal relationship with First Truth, but also it has an essential rapport with vision. It is the real beginning of eternal life, the pre-existence and anticipation of beatitude, for which man continually strives under the guidance of a loving charity.

The Classical Description of Faith

It is perhaps in his study of the classical formula of faith from the Epistle to the Hebrews[2] that we can find the secret of Thomas' faith, for here is found faith's true, existential dynamism for vision, its fundamental rapport with beatitude. The classical formula states that faith is the substance (hypostasis) or assurance of the things to be hoped for. It is the evidence (elenchos) or conviction of the things unseen. Thomas follows tradition in calling faith the substance or the foundation of the whole spiritual life, just as light is the substance or basis of color.[3] In his De Veritate he explains faith as the substance of things to be hoped for insofar as it is the first beginning of these things. Just as the foundation of a house or the hull of a ship is the substance or the first beginning of the completed structure, so faith is the real beginning of and initial participation in eternal life.[4]

Since eternal life consists in a full knowledge of God, there must pre-exist in faith some initial participation in this knowledge. It is this pre-existence which is the beginning of eternal life.[5] The inchoative knowledge mirrored in the human mind by the light of faith contains, in an incipient way, the things to be hoped for as the conclusions of science are contained virtually in their principles.[6]

Thomas often compared man's rapport with God in faith to that of a student with his teacher.

> Hence, in order that a man arrive at perfect vision of
> heavenly happiness, he must first of all believe God,
> as a disciple believes the master who is teaching him.[7]

In the liberal sciences, the principles must first be learned from the teacher. In these principles the whole science is contained in a germinal manner, just as conclusions are contained in their premises and effects in their causes. Thus he who learns the principles of science from his teacher, has the substance of it. Similarly one who believes God, has the substance of the full knowledge of vision which is contained virtually in his faith.

So in Thomas' explanation of faith as the substance of the things to be hoped for, we see faith's existential eschatology expressed as the anticipated possession, the pre-existing proportion, the incipient knowledge of the things to be hoped for. In faith, the hoped for things somehow subsist in us now.[8]

In the second part of the classical formula, faith is seen as the evidence or conviction of the things unseen. It is a proof from the infallible authority of God. It is a foretaste of the full knowledge of vision as the foreward of a book is a prelude to what follows. This second part of the Hebrews' formula complements the first so that both together show the rapport of the will and the intellect with their divine object in the act of faith. Faith is both the substance and the conviction of the future vision of the unseen but hoped for divine object.[9]

Thomas' Formula

Thomas took the Hebrews' description and expressed it in his own words, calling faith "the habit of the mind whereby eternal life is begun in us, making the intellect assent to those things which are not apparent."[10] Eternal life begins in us now with the habit of faith. Here is expressed concisely the existential and eschatological dynamism of Thomas' faith. Eternal life begins in us now and will be perfected and completed in the vision of beatitude.

Thomas frequently describes faith as a praelibatio or a fore-taste of vision.[11] This seems to indicate the savorous knowledge of the virtue of faith, the firm foundation of the spiritual edifice.[12] The knowledge of God, then, that we have through our faith is a

59

foretaste, a prelude, an anticipation, a guarantee, a beginning, a pre-existing proportion of that in which we will fully participate in vision.

First Truth

If faith is the beginning of eternal life, then the direct object of faith should be that whereby man is made one of the blessed. The divine object takes the prime place in Thomas' theology of faith, for it is First Truth who specifies the supernaturality of the act and habit of faith. Moreover, it is First Truth who determines that faith reside in the speculative intellect.[13] It is fitting that both faith and beatitude consist primarily in speculation, for the one is the beginning of the other. Thomas' theology of beatitude in contemplation is based on Aristotle.[14] The placing of faith in the speculative intellect ties faith in with beatitude and also gives Thomas' theology of faith an intellectual slant, although he gave an important place to the will, insisting that faith resided in the speculative intellect only insofar as it is moved by the will.[15]

Thomas teaches an object-centered faith. Following Aristotle, he describes the importance of the object in specifying the acts and habits.[16] It is the divine object, First Truth, who determines or specifies the supernatural nature of the act and habit of faith. He is not merely a passive object, but actively invites man to believe and enlightens his faith.

First Truth is the object and medium of our faith. The Old Testament tells us that Israel believed and relied upon Yahweh because he was true to his promises. He is the true God. Following this tradition, passed on by the Fathers and Theologians, Thomas calls First Truth--the true God, the exemplar and cause of all things that are true--the medium of our faith. He is the whole reason of our faith. He reveals himself to us and we know that he cannot lie. Upon this our faith is based. Credimus Deo. We believe God, First Truth, revealing.[17]

Nothing comes under a power, habit, or act, unless through the medium of the formal reason of the object, (mediante ratione formali objecti).[18] In faith, First Truth is the formal reason of the object; it is because of him that we believe.

Accordingly, if in faith we consider the formal reason of the object, it is nothing else than First Truth, for the faith

of which we are speaking does not assent to anything except because it is revealed by God.[19]

First Truth is the very medium of our faith.

Although we are led to creatures by reason of First
Truth, through it we are led mainly to First Truth, itself,
since it gives witness primarily about itself. So in faith
First Truth acts as medium and object.[20]

It is because of the infallibility of First Truth[21] that we give our
firm and certain assent of faith.[22]

It is First Truth who invites us and enlightens our way to
belief. The interior help of First Truth is the key to the dynamism
of Thomas' faith, for here First Truth specifies the act and habit
of faith, the habit of faith perfecting the intellect and acting as the
supernatural principle of the acts.

Thomas called First Truth's interior help in the act of faith,
the interior instinct, the divine calling, invitation, and motion.
It is Christ, First Truth, who invites, teaches, and illumines
man through the interior instinct,[23] which is more important than
external helps such as miracles and preaching.[24] The interior
instinct to believe seems to be something more than the habit of
faith, namely, whatever divine aid inclines man to believe.[25]
It is an interior speaking, inviting, whereby the unseen First
Truth calls man to himself.[26]

Following the gospels, the Fathers, especially Augustine, and
the Theologians, Thomas also called First Truth's interior help
the light of faith. Is the light of faith the same as the interior
instinct to believe? Thomas seemed to indicate a close link between the two.[27] In faith First Truth not only invites man to
believe, but also illumines his mind so that he can give a firm
assent to First Truth, even though he is unseen. He enlightens
man's intellect, stamps it with his seal, specifying the act of
faith as of and towards First Truth.[28]

The light of faith is really the habit of faith, itself,[29] illuminating the articles.[30] Yet even with this interior help,
man still does not see perfectly, not because of any defect in
the divine light, but rather because of man's imperfect participation in the light.[31] The light of faith does not destroy the
natural light, but rather strengthens it,[32] elevating man so that
he can see in a concrete manner that it is good here and now to
believe God.[33] Moreover, the light of faith helps man to see the

dynamic eschatology of faith, so that he can tend towards the vision of First Truth, and, understanding this tendency, he may adhere simply in First Truth through an assent proportioned to the dignity of God revealing. The light of faith for Thomas is the very habit of faith, conferring on the assent of faith the high-est firmness of adhesion, superior to that of natural certitude.[34]

Man of himself is insufficient to assent to the unseen and transcendent First Truth. He needs the help of First Truth to aid his assent by inviting and illuminating him interiorly so that he can adhere imperfectly in the unseen First Truth through faith in order to adhere in him perfectly in vision.

As in Thomas' discussion of the classical formula of faith, so also in his explication of the divine object, First Truth, the existential and eschatological dynamism of faith is evident. It is the same First Truth who is both the unseen object of faith here and now and who will be the seen object of beatitude. He it is who reveals himself to man externally and internally invites and enlightens man towards eternal life through faith.

Thinking with Assent

It is the inward invitation of the unseen First Truth which provides the act of faith with its eschatological drive, for the very heart of the act is a ceaseless striving to see the divine object. Augustine described the act of faith as thinking with assent, in which man, despite his firm assent, still thinks, seeking to understand the hidden mysteries of faith.[35] Thinking with assent is both existential and eschatological. What could be more existential than the act of thinking and what could be more eschatological than the dynamic striving for vision of the discursive thought of faith?

The thinking of the act of faith is not scientific thought which is the cause of the assent and ceases once the assent has been given. No, it is a discursive thought which perdures along with the firm assent. Faith is, in a sense, a medium between two thoughts. One inclines the will to believe, and this precedes faith. The other tends to the understanding of those things which it believes, and this is along with the assent of faith.[36]

The intellect does not rest satisfied in faith, it still thinks discursively and inquires about the things it believes even though its assent to them is unwavering. Since the understanding is dis-satisfied and terminated from without, a movement directly op-posite to what the believer holds firmly can arise.[37] The thinking of Faith is the movement of the soul while yet deliberating and not yet perfected by the clear vision of truth.[38]

The discursive thought of faith will remain restless and dis- satisfied until it can see First Truth in beatitude. This is an integral part of faith, distinguishing it from science and under- standing where the intellect rests satisfied; whereas the firm assent of faith clearly separates it from doubt and opinion.[39] Since the object is unseen, the intellect remains dissatisfied, for the intellect is made to see.[40] Thus our intellectual operation in faith remains imperfect.[41] Moreover, this imperfect knowl- edge is essential to our faith.[42]

But why does not God give man perfect knowledge of himself here below? Is this not a defect on God's part? The imperfect knowledge of faith is not due to any defect on the part of God, rather the fault lies in man whose weakened intellect cannot participate perfectly in God's knowledge here below. Discon- tented with this imperfect knowledge of faith, man restlessly strives to see the unseen object. Here is the kinetic eschatology of Thomas' faith, namely, the discursive thought ceaselessly yearning for vision. Through his faith, the beginning of eternal life, man seeks the full knowledge of beatitude, the perfection of eternal life.

While the intellect is assenting to the unseen First Truth, at the same time, urged on by the will, it strives earnestly for vision. So the act of faith is more than an intellectual assent. It is an affective knowledge, for in belief the will sustains, vivifies and informs faith by love.

Charity Perfects the Dynamism of Faith

After having discussed the object and act of faith in his Summa,[43] Thomas goes on to explain the habit of faith, the principle of the acts.[44] It is in the virtuous habit of faith, formed by charity, that we find the perfection of faith's eschatological dynamism, for it is charity which gives to the virtue of faith its perfect direction to beatitude.

In the act of faith, First Truth draws man to himself, man's in- tellect assenting at the command of the will. Yet the will must be rectified, perfected by charity in order to command the assent of faith and to direct it in a perfect manner towards the final vision. Charity rectifies the will in faith and in beatitude and thus serves as an effective and affective link between faith and vision.[45]

Charity informs the dynamism of faith, the loving will urging the intellect towards God (in Deum), in a perfect manner. Augustine describes this belief in God (credere in Deum) as a loving faith, accompanied by charity.[46] Besides that of charity, there is another élan which does not proceed from this virtue and which alone is essential to faith, for if the intellect is to assent, it must be moved by the will.

This initial affection for God in faith Thomas calls "a certain appetite for the promised good,"[47] distinguishing it from charity, which is a perfect and disinterested tendency. Credere in Deum for Thomas is not only that which is essential to faith and pertains to the will; it is also the virtue of charity perfecting the dynamism of faith in its proper movement towards its divine end.[48]

The initial movement of the will in faith, credere in Deum, is perfected by charity, the form of the virtues. In his theology of the virtue of faith, Thomas follows his teachings on the virtues in general, namely, that charity informs the acts of all the supernatural virtues, orientating them in a perfect manner to their last end. Without charity, these acts do not have their God-ward direction except in an incipient and imperfect manner. This ordination to the end is the form of the acts for form directs to end. The will initiates all moral acts and the object and quasi-form of the will is the will's end. In moral acts that which gives an act its order to an end, also gives it its form. Since charity gives form and direction to the acts of the other virtues, it gives form to them by applying them to its end.[49]

Charity acts in a similar manner towards the virtue of faith, informing the acts and ordering them to its end.[50] Thomas calls charity a kind of exemplary form[51] or an effective form of faith,[52] giving the acts of faith their perfect God-direction towards beatitude.[53] It is this dynamic faith, formed by charity, that is the foundation of the whole spiritual edifice culminating in glory.[55]

Personal Faith

Thomas' faith is dynamic in its definition, object, act, and formation. It is both an existential and an eschatological faith insofar as it is the real beginning of eternal life here and now. However, is not the faith of Thomas abstract and desiccated? Even the terminology smacks of the dialectic: substance, things to be hoped for, First Truth, formal object, act, habit, form. Medieval theologians have been accused of depersonalizing faith in their attempts to analyze it. Father Aubert writes that the Scholastics tended to emphasize the global aspect of faith so that faith became not so much a rapport between this single believer and God, but rather a collective relationship between the Church and God.[56]

Thomas Aquinas, too, has been accused of depersonalizing faith. It is true that Thomas took an object view of faith; it is true also that he abstracted from experiential circumstances in order to obtain a universal faith. Nevertheless, since he based his teachings on Scriptures and the Fathers, perhaps it would be within his mind to interpret some of his faith doctrine in a personalistic manner,[57] being careful not to interpret his writings according to problems that are more in common with our own times than with his.

Some would feel that the act of faith today is more of a personal decision for Christ than it was in medieval times. However, although Thomas analyzed faith in an abstract way, nevertheless, in the background is always the personal union between God and man. Thomas' faith is fundamentally a living, believing, experiential faith.

The personal God reveals himself to man and is believed. "Hence faith which through assent unites man to divine knowledge, has God as its principle object and everything else as a subsequent addition."[58] So the principle place in belief should go to the person to whom assent is given; secondary are the things that he reveals for our belief.[59] These revealed truths of faith come to us from God, who alone can see the divine secrets and teach them to us.[60] The personal God reveals himself to man because he loves him. Why then is the revelation obscure? Not because of a lack of love on God's part, but rather because of the weakness of man's intellect.

The object of faith, then, is a personal being, who is both truth and beatitude,[61] foreshadowing the personal beatific union of glory. Thomas' First Truth is not an abstract truth, but a subsistent Truth, personal God, under the title or aspect of First Truth. He is both the cause and the object of belief, inviting man to believe and illuminating him so that he can firmly assent and adhere in the unseen First Truth as the formal object of his faith.[62]

Thomas' faith is interpersonal. The divine Person reveals himself and the human person believes. In the background of Thomas' tract on faith it is man, the person, who is the principle of his acts, directing them freely towards his last end.[63] The whole man believes, not just his intellect and will. In the intercommunion of faith, love and knowledge are, in a sense, one, for both are essential acts of a person giving himself to God. As in the Hebrew "Amen," the whole man believes.

In revelation a personal, loving God gives his innermost secrets to man, who through his faith can enter into the privacy of the transcendent God. Man, the person, believes the personal God, who reveals himself to him. Thus faith is an interpersonal relationship between God and man similar to the personal exchange between a teacher and his student.[64]

Although the faith of Thomas Aquinas is not personal in the modern existential sense, nor does it stress the preconceptual intuition of the phenomenologists, it is, nevertheless, analogous to and compatible with today's developments in the theology of personal faith.

But is not Thomas' faith too intellectual? This was a criticism leveled by the Reformers. Even a casual look at the act of faith as taught by Thomas reveals the importance of the affective power, for it is only at the command of the will that the intellect assents.[65] Perhaps an ecumenical bridge between the "affective," more personal, faith of the Reformers with its Augustinian background and the "intellectual" faith of Catholics with its Thomistic roots can be found in a correct interpretation of both Augustine and Aquinas. In the writings of each of these giants can be found the importance of both the affective and the intellectual powers, moved and enlightened by God in faith. Certainly both would agree that fundamentally it is the person, who, using his faculties and inspired by divine grace, believes God.

Although Augustinian, Aquinas' faith is also Aristotelian so that the Reformers felt that in man's justification too much emphasis was placed on his cooperation and not enough on God's bountiful graces.[66] However in his tract on justification (ST 1-2, q. 113), Thomas leaves little doubt that in justification, not only grace but also faith is of God.

Finis

In conclusion, then, Thomas Aquinas teaches a dynamic faith, in which, drawn on by the interior invitation of the unseen First Truth, man gives firm assent and at the same time strives restlessly to see him. This basic dynamism, perfected by charity, a foretaste of beatitude, will never be satiated till man achieves the vision of and personal union with First Truth in eternal life, of which faith is the beginning and the anticipated possession.

1 For a fuller treatment of faith in St. Thomas, see The Beginning of Eternal Life, The Dynamic Faith of Thomas Aquinas (New York: Philosophical Library, Inc., 1968).

2 Hebrews 11, 1.

3 3S, d. 23, a. 1, ad 1.

4 DV, q. 14, a. 2.

5 Ibid.

6 In Hebr. 11, 1.

7 ST 2-2, q. 2, a. 3. Also: 3S, d. 23, q. 2, a. 1, s. 4; DV, q. 14, a. 10, 11; SCG, c. 152; In Hebr. 11, 1; ST 2-2, q. 4, a. 1, In Jn. c. 5, 1. 4, n. 5.

8 For further discussion of the eschatology of faith in Hebrews, see C. Spicq, L'épître aux Hébreux (Paris: Gabalda, 1953), pp. 336 ff; E. Grasser, Der Glaube im Hebraerbrief, Marburg (Marburger Theologische Studien, 2), Elwert, 1965, pp. 171-84.

9 DV, q. 14, a. 2; In Hebr. 11, 1; ST 2-2, q. 4, a. 1.

10 Ibid.

11 3S, d. 23, q. 2, a. 1, ad 4; DV, q. 14, a. 2, ad 9; CT, c. 1; SCG 4, c. 54; In Jn. c. 15, 1.3, n. 3.

12 In Jn. c. 3, 1. 3; In 1 Cor. c. 3, 1. 2.

13 ST 2-2, q. 4, a. 2, ad 3.

14 ST 1-2, q. 3, a. 5. Aristotle, Nic. Eth. 1. 10, c. 7, n. 9, (1178a, b). See D. Emmet, "Theoria and the Way of Life," JTS, XVII (April, 1966), 38-52.

15 ST 1-2, q. 56, a. 3; De Vir. q. 1, a. 7; DV q. 14, a. 4, ST 1-2, q. 57, a. 1.

16 ST 1-2, q. 18, a. 2; q. 54, a. 1, 2, 3. Aristotle, Politica, 3, 4, 2, (1276b, 31); Nic. Eth. 7, 8, 4, (1151a, 16); Meta, 5, 20, (1022b).

17 ST 2-2, q. 2, a. 2; also 3S, d. 23, q. 23, q. 2, a. 2, q. 2; DV q. 14, a. 7.

18 ST 2-2, q. 1, a. 3; q. 8, a. 3, ad 2.

19 In Boeth. de Trin. q. 3, a. 1, ad 4.

20 DV, q. 14, a. 8, ad 9.

21 ST 2-2, q. 2, a. 2; q. 4, a. 5, ad 2.

22 DV, q. 10, a. 12, ad 6.

23 3S, d. 23, q. 2, a. 2, s. 3; Qdl. 2, q. 2, a. 1, ad 3; In Jn. c. 6, 1. 5, n. 3.

24 ST 2-2, q. 10, a. 1, ad 1.

25 In Jn. c. 6, 1. 4, n. 7.

26 See J. Alfaro, "Supernaturalitas Fidei Iuxta S. Thomam,

II: Functio "Interioris Instinctus,'" Greg. XLIV (1963), 765-66.
   27 Qdl. 2, q. 4, a. 1, ad 3; In Boeth de Trin. 1, q. 1, a. 1,
ad 4. Father Alfaro, "Supernaturalitas fidei," calls the interior
instinct an actual motion of faith which proceeds from the habit.
It is the infused habitual inclination in second act, p. 763.
   28 Qdl. 2, a. 6, ad 3; In Boeth de Trin. 1, q. 1, a. 1, ad 4.
   29 3S, d. 23, q. 2, a. 1; In Boeth de Trin. 1, q. 1, a. 1,
ad 4.
   30 1S, prol.; q. 1, a. 3, q. 3, s. 2.
   31 DV, q. 14, a. 1, ad 5.
   32 ST 1, q. 12, a. 13.
   33 ST 2-2, q. 1, a. 5, ad 1.
   34 Alfaro, "Supernaturalitas fidei," p. 542.
   35 De Praedestinatione Sanctorum, c. 2, n. 5, (PL 44, 962).
   36 3S, d. 23, q. 2, a. 2, s. 1, ad 2.
   37 DV, q. 14, a. 1.
   38 ST 2-2. q. 2, a. 1.
   39 3S, d. 23, q. 2, a. 2, s. 1; DV, q. 14, a. 1; ST 2-2,
q. 2, a. 1.
   40 DV, q. 14, a. 1, ad 5; ST 2-2, q. 2, a. 3.
   41 SCG 3, c. 40.
   42 ST 1-2, q. 67, a. 3.
   43 ST 2-2, q. 1-3.
   44 Ibid., q. 4.
   45 Ibid., 1-2, q. 4, a. 4.
   46 In Jn., tr. 29, c. 7, n. 6, (PL 35, 1631).
   47 DV, q. 14, a. 2, ad 10; ST 2-2, q. 4, a. 7; q. 5, a. 2, ad
2.
   48 At times Thomas seems to identify credere in Deum with
formed faith: DV, q. 28, a. 4, ad 6; In Jn. c. 1, 1. 15; c. 6, 1.
13; In Rom. c. 4, 1. 2. However, in the Summa, he writes that
credere in Deum signifies the intellect as moved by the will in
the act of faith: ST 2-2, q. 2, a. 2. See J-M. Parent, "La signi-
fication du 'credere in deum' chez saint Thomas," ER, IX (1955),
149-55.
   49 ST 2-2, q. 23, a. 8, De Caritate, a. 3.
   50 3S, d. 23, q. 3, a. 1, q. 1; DV, q. 14, a. 5; ST 2-2, q. 4,
a. 3.
   51 DV, q. 14, a. 5.
   52 ST 2-2, q. 23, a. 8, ad 1.
   53 ST 1-2, q. 67, a. 6.
   54 3S, d. 23, q. 1, a. 1, ad 4; DV, q. 14, a. 2, ad 9; CT,
1; SCG 4, c. 54; In Jn. c. 15, 1. 3, n. 3.

55 <u>ST</u> 2-2, q. 4, a. 7, ad 4; also 1-2, q. 89, a. 2, ad 2; <u>In Jn</u>. c. 3, 1. 3.

56 R. Aubert, "Le caractère raisonnable de l'acte de foi chez les théologiens de la fin du XIIIe siècle," <u>RHE</u> XXXIX (1943), 22-99.

57 R. Aubert, <u>Le problème de l'acte de foi</u> (Paris: Warny, 1958), p. 622. Father Copleston in his <u>Contemporary Philosophy</u>, p. 104 (London: Burns and Oates, 1963), reminds us that "person" did not mean the same for medieval scholastics as it does for modern thinkers.

For the Scholastics "person" was the equivalent of human being, at least when applied to man. "For them (moderns) it (person) has a moral connotation and denotes what a medieval philosopher might have thought of a person who not only exists as a person, but also lives, acts, and chooses as a person, that is, in a way fitting a person." See Chapter IX, Part 2, for . Jean Mouroux' interpretation of Thomas' personal faith.

58 <u>DV</u>, q. 14, a. 8.

59 <u>ST</u> 2-2, q. 11, a. 1.

60 <u>SCG</u> 3, c. 154; <u>ST</u> 2-2, q. 6, a. 1.

61 <u>ST</u> 2-2, q. 5, a. 1.

62 The three-fold <u>credere</u> illustrates well the interpersonal relationship of faith. <u>Credo Deo</u>, I believe the personal God, First Truth, revealing. <u>Credo Deum</u>, I believe him as revealed. <u>Credo In Deum</u>, I believe in God, willingly assent to him. <u>ST</u> 2-2, q. 2, a. 2.

63 <u>ST</u> 1, q. 1; 1-2, prol; 2-2, q. 11.

64 <u>ST</u> 2-2, q. 2, a. 3.

65 <u>3S</u>, d. 23, q. 2, s. 1; <u>DV</u>, q. 14, a. 1, 4: <u>De Virt</u>. a. 7; <u>ST</u> 2-2, q. 1, a. 4; q. 2, a. 1, ad 3.

66 See R. Fife, <u>The Revolt of Martin Luther</u> (New York: Columbia University Press, 1957), p. 158.

CHAPTER V

Justification by grace through faith

FAITH IN THE REFORMATION

By the time of the Reformation, medieval scholasticism was fading fast. The Nominalists, distrusting the abstract universal terminology of the Scholastics, taught that since universals were only names, the concrete individual is what really matters. William of Ockham in the fourteenth century rejected the use of reason in matters of faith, an attitude popular with the Reformers, who, however, did not accept Ockham's teaching that man could of himself prepare the way for God's saving grace. Besides Nominalism, mysticism, with its personal experience of God, and Renaissance humanism, stressing the individual, rather than the institution, helped towards the dissolution of the medieval synthesis.[1] Against the Pelagian-like Nominalism, a new wave of Augustinianism arose, stressing man's helplessness and his complete dependence on God.

The Renaissance Church was badly in need of reform. Clerical and worldly, its princes were often civil rulers as well. Although there had been earlier attempts at reform, it was Martin Luther,

Augustinian monk and scripture scholar, who brought matters to a head by his teachings against the sale of indulgences. Inspired by the Psalms, Paul's Epistle to the Romans, and Augustine's On the Spirit and Letter, and reacting against the "good-work" oriented Church, and also the Nominalists, Luther taught a justification by the grace of God, experienced through faith alone. His treatises on faith, more scriptural in tone, lacked the abstract terminology of the medieval tracts. Moreover, his emphasis on the strength of God and the weakness of man in justification echoes Augustine in whose Anti-Pelagian works he saw the perfect interpretation of Paul.

JUSTIFICATION BY GRACE THROUGH FAITH[2]

Luther's strong biblical bent prompted him to deny practices in the Church, which he felt were not clearly delineated in the New Testament, for example: the sacraments, except for baptism and the Lord's Supper, the external organization of the Church, indulgences, Purgatory, veneration of the saints, and monasticism.

But it is in his theology of faith that Luther's scriptural training comes even more to the fore. Opposing the medieval concept of the righteousness of God expressing his justice, Luther preferred to describe it as his mercy. While lecturing on the Psalms and Romans and while reading Augustine, he clearly saw that the righteousness of God is primarily his grace, transforming man and making him righteous.

> At last, by the mercy of God, meditating day and night,
> I gave heed to the context of the words, namely, "In it
> the righteousness of God is revealed, as it is written,
> 'He who through faith is righteous shall live.'" There
> I began to understand that the righteousness of God is
> that by which the righteous lives by a gift of God, namely,
> by faith. And this is the meaning: the righteousness of
> God is revealed by the gospel, namely, the passive righteousness with which merciful God justifies us by faith,
> as it is written "he who through faith is righteous shall
> live." Here I felt that I was altogether born again and
> had entered paradise itself through open gates.[3]

For Luther righteousness is all from God so that man's works do not have the ultimate determination of his salvation. It is God's

71

grace alone which enables man to stand before the righteous God. For Luther righteousness, far from being a gift or a quality of man's soul, is the merciful cloak of God thrown over the naked shoulders of the shivering, shameful sinner. Luther tended to identify God's righteousness and his grace, which is shown by his treating of man as righteous.[4]

The central meaning of the Reformation is usually expressed in the phrase "Justification by grace through faith." That formula makes clear that the righteousness of God is seen most clearly in the grace by which we are accounted right and justified before God. It also points to, but inadequately expresses, the notion of faith as the matrix of the appropriation of grace. Faith is nothing else but the lively apprehension of grace made known and received. It is the stance of the believer as a result of the grace which he has known and in which he trusts. Therefore, the phrase "Through faith" is not to be understood as a means for apprehending grace, but as the mode of living by and in the power of God's graciousness.[5]

Thus the believer experiences God's merciful graciousness. Trust follows upon faith for even though the believer may not experience God's graciousness here and now, he trusts in God that he will again feel his divine mercy. Is this experiential faith of Luther a psychological event? All we can say is that it is personal faith and that the whole person is involved, body, soul, emotions, all. In this lively apprehension of God's love and mercy man is justified and made acceptable to God, and not by means of works or attempts at self-justification.

Freed from vain attempts at self-justification through sacraments and works, Luther no longer had to look to himself, but only to God. He considered the fundamental sin of man as that of self-reliance and boastful attempts at self-justification.

Was Luther's faith a moving from unbelief to belief?

The distinction which Luther knew, the difference between believing in the mere existence of God and the lively apprehension of His reality in Christ, corresponds in our day to the difference between denying His existence and affirming a genuine encounter with Him. For Luther, as for many others in his time, the belief that there was a God without knowing that He was a God for oneself was

72

tantamount to atheism, that is, acting as if His existence made no difference.[6]

This reminds one of Augustine's distinction between believing God (Deum), namely, believing that God exists, which even the demons do, and believing in God (in Deum), which is a personal loving relationship with God. [7]

Man cannot justify himself, he cannot will himself to righteousness, nor can he, of himself, overcome his estrangement from God.[8] God determines all. Man is helpless and must lean completely on God for his justification. This complete dependence, reliance on God, this firm certitude and confidence in God's saving mercy leads logically to the doctrine of predestination, which for Luther, far from being a source of fear, was a well-spring of the greatest hope.

> Predestination was a comfort to the believer. It was an affirmation on the part of the believer that God could be trusted, that He had a safe, sure destiny for us. Predestination was confessed by those who, by a miracle which they could only ascribe to God, discovered themselves delivered from the incapacities of their wills and now living in God's grace and promise. [9]

Luther's faith was not an intellectual decision, but a "fundamental re-orientation and re-direction of life. Thus the life of faith is the mode of existence which finds its vital source and center in God's forgiving and renewing grace."[10] As the living experience of God's merciful graciousness, faith must be dynamic, re-orientating life, flowering into good works. Faith for Luther cannot be reduced to reason and will, although it would be foolish to exclude these from the dynamism of his belief.

Faith and Good Works[11]

If everything depends upon God, then nothing is left for man. For Luther man's good works do not make him stand before God in the light of grace, for this would be self-reliance, self-justification, boasting, the greatest of sins. Luther, however, did not throw out all good works, but for him they were a fruit of faith rather than a cause of it. A man living righteously before the eyes of God should be driven to do good works. Indeed, a lack of such activity is a clear sign that this is not a man of faith, for it is in these works that faith fulfills the Law.

It is one thing to do what the Law commands and quite another to fulfill the Law. The works of the Law are useless if we feel its constraint and dislike it. How can God delight in works that come from a hostile heart? Joy is put in our hearts by the Holy Spirit through faith in Jesus Christ.

> We reach the conclusion that faith alone justifies us and fulfills the law. And this is because faith brings us the spirit gained by the merits of Christ. The spirit, in turn, gives us happiness and freedom at which the law aims. And this shows that good works really proceed from faith. That is Paul's meaning in chapter 3 (:31) when, after having condemned the works of the law, he sounds as if he had meant to abrogate the law by faith; but says that, on the contrary, we confirm the law through faith, i.e., we fulfill it by faith.[12]

Faith fulfills the Law. Moreover, it insures that all the credit for man's justification goes to God alone. The legalists do not give to God the glory he deserves, for they attribute salvation to their own works of the Law. There is a tendency in man to look at his good works and be gratified in his self-accomplishments. These works do not point to God, but to man, leading to a type of self-deification.

The Justified Sinner[13]

The believer is justified insofar as he stands in the light of God's grace and righteousness. Yet he is still a sinner as is evident by his continual falls. This is the dilemma of Luther, namely, fear of his own corruption as a sinner, yet certain, unwavering trust in God's mercy.

> The question at issue is that of the battle of the spirit struggling against the flesh, and finally killing outright the sins and passions that remain alive after justification. He (Paul) teaches that faith does not free us from sin to the extent that we can relax into laziness and self-assurance, as if sin no longer existed. Sin still exists; but on account of the faith that battles with it, is not held against us to our condemnation.[14]

74

It is Luther's certitude of God's saving <u>hesed</u>, despite his own sinfulness, that is at the heart of his theology of faith. God's mercy alone, applied to us in Jesus Christ, is the ground of our salvation. Incapable of this trust, our own works are only a fruit of it. If we cling strongly to God's mercy, then we are certain of our salvation, for God cannot deceive us. Thus doubts about our salvation mean lack of trust, or faith in God's mercy. True faith means absolute certainty of salvation, because our justification, grace, and salvation are of Jesus Christ, applied to us by God. True faith means that the individual is personally certain of his own salvation, trusting in God and his promises. Some say that this feeling of certitude in God's saving graciousness tends to make Luther's theology of faith too subjective, setting up a personalist structure of religion with man and his experience at its very foundation. McShane writes:

> He became an exaggerated subjectivist, too occupied with his personal commitments to God to reflect that for the successful implementation of Christianity, the subjective factors of religious experience should seek their interpretation in norms set by an objective, supra-personal authority.[15]

Perhaps Luther never thought of himself as a subjectivist, so engrossed was he in developing this personal relationship and commitment to God through his experience of faith. But one can see how it could lead to subjectivism and it may have been an early step towards what we call in modern times the triumph of subjectivity.

Faith and Reason[16]

> Here we see that every Christian is a true priest: for first he offereth up and killeth his own reason, and the wisdom of the flesh; then he giveth glory to God, that he is righteous, true, patient, pitiful, and merciful. And this is that daily sacrifice of the New Testament which must be offered evening and morning. The evening sacrifice is to kill reason; the morning sacrifice is to glorify God . . . Christian righteousness, therefore, as I have said, is the imputation of God for righteousness or unto righteousness, because of our faith in Christ, or for Christ's sake . . . This unspeakable gift therefore excelleth all reason, that God doth ac-

count and acknowledge him for righteous without any works, which embraceth his Son by faith alone.[17]

Luther's fundamental tenet that all depends upon God, nothing depends on man, leads logically to his distaste for the use of reason in things pertaining to faith. Gerrish writes:

> The ambivalence of Luther's attitude towards all three, (reason, philosophy, and Aristotle), is to be explained by reference to his dualism of an Earthly Kingdom, on the one hand, and a Heavenly Kingdom, on the other. The articles of belief cannot be arrived at by the exercise of natural reason. Neither is there any point in the attempt to buttress by reason what is already given in faith.[18]

Luther seems to hold for a clear Ockham-like separation of faith and reason.

Luther used Ockham, but developed his teachings further, accepting some, rejecting others. He attacked his exaltation of man's free will, but accepted his limitations on reason. Luther's distrust of reason, born of Nominalist teachings led him to dis-trust the Nominalists themselves. Moreover, habits of thought which he detected in the Nominalists, he seemed to see also in Thomas Aquinas, whose Aristotelianism had opened the way for legalism's corruption of the gospel message.[19] However, Aquinas also taught that the initiative in faith is from God and that no justifying good works can precede grace. Man can do nothing without God's assistance. No one can turn to God, unless God turns him to himself. Grace is given, not as a reward for natural works, but as a principle of merit.[20]

> For a full understanding of the Thomistic doctrine of justification by grace, we must stress, not only that grace (or, at least, "first grace"), cannot be merited by works, but also that grace is subordinated to meritorious works as means to end. And we do, after all, end up with a view of salvation different from Luther's. Perhaps the crucial difference lies in the fact that justification for Thomas is not yet salvation. It is only the beginning of the road. Nor is it the guarantee of finally arriving. For Luther, on the other hand, justification and salvation are virtually synonymous. Heaven is here. The pilgrim has arrived and lives already in the sphere of grace. There is no necessity for the Christian

to establish another relation with God, on the basis of merits. We might also say that for Luther eschatology is
"realized." The Christian has been translated already into
the kingdom of Christ (once and for all, eynmal), and his
standing there is entirely a matter of faith, not of merits
(sola fide).[21]

However, a close study of Aquinas' theology of faith reveals that
he too taught that faith is a real beginning, a foretaste, a guarantee, an anticipated possession of eternal life,[22] but a faith
which did not, nevertheless, preclude merit. Although faith is
the beginning of eternal life and has a strong eschatological dynamism, man is not yet in the state of final beatitude.
    Gerrish brings out three points of comparison between the
faith of Aquinas and that of Luther. First, Luther eventually
realized that he had departed not only from the "Modernist"
doctrine, but from Augustine as well.

It is as we see Luther struggling to distinguish his own
view of justification from Augustine's that his differences
from Thomas also become most apparent; for the Augustinian principle, that all our merits are gifts of God, is the
cornerstone of Thomas' doctrine of salvation.[23]

Secondly, Luther directly rejected Thomas' concept of faith
formed by love.[24] "Justification is through faith--yes, but faith
is a virtue, and its justifying power is in love which informs
it."[25] Thus justification would seem to be by love and not by
faith. Luther would have nothing to do with formless faith, although he was willing to allow a kind of "historic" or "acquired"
faith which is too weak to be a means of justification. Thomas's
fides charitate formata and Luther's fides salvifica have this in
common, namely, that they both flower into good works.[26]
    Thirdly, in the question of grace and merit, Luther felt that
the religious teachings of Paul had been sacrificed to the ethical
and metaphysical categories of Aristotle. Grace is the favor of
God, not a quality of the soul; it is a relation, not a substance.
Luther felt that Scholasticism's legalistic assumption of reason
had corrupted the simple faith of the gospels.

To sum up, against Thomas' attempt to wed grace and
merit, faith and works, stands Luther's sola gratia,
sola fide. And against Thomas' view of salvation as a

gradual process leading to eternal life stands Luther's eynmal, full righteousness (coram Deo) here and now. And the diagnosis of Thomas' error is that he tried to synthesize the Christian faith with Aristotelian philosophy.27

There had always been a reluctance among the Augustinians to accept Aristotle. However, Luther's basic distrust of reason, whether in Aristotle or Aquinas, is because reason is of man and cannot be of help in justification which is of God alone. For Luther reason is an earthly thing and tends to identify itself with the error of the "workmongers."28

CALVIN

Calvin, coming later than Luther, was the greatest systematic theologian of the Reformation. He translated many of Luther's ideas on faith and justification into his Institutes of the Christian Religion, which had a great influence on Reformed Protestantism.
Calvin, as Luther, placed the emphasis on God in man's justification. God through Christ takes the initiative in man's redemption. Man can do nothing, nor is he in any way deserving of the favor.

> The one thing that overwhelmed Calvin about the Christian faith was the good news of God's redemptive approach to sinful mankind in Jesus Christ. It was because he was so sure of this that he could talk of total depravity, of man's inability to save himself, and of God's justification of the sinner through faith in Jesus Christ.29

In his Institutes,30 Calvin bases his theology of faith firmly on the Word (III, 2, 6). "We hold faith to be a knowledge of God's will toward us, [received] from his Word. But the foundation of this is a preconceived conviction of God's truth." Merely to know God's will is not enough.

> But what if we were to substitute his benevolence or his mercy in place of his will, the tidings of which are often sad and the proclamation frightening? Thus, surely, we shall more closely approach the nature of faith; for it is after we have learned that our salvation rests with God that we are attracted to seek him. This fact is confirmed

for us when he declares that our salvation is his care and concern. Accordingly we need the promise of grace, which can testify to us that the Father is merciful; since we can approach him in no other way, and upon grace alone the heart of man can rest. (III, 2, 7)

This reminds one of Luther's experience of God's graciousness. For Calvin, merely hearing the Word is not sufficient, without the inner illumination of the Holy Spirit (III, 2, 33).

Calvin, as Luther, was impatient with the intellectual and speculative faith of the Scholastics. Faith is knowledge, but also confidence and assurance of the heart in God's mercy (III, 2, 33). Faith is both of the mind and of the heart. It is "a firm and certain knowledge of God's benevolence toward us, founded upon the truth of the freely given promise in Christ, both revealed to our minds and sealed upon our hearts through the Holy Spirit" (III, 2, 7). Strongly Pauline and Augustinian, many of Calvin's teachings on faith are reminiscent of Luther's. Besides man's corruption, God's mercy, and the centrality of the Word, Calvin emphasized a predestined faith, the experience of God's mercy, justifying, giving confidence and assurance of salvation. Calvin seemed to place a greater emphasis on the active life of faith which pervaded the whole Christian community.

TRENT

Clearly the Church had to act for it was being torn asunder by the rifts of the Reformation. Since Papal bulls and local synods were not enough, a general council was imperative. Luther himself had requested one in 1520 and the Diet of Speyer (1529) and the Recess of Augsburg (1530) had recommended it. Finally Paul III proposed a council in 1537 and agreed on Trent, a neutral spot on the border of Germany and Italy. However, the Protestant princes of Germany refused to attend, for they felt that they had already been condemned. Nevertheless, Paul still hoped to stem the tide of the Reformation. Beginning on December 13, 1545, the council's first five sessions covered scripture, tradition, and original sin.

Then after a long interval of political unrest, the decree on justification was adopted in the sixth session (January 13, 1547). Here is where we find Trent's teaching on the theology of faith. Trent agreed with the Protestants that justification begins with the grace of God, which touches the sinner's heart and calls him to repentance. It cannot be merited, but comes solely from God's love and mercy. Under the influence of actual grace, the sinner begins to turn towards God by acts of faith, sorrow, and love. Then God effects the spiritual renovation of man, that is, the remission of sin and the infusion of sanctifying grace.

Lutherans and Calvinists agreed with Catholics in attributing the beginning of justification to the grace of God alone. But the Lutherans taught that man can do nothing, since faith and justification can only be ascribed to God. Calvinists, however, admitted that man is active as well as passive under the influence of divine grace. Trent strongly affirmed man's cooperation in justification.

Some important chapters in Trent: Chapter Six[31] describes the part of man in the preparation for justification. He is awakened by grace and freely led on by God. He knows that he is a sinner. Yet, believing in revelation and the divine promises, he turns to God in hope. He detests sin, and, urged on by faith, hope and love, he firmly proposes to receive baptism. Chapter Seven[32] speaks of justification which is not only the removal of sin, but also sanctification and renovation of the inner man through the voluntary reception of God's grace. From an enemy of God, he now turns to be his friend. Justification is not merely imputed to man, he really is justified.

Chapter Eight[33] discusses in what manner man is justified by faith. Certainly faith, the beginning of his salvation, is the foundation and source of all justification. Man is justified freely for nothing precedes justification, neither faith nor works merit the grace of justification. Chapters Nine through Sixteen[34] warn against the doctrine of presumptuous trust (9). Here Trent insists that justification can be increased when faith acts along with works (10). The observance of the commandments is both necessary and possible. The just do not sin if they work for an eternal reward (11). Chapter Twelve cautions against the dangers of rash presumption in the doctrine of predestination. Sinners who lose justification can regain it through penance (14). By every serious sin grace is lost, but not faith, for unbelief is not the only mortal sin (15). Man is not overemphasized in Trent, for the strength of his merits comes from Christ. Moreover, his justice is likewise God's justice for he put it in man (16).

Faith is at the origin of the process of justification. Trent does not give a formal definition of faith, but describes it, not as an act of confidence, but of the intellect submitting to God and recognizing the truth of that which he reveals. De facto, many of these truths are promises, which do elicit confidence. The religious value of faith is not only in speculative knowledge about God, but also in a real assimilation of the Christian to Christ. Faith is at the very root of justification. Without it, it is impossible to please God. Moreover, it is not only the beginning, but perdures through justification.

Trent gives many of the qualities of faith. It is supernatural, entirely under the influence of the Holy Spirit. It is free. Faith is an orientation of man towards the God of promises and its certitude is based on his veracity. The first infusion of faith in justification unites the believer to Christ. The sinner has true supernatural faith, although it is dead. However, only living faith can be an effective principle of divine life for the believer.

CONCLUSION

At the risk of over-simplification, it would be good to try to summarize some thoughts about the Reformers' theology of faith and that as announced by the Council of Trent. Reacting to the laxity of the good-work-orientated Church of his time, and also to Pelagian-tinged Nominalism, and influenced by Paul and Augustine, Luther felt that the human element had been over-emphasized, to the neglect of the divine. In a sense Luther over-reacted, for his theology of faith went to the other extreme, namely, denying the power of man to cooperate in faith and attributing all to God. If everything is due to God, then man can do nothing. Luther taught the Pauline theme that justification is by grace through faith and not by works. Good works are necessary, not as a means of justification, but rather as signs of faith, for true faith must burst forth in fruit.

Opposing the medieval idea of God's righteousness as his justice, Luther taught it as his mercy. Grace is not an internal modification of man's soul, but is God's merciful graciousness towards the sinner, through which man is accounted as right and justified before God. Faith is the lively experiential apprehension of God's graciousness, made known and received and in which man trusts. Freed from works and the need and worry of self-justification, he now lives in the power of God's graciousness. Reacting to the more intellectual faith of Scholasticism, Luther taught a living experiential faith founded on God's gracious mercy. Man is justified and at the same time a sinner. Keenly aware of man's sinful nature, Luther was just as certain of God's saving graciousness. God's mercy alone, applied to us in Jesus Christ, is

81

the basis of our salvation, giving a personal certainty of salvation, and a strong feeling of predestination. Luther's dualism, that is, the Earthly Kingdom vs. the Heavenly, led to his distrust of any thing that smacked of the secular, for example, philosophy, good works, organized church, hierarchy, sacraments. His distrust of reason in matters of faith and his teaching of God's acceptance of man and his non-imputation of his sins reflect Ockham. In general, Luther's theology of faith set the pace for later Protestant theologians such as John Calvin.

The Council of Trent countered Protestant doctrines on faith, with a re-emphasis on the part that man plays in salvation. It is true that justification is from God alone, but man is free to reject it. Moreover, with God's help he can perform acts leading up to the act of faith. Yet neither faith nor justification can be merited. Trent insisted on the intrinsic change in man through justification, not merely the extrinsic non-imputation of sin and the imputation of righteousness. Trent identified justification and sanctification. And, while admitting that the justified man is a sinner, that is, one who had sinned and was capable of sinning again, denied that he was, de facto, in sin.

Although opposing Luther's personal confidence in God's graciousness as presumptuous, the council however agreed with Luther that faith plays an essential role in man's justification. Moreover, man can not only prepare for faith with God's help, but also he can really merit through the merits of Christ by good works done along with faith.

Luther and the other Reformers had forced the Church to clarify her stand on many issues including the sacraments and justification. This led the way to a whole new trend in piety, emphasizing man's part in salvation in cooperation with God and man's real sanctification through justification by the infusion of sanctifying grace with its accompanying virtues and gifts.

Notes

1 See J. Dillenberger and C. Welch, Protestant Christianity (New York: Charles Scribner's Sons, 1954), pp. 5-10.
2 For English translations of Luther's writings on this topic, see Luther's Works, J. Pelikan and H. Lehmann, gen. eds., 55 vols. (Philadelphia: Muhlenberg and Fortress; St. Louis: Concordia Publishing House). This series referred to here as "P." Also see Martin Luther, Selections from His Writings, J. Dillenberger, ed.

(Garden City: Doubleday and Company, Inc., 1961), referred to here as "D." Specific works treating of justification by grace through faith are: Preface to Romans, D 22, P 35, pp. 368-69. Freedom of the Christian, D 56, 66-67; P 31, pp. 347-48. Preface to the Latin Writings, D 11-12. Pagan Servitude of the Church, D 300-01. Lectures on Galatians, P 26, pp. 347-48.

3 Preface to Latin Writings, D 11.

4 D, xix.

5 D, xxv & xxvi.

6 D, xxvii.

7 See Chapter III.

8 Bondage of the Will, D, pp. 167-203.

9 D, xxviii.

10 Ibid.

11 Preface to the New Testament, D 17-19; P 35, pp. 258-60; Preface to Romans, D 27-29, P 35, pp. 373-74. Preface to the Epistles of James and Jude, D 35-36, P 35, pp. 395-98. Pagan Servitude of the Church, D 282-83, P 36, pp. 46-48. Commentary on Galatians, D 100-26, P 26, pp. 4ff.

12 Preface to Romans, D 21-22; P. 35, pp. 386ff.

13 Ibid., D 22-29, P 35, pp. 372-74. Commentary on Romans, W. Pauck, tr., LCC, Vol. XV (Philadelphia: Westminster Press, 1961), pp. 120f.

14 Preface to Romans, D 29.

15 E. McShane, "Martin Luther," Thought, XLI (Spring, 1966), 110. See also J. Lortz, Die Reformation in Deutschland (Freiburg: Herder and Herder, Inc., 1948), Vol. I, pp. 160ff. Also P. Hacker, Das Ich im Glauben bei Martin Luther (Graz: Styria, 1966).

16 Commentary on Galatians, D 127-31.

17 Ibid., p. 131.

18 B. Gerrish, Grace and Reason (Oxford: Clarendon Press, 1962), p. 41.

19 Ibid., p. 114.

20 Thomas Aquinas, Summa Theologiae, 1-2, q. 109-14.

21 Gerrish, Grace and Reason, pp. 125-26.

22 See Chapter IV.

23 Gerrish, Grace and Reason, p. 126. Thomas, ST 1-2, q. 114.

24 See Chapter IV.

25 Gerrish, Grace and Reason, p. 126.

26 Ibid.

27 Ibid., p. 134.

28 Ibid., p. 113.

29 H. Kerr, A Compendium of the Institutes of the Christian Religion by John Calvin (Philadelphia: Westminster Press, 1964), v.

30 Quotes from Calvin: Institutes of the Christian Religion, ed. J. McNeill, tr. F. Lewis, LCC, Vols. XX, XVI (Philadelphia: Westminster Press, 1964).

31 DS 1526, TCT 562.

32 DS 1530, TCT 564.

33 DS 1532, TCT 565.

34 DS 1533-45, TCT 566-73.

CHAPTER VI

Reasonable faith

THE ENLIGHTENMENT TO VATICAN I

The Reformers had exalted the role of divine graciousness in man's salvation and had reduced to almost nothing the part of man. Up God, down man. This over-emphasis on faith was to bring a later reaction in the form of the Enlightenment of the eighteenth century, when the balance swung from faith to reason. Up man, down God.

ENLIGHTENMENT

The Enlightenment, a popular movement in eighteenth century Europe, whose aim was to make reason the absolute ruler of human life, had roots going back to Renaissance humanism. It emphasized the natural man and his unaided attainments. And although it was not necessarily anti-religious, it did tend to rebel against the dualism of Augustine, Luther, and the Pietists, and the repressive other-worldliness of ecclesiastical tradition. The Enlightenment not only fostered intellectual revolution, but political, economic, and scientific, as well.

In the spirit of toleration following the seventeenth century persecutions, a number of philosophies and intellectual trends arose which influenced the spread of the Enlightenment and later rationalism. The Deists held that God had created the world and then turned it over to natural laws and human management. Pietism opposed the intellectualism of orthodoxy, and, although it objected to the exaggerated reason of the Enlightenment, it was similar insofar as it emphasized the inner light, which bore some resemblance to the light of reason. The rise of natural science was an important factor. Galileo and Newton had given scientific explanations of the cosmos. Man now felt at home in the world, since he didn't need divine help to run it, nor did he need divine revelation to help him understand it. Coming into his own, man no longer considered himself corrupt and in need of grace. The sense of divine creation was lost in the popular nineteenth century evolutionary theories.

Growth of Rationalism

French Rationalism always seemed hostile to the faith. René Descartes insisted that only clear ideas should be received. Needless to say, much of revelation would not fit this pattern. Moreover, the French Encyclopedists and Voltaire argued against supernatural miracles.

In England Bacon's inductive reason and Hobbes' materialism led the way. Locke tried to formulate a science of human nature and society with ethics as the essence of Christianity. The Deists of the beginning of the eighteenth century challenged the infallibility of the Scriptures. Hume, favoring absolute empiricism, questioned the belief in miracles which cannot be demonstrated. But he also undermined the very foundations of Deism and science by asserting that man can only observe a succession of events without attaining their causal connection.

In Germany Leibnitz taught that God's ways with man are both rational and good. Thus human freedom can be reconciled with divine omnipotence and omniscience, and evil with divine goodness. His disciple, C. Wolff, the father of German Rationalism, built up a system of natural theology by means of a deductive logic independent of revelation. J. Semler, professor at Halle, tried a rationalistic approach to the Bible, and G. Lessing substituted for Christianity a purely Deistic belief in morality and a supreme being. Thus the rationalistic trend spread rapidly in Germany.

Kant

Kant helped bring the rationalist movement to a climax. In his
Religion Within the Bounds of Reason Alone (1793), he tried to
show the limitations of rationalistic religion, for man cannot of
himself find the essence of things or of God. Directing his Critique of Pure Reason against the rationalism of Wolff, Kant explains in the section on "Transcendental Dialectic" why rational
psychology, cosmology, and theology as discussed by Wolff are
impossible. Mere reason is not sufficient for cognition of absolute being, God, soul, and world--transcendental ideas--for
reason can only reach objects which lie within experience and
thus cannot recognize the nature of things in themselves. Its
sole task in theoretical cognition is to spell the phenomena in
order to be able to read them as experiences.

Opposing the metaphysical rationalism of Descartes, Spinoza,
Leibnitz and Wolff, Kant retained the fundamental idea of the older
rationalism, namely, that reason can recognize completely only
that which it can produce according to its own design, so we know
a-priori only so much of things as we ourselves put into them. We
must deal with experience itself. The understanding is able to recognize a-priori and to anticipate the form of experience insofar as
it constitutes this form. It is itself "the legislation for nature," but
only insofar as we understand by "nature" not the subsistence and
constitution of absolute objects, but the order and regularity of
empirical phenomena. Rational cognition becomes fruitful only
where, instead of dwelling on noumena, it concerns itself with phenomena, for only through pure intuition does cognition by understanding or cognition by pure reason receive a real content.

The mistake of Empiricism, according to Kant, consists in overlooking the intellectual factor which is indispensable for any cognition of the objects. The mistake of Rationalism was in overesti-
mating this factor and insulating it from sensible conditions upon
which its application depends. Leibnitz had intellectualized the phenomena, just as Locke had sensualized the concepts of understanding, regarding them as nothing more than empirical or abstracted
concepts of reflection. Scientific Rationalism taught that experience
is possible only through the representation of a necessary connection
between perceptions, based on the supposition that the world is the
work of an infinite intellect. Kant removed Rationalism from dependence on dogmatic metaphysics, maintaining that the truth of
experience is self-sufficient, although its form and order are based
on the general orderliness of the understanding.

Kant climaxed the Enlightenment attitude towards religion, distinguishing clearly between the phenomena of experience and the noumena known through pure reason. Knowledge of the world cannot lead to knowledge of God. Religion must be based on the apprehension of the moral law, for God and immortality are postulates of moral experience. In a sense, this seems to be a type of natural religion, for religious beliefs are based upon the dictates of practical reason, moral experience. Kant rejected nature as the prime datum of religious beliefs, rather grounding religion in immediate experience. His experiential religion lays the groundwork for future developments in the theology of personal, existential, and phenomenological faith.

Hermes

Hermes (d. 1831) was a German priest and professor at Munster, who although in some ways opposed to Kant and Fichte, in other ways was strongly influenced by them. He taught that our knowledge is subjectively true when we are convinced in our own minds that it coincides with its object, so that the necessity of our conviction is the criterion of objective truth. Belief in a truth is of the theoretical reason, while the accepting of the truth is of the practical or the obligating reason. Doubting everything which was not self-evident, Christians should hold themselves loose from the faith which they had been taught until it has been demonstrated to their satisfaction by reason.

Hermes called faith a state of certitude and of persuasion in rapport with the truth of the thing known, a state to which we are led by the necessary assent of the theoretical reason or by the necessary consent of the practical reason. Thus faith for Hermes would seem to be a necessary conclusion about God or revelation, truths known through revelation and reason in the speculative and in the practical reason.

The authority of God is only one motive of credibility. The last veritable motive of faith is the physical and moral necessity of believing, constituted by reason. Hence man should be ready to follow reason, whether or not it is in contradiction with revelation, for otherwise one would sin against reason. This doctrine clearly endangered the liberty and the supernaturality of faith. Hermes taught a two-fold faith, namely: the faith of knowledge or natural reason, and the faith of the heart or will, a supernatural, living faith, which succeeds the faith of knowledge. This latter is a total submission to God, gratuitous, and in conformity with the truths obtained from natural reason. Actually a similar two-fold faith can be found in some medieval authors as well, although for them supernatural faith transcends reason.

In 1833 Rome criticized Hermes for his teaching that one should throw his faith in doubt in order to understand it better and for his renunciation of the traditional proofs of God and of miracles. These and other doctrines of his could lead to a dangerous scepticism about revelation and the supernatural. Hermes has been called a Semi-Rationalist, one of the many offshoots of the Rationalistic and Positivistic trends of the time.

OTHER NINETEENTH CENTURY TRENDS

The spirit of the times was one of secularization with the emphasis on science and reason and with a lessening stress on the other world of faith and eschatology. Many products arose from this environment, not only the Rationalists, but Positivists and Empiricists as well.

Positivism was promoted by A. Comte (1798-1857), one of whose tenets was that theological and metaphysical knowledge should be discarded in favor of a third type of knowledge based on experience and observation. Man now no longer looked for causes, but only for the laws that govern all phenomena and their sequence. The sciences that would discover and verify these laws were mathematics, astronomy, physics, chemistry, biology, and sociology. In later years Comte developed a religion of humanity, in which the genius of man took the place of God. Positivism had a great influence in fourteenth century Europe and America.

The emphasis on man and material in reaction to the old, established eschatological churches can also be seen in Feuerbach, Marx, Nietzsche, and, of course, today it is being resurrected by the radical theologians who are proclaiming the death of God. So we certainly cannot bury the eighteenth and nineteenth centuries as irrelevant today.

The Traditionalists quickly rose to the defense of the handed-down religion. However, they went too far in the opposite direction, denying the capacity of man to know without God's help. For them intellectual cognition was reduced to belief in truth communicated by revelation from God, and received by the traditional instruction through the medium of language which was originally a supernatural gift. The Fideism of Bautain bore similarities to Traditionalism: for example, its strong reaction to Rationalism and its over-emphasis on faith to the neglect of reason.

The modified Traditionalism of M. Bonnetty restricted the absolute necessity of traditional instruction from revelation to metaphysical, religious, and moral truth, admitting that the human intellect can discover other truths by its own power.

THE FIRST VATICAN COUNCIL

The eighteenth and nineteenth centuries were times of revolution, political, industrial, and intellectual. Old kingdoms were out, democracies and republics were in. Italy itself, under the leadership of Garibaldi, was fighting for unification which would soon mean the dissolution of the Papal States. Vatican I, belonging to a new age of the world, has been called the first modern council. Travel and communications were easy; journalists quickly brought the news to the people.

Pius IX, ruling 18,000 square miles of the Papal States in Central Italy, was quite conscious of the harm done to the Church by revolutions and the God-less ruling in some Christian states. He was also keenly aware of the intellectual and religious trends of the times. In 1864 he condemned Rationalism, exaggerated Traditionalism, Indifferentism, Socialism, Communism, and some problems arising out of Church-state tensions. Many of these issues would come up again in Vatican I.

Pius IX's bull Aeterni Patris (1868) gave the purpose and plan of the First Vatican Council. Topics to be reviewed were clerical life, marriage, education of youth, church and state. Commissions were set up to condemn Rationalism, restate the Catholic faith, revise canon law, clerical life, and so forth. One hundred experts set up fifty-one drafts of decrees, only two of which were ultimately passed in what was to be an abortive council.

Dei Filius[1]

When the Dogmatic Constitution on the Catholic Faith, Dei Filius, was first presented to the bishops, they felt it was too long and involved and sent it back to be redesigned by Kleutgen and Gay. Improved by many amendments--for example, "error" replaced "anathema"--the revised constitution defended the fundamental principles of Christianity against the errors of Rationalism, Materialism, and Atheism.

Chapter One[2] defends the personal God who created freely out of nothing and foresees and guides all in his divine providence towards their final end. Moreover, the council fathers condemn

90

the Materialists' doctrine that only matter exists and the Panthe-
ists' teachings that the substance of God is the same as the substance of all things or that finite things emanate from divine
substance.

Chapter Two[3] speaks of natural and supernatural knowledge
of God. Against the Fideists and the Traditionalists the fathers
teach that God can be known with certainty through natural reason.
Against the Rationalists they maintain the necessity of revelation
through Scriptures and tradition. Man can be raised above nature
by divine power to knowledge and perfection higher than nature.

In defining faith in Chapter Three,[4] Vatican I repeats the main
ideas of Trent; namely, faith is a supernatural virtue, infused,
under the action of provenient and helping grace. Because of the
infallible authority of God revealing, man's reason is subordinate
to the Uncreated Truth, the First Truth of Augustine and Aquinas.
Reason is not the supreme rule of all truth, for it accepts and
uses other means of knowledge which will permit it to enter into
contact with the whole truth. Repeating an earlier tradition beginning with Scriptures and carrying through the Fathers and
Theologians, and echoing Thomas' "faith is the beginning of eternal life," Vatican I calls faith the beginning of man's salvation.

We believe, not because of the intrinsic truth of things as
seen by the light of natural reason, that is, because of an intrinsic evidence naturally acquired by experience or by philosophical
demonstration. Rather we believe because of an intellectual motive
extrinsic to the object, namely, the authority of God who makes
it known by revelation and who can neither deceive nor be deceived. Upon this infallible authority is the certitude of faith
based, a certitude stronger than that of science, even though the
object is unseen.

Chapter Three[5] insists that the virtue of faith is reasonable,
supernatural, free, and necessary. Miracles are not only possible,
but actual as confirmation of revelation. Human reason is not
completely independent of faith so that faith cannot be demanded
by God. Hence the free assent to Scripture and tradition aided by
external and internal graces is not produced by reason alone.
Against Hermes the Fathers teach that Catholics, freely assenting to the truths of revelation, should not doubt their faith until
they have received a scientific demonstration of credibility.

Chapter Four[6] treats of faith and reason. The mysteries of
faith cannot be grasped by natural reason. But revealed truth can
never contradict reason, nor can reason go against faith. Faith
and reason support each other in many ways. Thus reason, de-

monstrating the foundations of faith and enlightened by the light
of faith, pursues the science of divine things. And faith, setting
reason free, guards it from error and furnishes it with exten-
sive knowledge. Faith is not a philosophical system fashioned
by the human mind, but a divine deposit entrusted to the Church
for interpretation and protection. It is wrong to say that there
are no mysteries in divine revelation and that all doctrines of
faith can be understood or demonstrated from natural principles
and reason.

CONCLUSION

There is a relevance of eighteenth and nineteenth century Rationalism and Vatican I for today, for the exaggerated humanism
of the radical theologians seems to lean heavily on Hegel, Feuerbach, Nietzsche, and others of this age. The transcendent God is
dead, they tell us, as is the Church, eschatology and faith. Leaving
behind the dead problem-solving God, self-sufficient man must
rely only on his native intellect, his advanced scientific skills and
knowledge for the betterment of himself and the world. In flight
from weak immature faith, man has now come of age. The old
antithesis of faith and reason is still there, but in a much more
radical form. Man must say "No" to faith and say "Yes" to his
own natural reasoning powers. But the old wisdom of Vatican I
must be preserved. Faith and reason are both necessary to man
for each aids the other towards eternal life.
    Vatican I affirms what had always been taught by the Church,
namely, faith is the free response of man to the manifestation of
divine truth. It is a meritorious submission of his intellect before
the infinite authority of his Creator, the exterior testimony of
God revealing and the interior grace enlightening the mind and
inclining the will. Faith is a free and virtuous adhesion which is
a work of grace and not merely the rational examination of human
doctrine. The Church has always safeguarded the rights of reason
in the act of faith, but puts in the forefront the rights of grace and
the moral aspect of the act of faith. Although God takes the initiative in faith, man is free to reject his gift. Thus God and man
cooperate in the act of faith.
    Nineteenth century Rationalism tended to generate a rational-
istic apologetic which in attempting to show the reasonableness
of faith and revelation sometimes fell into the error of trying
to prove from reason the divinely revealed mysteries. Faith as
an intellectual assent to the handed-down propositions, based

on solid rational preambles characterized the main apologetical and catechetical thrust until nuanced by the more recent emphasis on personal faith.

Notes

1 DS 3000-3045, TCT 354-362, 58-85.
2 DS 3001-3003, 3021-3025, TCT 355-362.
3 DS 3004-3007, 3026-3029, TCT 58-62.
4 DS 3008, TCT 63.
5 DS 3009-3014, 3031-3036, TCT 64-74.
6 DS 3015-3020, 3041-3043, TCT 75-85.

CHAPTER VII

I and thou

SCHLEIERMACHER TO BUBER

In this chapter and the following two we will see the strong modern influence of the subjective, the personal, existential, I-Thou approach to faith. Beginning with the Pietists and Schleiermacher, we will then see Kierkegaard, Buber, Barth, Bultmann, and others. Personal faith has strong biblical roots, as we have seen in earlier chapters. The Fathers taught it, as did the early medieval theologians. It is even perceptible to the perceptive behind the abstract terminology of Aquinas. In Luther and the Reformers it is the experience of God's graciousness. Many Protestant theologians from Luther on down have opposed the abstract, noetic faith of the Scholastics with the personal and experiential. From the time of Kierkegaard, modern existentialists have contributed much to the development of the theology of personal faith.

1 FRIEDRICH SCHLEIERMACHER (1768-1834);
CONSCIOUS ABSOLUTE DEPENDENCE ON GOD

Eighteenth century Pietism reacted strongly to German Lutheran Scholasticism. In order to bring back the experiential faith in the living Christ, Philip Spener and August Francke instituted collegia pietatis dedicated to the love of God in Jesus Christ, known and experienced by the believer in the New Testament. In this experience the believers are justified and, as priests, give good example to each other, the personal feeling of the presence of Christ transforming their lives. Pietism's new emphasis on the gospels opposed the abstract speculations of the Protestant Scholastics, for whom theology had become a substitute for faith, the living experience of Christ.[1]

Schleiermacher, as Kant, had a Moravian pietistic background. He also came into contact with the thought of the Enlightenment and with its Romantic reaction, which emphasized imagination, creativity, freedom, individuality, the life of the spirit, in contrast to the rational and the speculative.

Schleiermacher taught a religion of the inner emotions, not a way of thinking, or a creed of truths, or an ethical code of laws. Belonging to the area of feeling or affection, religion is a primal and immediate awareness, a direct experience of God, similar to that of mysticism. From this basic Christian experience all dogmas must flow. Answering the Romantics' criticism of religion and Kant's critique of knowledge, Schleiermacher maintained that the essence of religion is feeling (Gefuhl) or the immediate consciousness of absolute dependence on God. Concepts such as God's eternity, omnipotence, and creation are derived from this experience.

Kant had anticipated this emphasis on the subjective in theology; Schleiermacher made it explicit as the beginning point from which Church doctrines flowed. The Bible and tradition are nothing more than records of this internal experience. Schleiermacher has been called the Father of Modern Theology because of his pioneering approach. Certainly he led the way to the liberal trends and the theology of religious experience so popular in the nineteenth century.[2]

The Christian Faith (1821)[3]

Piety

Schleiermacher defines the Church from his basic teachings on piety.

95

The piety which forms the basis of all ecclesiastical com-
munions is, considered purely in itself, neither a Knowing
or a Doing, but a modification of Feeling, or of immediate
self-consciousness. (5)

Earlier he had expressed a similar thought in his On Religion:
Speeches to Its Cultured Despisers (1799).[4] Schleiermacher's
affective line reflects his pietistic training, his Platonic studies,
and the Romanticism of the times. The Church for him was a communion of piety rather than a gigantic impersonal institution. Is
the "feeling" of Schleiermacher the same as his self-consciousness?
Self-consciousness seems to make feeling more explicit, for there
can be feeling in unconscious states. Moreover, this self-consciousness is immediate, that is, not mediated by a self-contemplation
(Christian Faith, 6).

How does Schleiermacher's piety differ from other feelings of
man?

The common element in all howsoever diverse expressions
of piety, by which these are conjointly distinguished from
all other feelings, or, in other words, the self-identical
essence of piety is this: the consciousness of being absolutely dependent, or, which is the same thing, of being in relation with God. (12)

The feeling of dependence is united closely to a feeling of freedom

in the sense that not only the subject, but the corresponding
other is the same in both. Then the total self-consciousness
made up of both together is one of Reciprocity between the
subject and the corresponding other. The feeling of absolute
dependence is expressed inwardly as a consciousness of God.
. . . And that feeling, whenever it attains to a certain clear-
ness, is accompanied by such an expression, but is also
combined with, and related to, a sensible self-consciousness.
Then the God-consciousness which in this way has arisen will,
in all its particular formations, carry with it such determination as belongs to the realm of the antithesis in which the
sensible self-consciousness moves. (25)

Communion

Religious self-consciousness leads to fellowship and communion as was evident in the <u>collegia</u> of the Pietist movement.

> The religious self-consciousness, like every essential element in human nature, leads necessarily in its development to fellowship or communion; a communion which, on the one hand, is variable and fluid, and, on the other hand, has definite limits, i.e., is a Church. (26)

> Fellowship, then, is demanded by the consciousness of kind which dwells in every man, and which finds its satisfaction only when he steps forth beyond the limits of his own personality and takes up the facts of other personalities into his own. It is accomplished through the fact that everything inward becomes, at a certain point of its strength or maturity, an outward too, and, as such, perceptible to others. (27)

Thus arise feelings of brotherly love and the priesthood of the brethren.

The Christian communion is distinguished from others by its faith in Jesus as the Redeemer.

> In the same sense we spoke above of faith in God, which was nothing but the certainty concerning the feeling of absolute dependence, as such, i.e., as conditioned by a Being placed outside of us, and as expressing our relation to that Being. The faith of which we are now speaking, however, is a purely factual certainty, but a certainty of a fact which is entirely inward, that is to say, it cannot exist in an individual until, through an impression which he has received from Christ, there is found in him a beginning--perhaps quite infinitesimal, but yet a real premonition--of the process which will put an end to the state of needing redemption. But this term "faith in Christ" here (as the term 'faith in God' formerly) relates the state of redemption, as effect, to Christ as cause. That is how John describes it. And so from the beginning only those people have attached themselves to Christ in His new community whose religious self-consciousness had taken the form of a need of redemption, and who now became assured in themselves of Christ's redeeming

power so that the more strongly these two phases appeared in any individual, the more able was he, by representation of the fact (which includes description of Christ and His work) to elicit this inward experience in others. Those in whom this took place became believers, and the rest did not. This, moreover, is what has ever since constituted the essense of all direct Christian preaching. Such preaching must always take the form of testimony; testimony of one's own experience, which shall arouse in others the desire to have the same experience. (68-69)

The kerygma for Schleiermacher is preaching the Christian experience to others, a handing on of the inward feeling of faith. Unless a man has this interior experience of the Holy Spirit, miracles and prophecies cannot produce it. Scriptures themselves and all dogmatic development are fruits of this inner life.

Schleiermacher's doctrine of faith as an inward experience, feeling, or consciousness of our absolute dependence on God, had a great influence on subsequent teachings on religious experience in the nineteenth century. He was one of the pioneers in the modern theology of personal faith. His importance to the development of Protestant thought has been compared to that of Kant.

2 SOREN KIERKEGAARD (1813-1855);
THE LEAP OF FAITH

Kierkegaard reacted against both Hegel's objectivism and Schleiermacher's feeling of dependency, which he felt led more to religiosity than to religion. Kierkegaard criticized sharply the objective, depersonalized, Hegelian Christian church of his time. Sure that the Christianity of the New Testament no longer existed, he desired to leap across the dead bones of Christendom to contemporaneousness with Christ.

In nineteenth century Lutheran theology, the philosophies of Kant and Hegel had all but taken over with their dry and uninspiring philosophical speculations. Kant had destroyed the epistomelogical presuppositions of orthodoxy. "The only way that evangelical theology would be able to reassert itself was by developing a new philosophy to counter the various blends of Kantianism, Hegelianism, Spinozism that had crowded out the Christian theological witness."[5] In Kierkegaard Lutheranism produced a giant who revolutionized philosophy and theology, recovering the deep evangelical insights of Luther. In fact, Kierkegaard's attitude towards

Hegel reminds one of Luther's attack on Aristotle. Against objective spectator science and speculative philosophy, Kierkegaard proposed a subjective existentiality and total commitment to the Absolute, building Luther's existential insights into a working philosophy.[6]

Kierkegaard felt that modern philosophy was pagan. Against Cogito, ergo sum he placed Credo, ergo sum. Objective knowledge, he felt, was grounded in the dialectical negation of faith and thus opposed to the subjectivity of faith. Hence God and the concrete existing individual were banished from the world of the universal. Since the existing individual is incommensurate with objective reality, to know objectively is to cease to exist subjectively and vice versa. So existence in faith is antithetical to existence in objective reality. And true faith is a radical inwardness whose subjectivity negates objectivity.[7] "The degree of involvement of the subject increases to the extent that objective certainty diminishes. Subjective interest in the act of faith reaches its peak when every shred of objective certainty disappears."[8] Faith tends to become reasoned and objective so that it must be constantly interiorized.

Correlative to individuality, subjectivity is the individual before God. "The individual man must learn to dare to be himself before God. If he is to be a Christian, he must not forget 'What his name is before God.'"[9] Christianity, therefore, is not just a doctrine to which one assents, but rather it is an existential communication to the individual and never allows him to stand as a disinterested spectator.[10]

In describing man's ascent to faith, Kierkegaard outlines three stages of life[11]--aesthetic, moral, and religious--whereby, escaping from the material world, one unites himself by choice with the Infinite. Leaving behind the aesthetical world of pleasure, he chooses the higher ethical stage of life. An example of this higher moral life is Judge Williams who, in contrast to John the Seducer, strives for an abiding marital love, where past, present, and future are united in an ethical continuity springing from an internal earnestness and sincerity rather than merely based on an exterior code.

Contrasting with the religiosity of the ethical stage is the mode of Christian faith whereby man renounces the temporal world and conscious of his eternal validity makes his leap of faith. And so he sees the true value of the finite world in relation to the infinite, as Abraham, by giving up his dearest possession, Isaac, found him again in his leap of faith. Kierkegaard felt that he himself had never reached this third stage. Perhaps his humble estimate of himself meant that he really had.

a Journals (1834-1855)[12]

Faith and the Absurd

The relation of faith to the absurd is one of the central themes of Kierkegaard's theology of faith, for to the outsider, to the non-believer, to reason, faith seems absurd and paradoxical. The absurdity of faith is that, despite the total otherness of man, God still comes into contact with him, that God became man. This to the unbliever and to reason is absurd.

> And, therefore, faith hopes also in this life, but be it noted, by virtue of the absurd, not by virtue of the human understanding, otherwise, it is merely wisdom, not faith. Faith is, therefore, what the Greeks called divine folly, that is, not merely an intellectual observation, but something which can be directly carried out. (5/17/1843, 445 & 446)

> The "immediate" believer cannot apprehend the thought that the content of faith is, for the reason and for the third person who is not the believer, the absurd, and that to become a believer every one must be alone with the absurd.

Hence the confusion in speaking about faith, for the believer cannot stand this "double-vision--namely, that from the other side faith is seen as the absurd. This is the tension which is a part of the life of faith" (1850, 1084).

Faith and Works

Kierkegaard, as Luther, taught the importance of good works as a fruit of faith, but not as a merited right to a reward.

> Good works, in the sense of merit, are naturally an abomination to God, nevertheless, good works are required of men. But they should be and yet not be. They should be and yet man should be humbly ignorant of their existence, or

that they have any importance. It is like a right which is only a right under particular conditions of service: thus good works should be served in humility, in faith. (1/24/ 1847, 637)

Otherwise we are like children who give our parents a gift bought with money which our parents have given us. As Paul says (1 Cor 4:7): "What have you that you did not receive? If then you received it, why do you boast as if it were not a gift?"

Uncertainty of Faith

Although in faith man stakes everything on Christ, he cannot acquire an immediate certainty about his faith, "for to believe means precisely that dialectical hovering which, although in fear and trembling, never despairs. Faith is an infinite self-made care as to whether one has faith--and that self-made care is faith" (5/13/1848, 763). Kierkegaard's dialectical hovering reminds one of the restless dissatisfaction of the discursive thought of faith in Aquinas.[13] This restlessness, fear and trembling, are a necessary part of the risk of faith.

The believer stakes his whole life on the "if" of faith, risking his life and thus proving his faith. Rather than proving it first and then believing, he risks and believes first. In belief one's life becomes a daily test or risk (1850/1044). Yet although faith is a risk and trial, it is not anxiety and despair, which are products of sin and the lack of faith. One must leap from sin and unfaith to faith, the God-given "comforted despair."

The believer. . . believes that God does so in order that he should stand the test. Alas, and in a certain sense: it follows from this that unbelief, melancholy, anxiety, and so on, usually succumb, because they weaken themselves beforehand, and as a punishment for thinking evil of God; whereas faith is readily victorious. (1850, 1064)

The man in dread must hold firmly to the conviction that God is love, only then will he succeed in establishing a concrete relationship with God.

101

Personal, Existential Faith

Faith is not an intellectual process as in Greek philosophy.
Rather for the Christian it belongs to the existential order. God
does not teach doctrines to believe intellectually, as a professor
would do. Since it is existential, faith is not intellectual knowledge, but a relation of personality to personality. What is personality? It is not a collection of doctrines nor something to which we
may have ready access. Rather it is bent in on itself, something
hidden, mysterious.

> Personality is that which is within to which a man, himself
> in turn a personality, may be related in faith. Between
> person and person no other relation is possible. Take the
> two most passionate lovers who ever lived, and even if
> they are, as is said, one soul in two bodies, this can never
> come to anything more than that the one believes that the
> other loves him or her.[14]

Faith is to be found in the personal relationship between the
personal God and the believing human person.

b Fear and Trembling (1843)[15]

Kierkegaard wrote this little volume in a period of struggle
after his break-up with his fiancée. Some feel that his description of Abraham's sacrifice of Isaac is symbolic of his sacrifice
of his dearest Regina.

Abraham

By faith Abraham, the father of all believers, left Ur for the
land of promise, by faith he believed God's promise of numerous
progeny.

> Then came the fullness of time, if Abraham had not be-
> lieved, Sarah surely would have been dead of sorrow, and
> Abraham dulled by grief, would not have understood the
> fulfillment, but would have smiled at it as a dream of youth.
> But Abraham believed, therefore, he was young; for he who
> always hopes for the best becomes old, and he who is always
> prepared for the worst, grows old early. But he who believes,
> preserves an eternal youth. . . The miracle of faith consists

in the fact that Abraham and Sarah were young enough to wish, and that faith had preserved their wish and therewith their youth. (22-23)

But then came the greatest test of faith, the command to sacrifice Isaac. Although in fear and trembling, Abraham never ceased to believe and this by virtue of the absurd for all human reasoning had long since ceased to function (48).

A Work of Art

Some people think that faith is something crude and clumsy, appealing to those of dull nature. But really the act of faith is a work of art. "The dialectic of faith is the finest and most remarkable of all; it possesses an elevation, of which indeed I can form a conception, but nothing more. I am able to make from the springboard the great leap whereby I pass into infinity" (48-49). Abraham made this great leap and so became the father of all believers.

Faith, Difficult

Kierkegaard felt that he himself had not yet made the difficult movement to the third stage of life, faith. This affirmation was a personal matter between him and God, the object of his faith. Certainly no one should consider the leap of faith something lowly and easy to perform, for it is really the greatest and the hardest (74-75).

Faith is paradoxical insofar as the individual, as the particular, is higher than the universal. "Yet in such a way, be it observed, that it is the particular individual who, after he has been subordinated as the particular to the universal, now through the universal becomes the individual who as the particular stands in an absolute relation to the absolute" (82). Abraham paradoxically overcame the universal law by his individual faith, and this by virtue of the absurd, for it is absurd that he the individual should be higher than the universal (83).

c Concluding Unscientific Postscript (1846)[16]

In what Kierkegaard thought would be his last work, a sequel to his Philosophical Fragments, he pursues his favorite topic, the subjective vs. the objective.

Leap of Faith

The leap of faith, from unbelief to belief, can be endangered by objective dialectical analysis which can change faith, "into un-certainty of an entirely different order, replacing its passionate conviction by those probabilities and guarantees which he rejected in the beginning when he made the leap of faith, the qualitative transition from non-belief to belief" (15). The leap of faith is more difficult if the matter has already been decided. When one is not a Christian and confronts the decision to become one, Christianity helps one to be aware of his decision. And the dis-tance between is a help, the preliminary running start making the leap easier. But if one already stands as a Christian, it is much harder to make the leap. "It is easier to become a Christian when I am not a Christian, then to become one when I am one" (327). This is certainly borne out by experience, for it is most difficult for a born-Christian to experience a real conversion in later life.

Faith Does Not Need Proof

Faith should consider proof as an enemy. When faith feels ashamed as a young woman who is embarrassed about her lover and so must have proof of his value, when faith begins to lose its passion, it demands a proof so as to appear more respectable to the unbeliever (31). There is a real danger in trying to answer rationalists with rationalistic arguments for faith, for in the process, faith itself is often lost.

> Suppose a man wishes to acquire faith; let the comedy be-gin. He wishes to have faith, but wishes also to safeguard himself by means of an objective inquiry and its approx-imation-process. What happens? With the approximation-process the absurd becomes something different; it now becomes probable, it becomes increasingly probable. Now he is ready to believe it, and he ventures to claim for him-self that he does not believe as shoemakers and tailors and simple folk believe, but only after long deliberation. Now he is ready to believe it. And lo, now it has become pre-cisely impossible to believe it. Anything that is almost pro-bably probable, or extremely and emphatically probable, is something he can almost know. -- But it is impossible

to believe, for the absurd is the object of faith, and the
only object that can be believed. (189)

Aquinas also distinguishes between faith and science. The object of faith is unseen, whereas the object of science is seen.
Nothing can be seen and believed simultaneously except under
the general aspect of credibility.[17]

Object of Faith, The Reality of Another

The object of faith is a person, not merely objective truths.
If the object of faith were a doctrine to be learned, faith would
be an intellectual relationship and we would have to be careful
not to err. Moreover, if the object of faith were a teacher with
a doctrine, the doctrine would be more important than the
teacher and the relationship would again be intellectual. But the
object of faith is the reality of the teacher, that the teacher really exists.

The object of faith is hence the reality of the God-man in
the sense of his existence. But existence involves first
and foremost particularity, and that is why thought must
abstract from existence, because the particular cannot
be thought, but only the universal. The object of faith is
thus God's reality in existence as a particular individual,
the fact that God has existed as an individual human being.
(290)

Definition of Faith

Faith is the objective certainty due to the repulsion of the
absurd held fast by the passion of inwardness, which in
this instance is intensified to the utmost degree. (540)

This formula only fits the believer, not a lover or a thinker,
but only the believer in his relationship to the paradoxical absurd. Faith cannot be considered as provisional in nature,
something to be resolved in a higher type of knowledge. Far
from resting content with unintelligibility, faith has a repulsion
from it, which is the very expression of its passion.

d Works of Love (1847)[18]

In Part II of this collection of discourses Kierkegaard treats of the love that believes all things, and yet is never deceived, the strong biblical loving belief.

Mistrust Believes Nothing At All

Commenting on Paul's "Love . . . believes all things" (1 Cor 13:7), Kierkegaard explains that there are other foundations of belief besides love, namely, frivolity, inexperience, and simplicity, which believe for reasons of vanity, conceit, and flattery. Mistrust, however, believes nothing at all. In this it is very close to evil.

> To believe nothing is right on the border where believing evil begins. The good is the object of faith, and, therefore, one who believes nothing, begins to believe evil. To believe nothing is the beginning of being evil for it shows that one has no good in him, since faith is precisely the good in man. (220)

Often mistrust is based on the evil in a man, which he suspects is in others also. To the world loving belief appears to be the height of foolishness. But this is a misunderstanding, for it crosses out "Love" and underlines the foolishness, "the believing of all things" rather than emphasizing the love which believes all things (220).

True Love Cannot Be Deceived

> Amazing! To believe nothing in order to never be deceived-- this seems to make sense. For how would a man ever be able to deceive some one who believes nothing! But to believe everything and thereby, as it were, to throw oneself away, fair game for all deception and all deceivers, and yet precisely in this way to assure oneself infinitely against every deception, this is remarkable. (221)

Yet even though he is not deceived by others, the man of mistrust is really deceived by himself for by believing nothing, he is tricked out of the blessedness of devotedness and love. The only sure way of never being deceived is to believe all things in love (221-222).

106

It is true that a lower type of love can be conceived where love is given and received on a commercial basis. However, the true lover loves all and does not demand reciprocating love. One cannot deceive the true lover, for he who tries it only deceives himself.

> By his attempt the deceiver becomes contemptible, and the lover preserves himself in love, abides in love and consequently in possession of the highest good and the greatest blessedness--therefore, he certainly is not deceived! The deceiver, however, deceives himself. He does not love, and thereby he has deceived himself out of the highest good and the greatest blessedness. (225)

Although the deceiver wants to trick the lover out of his love, this cannot be done, since the true lover does not in any way demand reciprocity. He can no more be deceived out of his love than one can be tricked out of a gift of money which he offers. "The true lover protects himself by believing all things--consequently by loving the deceiver" (228). The self-lover considers himself deceived when his love is not reciprocated. Not so the true lover who considers it a victory to continue loving the deceiver. Believing all, he is never deceived.

Conclusion

Kierkegaard is of salient importance in the development of modern Protestant theology of faith. The Father of Existentialism, he took up the subjective, personal line, going back beyond Luther to the New Testament, and opposed to the abstract Hegelian idealism. We will see his influence in such men as Buber, Barth, Bonhoeffer, and Marcel.

3 MARTIN BUBER (1878-1965);
   I AND THOU

Although most of the selections in this work on faith are from Christian sources, our study would not be complete without the distinguished Jewish theologian Martin Buber, for Buber's I and Thou[19] made a profound impression on the Christian world of faith especially in men such as Karl Heim, Friedrich Gogarten, Eberhard Grisebach, Rudolph Bultmann, Karl Barth, Paul Tillich, Reinhold Niebuhr, and others. A poet writing in images, Buber has a directness, an appeal to the here and now, a personal theme, which one might say is characteristic of Hebrew faith. Buber's faith is existential, reflecting Kierkegaard.

a I and Thou (1923/1957)

In this little epoch-making book we find Buber's greatest contribution to the theology of faith. His "I-Thou" theme has been strongly influential not only in theology, but in philosophy and psychology as well. Besides Kierkegaard's personalism and Dilthey's also, Buber echoes to some degree Nietzsche's criticism of the shallowness and hypocrisy of the traditional western values and his attempt to transcend them by affirming life and its elemental forces. Buber also shared the mystical trend of Hasidism leading to a personal affirmation of Jewish faith. But as he became more existential-minded, Buber became less and less interested in the mystical elements of Hasidism.[20] In I and Thou, first published in German in 1923, he criticized the mystical approach to unity and instead spoke of a relationship of love --similar to that between man and wife--as the real clue to the meaning of existence. Needless to say, this is a strongly biblical theme.

Buber's "I-Thou" philosophy directs itself towards real questions engaging the whole person, not just his intellect. Philosophical problems concerning the nature and destiny of man cannot be properly considered apart from concrete situations. Buber's emphasis on the life experience is certainly the foundation stone of his philosophy. His uniting of existentialism with the world-affirming spirit of Judaism is his outstanding contribution to contemporary thought.[21]

Buber's main theme in I and Thou is that there are two fundamental attitudes, or relations, in human experience. The first is a personal relationship of one subject with another subject, "I-Thou." The second is a contact with experienced objects, "I-It." The second attitude is that of the scientist whether he is dealing with people or things. In the "I-It" relationship, the "I" holds back seeking to control the object of its attention, but never accepting the other just as it is in itself. The danger for man is to become exclusively preoccupied with "I-It" to the exclsuion of "I-Thou."[22]

"I-Thou" is most fully expressed by the mutual love of husband and wife, where each "I" reveals himself to his "Thou." Since the whole person is involved, not just the intellect or the senses, the

"I-Thou" relationship is spoken with the whole being (3).

There is a tendency in each man to treat another man as an "It." For example scientists, politicians, employers, educators often treat people as things, commodities, objects to be used. There can be a failure in charity, love, in treating a fellow man as an "It" and not as a "Thou."

Buber relates every "I-Thou" encounter to the "Eternal Thou," God, who by his very nature never ceases to be a "Thou" for us. The "Eternal Thou" is never absent, but man can absent himself from him. Although we cannot measure or define him, we can hear his voice and answer him in obedience. In every true meeting with a "Thou," we catch a glimpse of the "Eternal Thou."[23] The bible is a history of this, for the "I-Thou" relationship between Israel and Yahweh must be expressed in love of one's neighbor. In the "Eternal Thou" the extended lines of these human personal relationships meet and are consummated.

Buber does not speak of God as an idea or as a principle, but as a person who comes into direct contact with man through his creating, revealing, and redeeming acts. Thus man can have a direct relationship with him. When we turn towards God, we do not turn away from other "Thou's" but rather bring these "I-Thou" relationships to fulfillment in God.

So for Buber "I-Thou" does not mean turning away from the world, but rather finding a true "I-Thou" relationship with it and so with the Eternal Thou.

> Buber has defined evil as the predominance of the world of It to the exclusion of relation, and he has conceived of the redemption of evil as taking place in the primal movement of the turning which brings man back to God and back to solidarity of relation with man and the world. Relation is 'good' and alienation 'evil.' Yet the times of alienation may prepare the forces that will be directed, when the turning comes, not only to the earthly forms of relation, but to the Eternal Thou.[24]

Buber gave a strong impetus to the modern theology of personal faith. His faith is a dialogue, a direct, personal, mutual relationship with God, for he felt that God has put man on earth in order to have this personal relationship with him. However, many today are challenging the possibility of calling God a Person. Buber clarified his position in his 1957 postscript to I and Thou.

The description of God as a Person is indispensable for every one who like myself means by "God" not a principle . . . nor an idea . . . but him who . . . enters into a direct relation with us men in creative, revealing, and redeeming acts, and thus makes it possible for us to enter into a direct relation with him. This ground and meaning of our existence constitutes a mutuality, arising again and again, such as can subsist only between persons. The concept of personal being is indeed completely incapable of declaring what God's essential being is. But it is both permitted and necessary to say that God is also a Person. (135)

God's infinite attributes include not only spiritual being, and natural being, but also personal being.

As a Person God gives personal life, he makes us as persons become capable of meeting with him and with one another. But no limitation can come upon him as the absolute Person either from us or from our relations with one another. In fact, we can dedicate to him not merely our persons, but also our relations to one another. The man who turns to him, therefore, need not turn away from any other "I-Thou" relation. But he properly brings them to him and lets them be fulfilled "In the face of God." (136)

God's speech penetrates our daily lives in biographical and historical events.

Happening upon happening, situation upon situation, are enabled and empowered by the personal speech of God to demand of the human person that he take his stand and make his decision. Often enough we think that there is nothing to hear, but long before we have put wax in our ears. (136 and 137)

b Two Types of Faith (1950)[25]

Here Buber contrasts Hebrew faith as found in Phariseeism and in the teachings of Jesus with that of Hellenistic Judaism as seen in Paul and John. Hebrew faith, emuna is a complete personal confidence in some one, an "I-Thou" relationship, whereas pistis, is more the acceptance of a thing. The origin of emuna is in the history of the Jewish nation, whereas pistis is more of an individual event (170). The story of Israel is a history of faith events. However, as Judaism loses its sense of community, personal faith is endangered.

> Therefore, the danger which threatens personal faith is to become impoverished in its essential spontaneity in the time of eclipse and in its place to be succeeded by elements of pistis, in part a logical and in part a mystical experience. (171)

Buber distinguishes further the two types of faith, Jewish and Christian. In the first, one "finds himself" in the relationship of faith, in the second, he is "converted" to it. The Hebrew who finds himself in faith, does so as a member of the covenant community. The Christian is converted as an individual and the community is formed from the converted individuals (9). Thus the Israelite community of faith is contrasted with the new community of Christians. Hebrew faith in God was born

> from the tribe-forging and nation-forging migrations which were experienced as guided by God. The individual finds himself within the objective race-memory of such guidance and of such a covenant. His faith is a perseverance in trust in the guiding and covenanting Lord, trusting perseverance in the contact with Him. (10)

There was some modification of this attitude in the diaspora, but not in its inner nature.

Christianity began as diaspora and mission. Jesus calls men to turn to the Kingdom of God. Salvation is here.

> To the one to be converted comes the demand and instruction to believe that which he is not able to believe as a continuation of his former beliefs, but only in a leap. To be sure the inner precinct of faith is not understood as a mere believing that something is true, but a constitution of existence. But the forecourt is the holding of that which has hitherto been considered not true, indeed quite absurd, and there is no other entrance. (10 and 11)

This passage clearly reflects Kierkegaard, for whom the leap was not to an absurd proposition, but rather to the paradoxical person of Christ, the God-man.

Buber contrasts the Jewish emuna, the faith of confidence, which is seen in the New Testament where faith is spoken of in the active form "to believe," (e.g., Mark 9:23, "All things are possible to him who believes") with pistis (as found in Romans 10:9, "Believe in your heart that God raised him from the dead").

> And this faith is a "Believe that" in the pregnant sense of the word, which is essentially different from the faith of the Jews that on Sinai a divine revelation took place, as it signifies the acceptance of the reality of an event, which is not destined, like the former, to confirm and strengthen the hereditary actuality of faith of the Jewish person who hears it, but fundamentally to change it. (97 and 98)

Certainly Buber is right. Christian faith is primarily a conversio, a metanoia. But it is not merely an intellectual decision, a change of mind as when one changes an opinion. Rather it is a complete conversion to, commitment to, the person of the risen Christ.

Does the Christian believe that Christ has risen, or rather does he believe in the risen Christ? We cannot separate the person believed from his kerygma. There is not here a switching of allegiance from Yahweh to Jesus Christ, for the belief is that Yahweh has raised up Jesus, his Son. New Testament pistis, if accepted as "believing that" is based on the confidence of emuna, which precedes it. For Paul pistis is man's concrete relationship to Christ in confidence, hope, fidelity, and obedience. Ingo Hermann writes:

> The narrowing down of the pistis concept to an act of faith that merely accepts a thing as true, and thus merely intellectually conceived, cannot be justified on the basis of the material available. Pauline faith in particular is not merely dogmatic faith.[26]

The conversion of faith is a movement from self-reliance to obedience in confidence, involving both emuna and pistis. Hermann rightly criticizes Buber for limiting pistis principally to "belief that." Certainly there was some Greek influence on Paul and John, but their training was essentially in Hebrew thought. Paul's Pharisaic education showed through in his beautiful tracts on faith where pistis would seem to be almost the equivalent of emuna.

Conclusion

The personal faith relationship of the Old Testament between Israel and Yahweh was described by the Prophets as having the intimacy of a marriage union, whose love, knowledge, and fidelity typify the interpersonal relationship between Israel and her God. Buber distinguishes clearly between this Jewish faith and the seemingly intellectual faith of Paul. But others would say that the personal biblical emuna shines through Paul's pistis as the personal Christian commitment to Jesus Christ.

Buber, carrying on the biblical "I-Thou" theme and combining it with the personalism of Kierkegaard and Dilthey has added much to the modern development of interpersonal relations in general and of personal faith in particular, which we will see in such contemporary giants as Karl Barth, Rudolf Bultmann, Paul Tillich, Dietrich Bonhoeffer, and Gabriel Marcel.

Notes

1 J. Dillenberger and C. Welch, Protestant Christianity (New York: Charles Scribner's Sons, 1954), pp. 122-27.

2 Ibid., pp. 182-89.

3 The Christian Faith, Vol. I (New York: Harper & Row Publishers, 1963). Page numbers of the work under discussion will be in parentheses throughout the next three chapters.

4 J. Oman, tr. (New York: Harper & Row Publishers, 1958), p. 36.

5 J. Pelikan, From Luther to Kierkegaard (St. Louis: Concordia Publishing House, 1950), p. 113.

6 Ibid., p. 115.

7 William Hamilton, Radical Theology and the Death of God (Indianapolis: Bobbs-Merrill Company, Inc., 1966), p. 97.

8 Louis Dupre, Kierkegaard as Theologian (New York: Sheed and Ward, 1963), p. 135.

9 V. Lindstrom, "The Problem of Objectivity and Subjectivity in Kierkegaard," tr. N. Enkvist, A Kierkegaardian Critique, H. Johnson and H. Thulstrup, eds. (New York: Harper & Row Publishers, 1962), p. 237.

10 Ibid., p. 239.

11 Either/Or (1843) and The Stages of Life (1845) describe the first two stages, whereas Fear and Trembling (1843) and Repetition (1843) illustrate more the mode of Christian faith.

12 A. Dru, tr. (London: Oxford University Press, 1951). In the parentheses after the quotes, the first series of numbers refers to the date of the entry, the second number refers to the passage in Dru's edition.

13 See Chapter IV.

14 The Last Years, Journals, 1853-1855. R. Smith, tr. (London: Collins, 1965), pp. 99-100.

15 W. Lowrie, tr. (Princeton, New Jersey: Princeton University Press, 1952). See also Concept of Dread (1844) and Sickness Unto Death (1849).

16 D. Swenson, tr. (Princeton, New Jersey: Princeton University Press, 1941).

17 See Chapter IV, also Aquinas, ST 2-2, q.1, a. 4 & 5.

18 H. & E. Long, tr. (New York: Harper & Row Publishers, 1962). Page numbers in parentheses.

19 R. Smith, tr. (New York: Charles Scribner's Sons, 1958).

20 M. Diamond, Martin Buber, Jewish Existentialist (New York: Oxford University Press, 1960), p. 3.

21 P. Pfeutze, Self, Society, Existence (New York: Harper & Row Publishers, 1961), p. 143.

22 Ibid. For further development of Buber's interhuman relationship see Between Man and Man, R. Smith, tr. (London, 1947).

23 P. Pfeutze, Self, Society, Existence, p. 154.

24 M. Friedman, Martin Buber, The Life of Dialogue (New York: Harper & Row Publishers, 1960), p. 76.

25 N. Goldhawk, tr. (New York: Harper & Row Publishers, 1961).

26 The Experience of Faith, D. Coogan, tr. (New York: P. J. Kennedy & Sons, 1966), p. 67. See also R. Smith, Martin Buber (Richmond, John Knox Press, 1967), p. 40.

CHAPTER VIII

Christ alone

BARTH TO BONHOEFFER

1 KARL BARTH (1886--);
SOLA FIDE, SOLUS CHRISTUS

In what has been called a Theology of Crisis, Barth strongly criticized liberalism for minimizing God's transcendence and so for minimizing faith. In trying to make religion more relevant with the aid of science, historical method, and philosophy, the liberals had reasoned away the great and infinite distance be- tween God and man so that the leap of faith was no longer neces- sary. For Barth faith is an existential giving of self, not a leaning upon history or science or philosophy. God intervenes in a vertical and punctual manner in man's life; his revelation is a breath-taking event in which he continuously gives himself to be known and loved. In the beginning Barth used Kierkegaard; however, in his later works he regarded existentialism as a remnant of Pietism.[1]

In the Twenties and early Thirties Barth collaborated with Brunner, Gogarten, Thurneysen, and others in the Neo-Orthodox school. Firmly resisting liberal theology, they insisted on the bi-polar dialectic between God and man. God is totally other, incon-ceivable, incomprehensible; man is fallen, sinful, mortal. Yet man can see the shining light of God's revelation in Jesus Christ whom he accepts in obedient faith.[2] As the years went by, Barth's early dualistic and sometimes polemical style gave way to a more synthetic, Christo-centric approach to theology.[3]

a The Epistle to the Romans (1918)[4]

This is Barth's famous early commentary on Romans, where he first took the liberals to task for minimizing God's transcendence.

What Is Faith?

Faith is awe in the presence of the almighty God. Although it loves God, it is keenly aware of the distinction between God and man and God and the world. Affirming the resurrection as the turning point of the world, at the same time, it affirms the divine "No" in Christ.

> He who knows the world to be bounded by a truth that con-tradicts it; he who knows himself to be bounded by a will that contradicts him, he who, knowing too well that he must be satisfied to live with this contradiction and not attempt to escape from it, finds it hard to kick against the pricks (Overbeck); he who finally makes open confession of the con-tradiction and determines to base his life upon it--he it is who believes. The believer is the man who puts his trust in God, in God Himself, and in God alone; that is to say, the man who, perceiving the faithfulness of God in the very fact that He has set us within the realm of that which contradicts the course of this world, meets the faithfulness of God with a corresponding fidelity. (38-39)

The believer discovers God's saving grace in the gospel, marking the advent of eternal blessedness and giving the courage to stand and watch. Here is a free choice between scandal and faith, a choice which is presented to him everywhere and at every moment. Although feeling, conviction, perception, moral life, and piety ac-company faith, they are merely unimportant signs of faith and so should not be confused with it. Faith lives on its own because it lives on God (40).

Faithfulness of God in Jesus Christ

Our faith is based on the faithfulness of God. God's righteousness is made manifest through his faithfulness in Jesus Christ.

> The faithfulness of God is the divine patience according to
> which he provides, at sundry times and at many diverse
> points in human history occasions and possibilities and
> witnesses of the knowledge of His righteousness. Jesus of
> Nazareth is the point at which it can be seen that all other
> points form one line of supreme significance. (95)

God's faithfulness is established when we find Christ in Jesus.
Our discovery is authorized because every manifestation of the
faithfulness of God bears witness to what we have encountered
in Jesus. We believe in God because he is faithful. And we believe in Jesus Christ because God's faithfulness is manifest in
him.

Faith Is Conversion

In faith man stands naked before God, completely impoverished
that he may gain the kingdom of heaven; "It is the attitude of the
man who for the sake of Jesus has lost his own soul" (98). Faith
is the faithfulness of God which is hidden beyond all human ideas,
reasonings, and positive religious achievements. Faith is not
something that we have as an assured possession. Rather it is a
leap into the unknown, a flight into the empty air (98).

By Faith Alone

Faith marks the new order where self-recognition and boasting
ends and God's righteousness begins. Faith is not a foundation
built by man or a system according to which we live. From the
human point of view, religion, law, and method of life become
anarchy and abyss, but the law of God's faithfulness is where we
are established in God.

> This 'moment' of the movement of men by God is beyond
> men, it cannot be enclosed in a system or a method or a
> 'way,' it rests in the good pleasure of God, and its oc-
> casion is to be sought and found only in Him. 'The law of

the spirit of life' (8:2) is the point of view--by which all human boasting is excluded. (110)

We cannot escape the paradox of faith for by faith alone does man stand before God. God's faithfulness can be believed only because it is this. If it were more, it would be less (112).

We Believe We Shall Also Live

Faith is the beginning and the end, assuring that man's invisible existence in God is based on reality. Faith is the giant irrevocable step over the chasm separating old and new. It is bi-polar and paradoxical.

Faith presents itself in a series of paradoxes: human vacuum--divine fullness; human speechlessness, igno- rance, and expectation--divine words, knowledge, and ac - tion; the end of all things human--the beginning of divine possibility. Faith is the divine revolution and upheaval by which the well-known equilibrium between 'Yes' and 'No'; grace and sin, good and evil, is disturbed and overthrown. (201)

The believer, dying in Christ, sees in the Cross a chance to grasp the insecurity of human existence as a divine necessity moving beyond insecurity. It is through faith that our existence in God comes onto the horizon. By our faith we take the great step of conversion which is irrevocable since it will allow no turning back. In faith there is not only emptiness, but also full- ness, not only our own belief, but also God's faithfulness. What do we believe?

We believe that Christ died in our place, and that there- fore we died with Him, we believe in our identity with the invisible new man who stands on the other side of the Cross. We believe in that external existence of ours which is grounded upon the knowledge of death, upon the Resur- rection, upon God. We believe 'That we shall also live with Him.' (202)

Dialectical faith links God and man in eternal life.

b Anselm: Fides Quaerens Intellectum (1931)[5]

Going back to Anselm and Augustine, Barth finds the key to his theology in inquiring faith, not in the arguments of reason.

Theology, Intellectus Fidei

Anselm was deeply concerned with the Intellectus Fidei, for example, Fides Quaerens Intellectum was the original title of his Proslogion. The Intelligere of faith is desired by faith and leads to probare and laetificare. This is a spontaneous desire, for the quaerere intellectum is really immanent in faith. So faith does not require proof, it merely desires it insofar as it wants intelligere.

> For Anselm 'to believe' does not mean simply a striving of the human will towards God but a striving of the human will into God and so a participation (albeit in a manner limited by creatureliness) in God's mode of Being and so a similar participation in God's aseity, in the matchless glory of his very Self and therefore also in God's utter absence of necessity. (17)

Theology presupposes faith and so cannot lead to faith, confirm faith, or remove doubt. It would be profitable for those engaged in the teaching of theology to read and reread Barth's writings on the intellectus fidei.

The Nature of Faith Seeks Knowledge

Faith seeks knowledge of God, the Truth. In Anselm's affective faith, tendere in Deum, the Word encounters us as Imago summae essentiae. Thus the completeness of man's likeness to God is restored to him through faith. The intelligere of faith gives us the potentiality of advancing towards vision. It is itself a similitude of the vision and perhaps, in a sense, the beginning of the vision, leading men, not beyond, but right up to the limits of faith.

> Intellectus is the limited, but fully attainable, first step towards that vision which is the eschatological counterpart of faith. Therefore fides is essentially--quaerens intellectum. (21)

119

And Anselm urges us to seek the intelligere of the things that we believe, hungering for the ratio fidei.

Ratio Fidei

Anselm tells us that as there is no self-redemption, so there is no self-rescue from irrationality to rationality, from stupidity to wisdom. But when the ratio fidei rises out of the irrationabilitas becoming vera ratio, then this is the work of the self-illuminating ratio veritatis enlightening the noetic ratio from above. This is the work of the ratio fidei itself.

As theology cannot anticipate the move from insipiens to fidelis, so it cannot dissolve the right order between the faith and knowledge of the believer by which faith must be obedience to authority which is prior to knowledge (64).

Anselm's Fides Quaerens Intellectum has proved to be the foundation of Barth's approach to theology. As he wrote in the preface of the second edition:

> Most of them [commentators] have completely failed to see that in this book on Anselm I am working with a vital key, if not the key, to an understanding of that whole process of thought that has impressed me more and more in my Church Dogmatics as the only one proper to theology. (11)

c Church Dogmatics (1934-1958)[6]

Object of Faith, Jesus Christ

Faith is what makes a man a Christian, and is the basis of the Christian existence of the individual. Barth, as Aquinas, teaches the importance of the object of faith.

> Faith stands or falls with its object. It is a subjective realization, that is, as a human activity, it consists in the subjectivization of an objective res which in its existence and essence and dignity and significance and scope takes precedence of this subjectivization and, therefore, of the human subject and his activity, his faith. (IV, i, 742)

Through faith the Christian enters into relationship with the divine object, Jesus Christ, the person present. Faith for the Christian is orientation to Christ, for the man who believes looks to Christ and is wholly dependent on him, renouncing all self-determination and all control of his own center. Since the man of faith has found in Christ his true center which is outside of himself, he must cling to him and depend on him so that any other orientation must be subordinate to this (IV, 1, 743-44).

Faith is not only related to Jesus Christ, its object, but it is based on him, originating from the point to which it is orientated. The very necessity of faith lies in its object in whom faith takes place for each believer. Confronting man as an absolute superiority, the divine object rejects every sin and disbelief so that man is born again in obedience and in the freedom of faith. "This object of faith is, in fact, the circle that encloses them all, and which has to be closed by every man in the act of faith" (IV, 1, 747). Barth's circle of faith begins and ends with Jesus Christ, encompassing man and completed in the act of faith. In the "No" and "Yes" of faith in Jesus Christ, the root of unbelief is pulled out and replaced by the root of faith, making unbelief impossible.

The Holy Spirit is the power in which Jesus Christ makes a man free for his choice of faith. He is the power in which the object of faith has also its origin and basis. Faith is his work and gift, confessing itself

> as the human decision for this object, the human participation in it which he makes in his own free act but which he can only receive, which he can understand only as something which is received, which he can continually look for as something which is received again and which has to be confirmed in a new act. (IV, 1, 748)

Since the strength of faith lies in him who is believed, it is as simple and wonderful as the discovery of a child who finds himself in his father's house or in his mother's lap.

Personal Faith

Because faith is orientated to and based on Jesus Christ, in it the subject is completely renewed, brought into peace with God from his struggle against him and so he becomes a partaker of the salvation given to him (IV, 1, 750). The Christian with his personal faith as a member of the Mystical Body is in direct contact with the head. This means that the individual Christian can only believe in and with the community. However, "the creaturely subject constituted in the being and work of Jesus Christ and awakened as such by the power of the Holy Spirit, is in the last resort the individual Christian in the act of his personal faith" (IV, 1, 751).

> If there is no Christian I and Thou and He outside the two-fold, Christ-centered circle of the We and You and They of the race and the community, then the general no less than the particular is an abstraction not to say an illusion, since it does not become event in the Christian I and Thou and He, in the personal faith of the members of the body of Christ. (IV, 1, 751)

Although the Christian believes within the community, community faith is dependent on the personal faith of its members. The faith event of the individual member is not merely cognitive in character, for it posits a new being, a new creation, a new birth. Since the believer is encircled by Christ, his faith originating and orientating towards him is not merely intellectual, but creative.

Faith is the relationship between Jesus Christ and the individual man. Not only does Jesus Christ confront the community, but also the individuals in it. "'Jesus lives'--and I with Him--which means that from all eternity God has thought of me, elected me, acted for me in Him, called me to Himself in Him as His Word" (IV, 1, 753). Each faith relationship is unique, for each believer is uniquely this man, both in relation to God and in relation to his fellow men. Jesus Christ is Mediator, Savior, and Lord just for him. Christ died for his sins, for him God raised him up. By his faith the believer recognizes and confesses that Jesus Christ is for him. And in this is his new birth. "There is no pro nobis or propter nos homines which does not include in itself and is not enclosed by pro me" (IV, 1, 755).

The Act of Faith

The act of faith is

> the act of the Christian life to the extent that in all the activity and individual acts of a man it is the most inward and central and decisive act of his heart. The one which-- if it takes place--characterizes them all as Christian, as expressions and confirmations of his Christian freedom, his Christian responsibility, his Christian obedience. (IV, 1, 757-58)

The act of faith is the acknowledgment, recognition, and confession of God, which are included in and follow from the fact that
it is a free act of obedience. Man's encounter of faith is fundamentally an obedience to Christ, rather than an acceptance of
certain statements which attest and proclaim him.

The Living Knowledge of Faith

The knowing of faith is not an abstract cognition, since it is
only one element in the active recognition of faith. It decides the
meaning and direction of faith, showing us what must be the object and origin of the recognition of faith. The knowing of faith
is related to its object. Objective and theoretical, it is also
practical, knowing and recognizing and acknowledging that Jesus
Christ is and does for me--that he is my Lord (IV, 1, 765). This
is not an abstract or dead knowledge, but a concrete, living,
existential knowledge, which is the active recognition of faith, a
personal knowledge which moves the Christian to shape his existence to parallel that of the Lord.

"Faith in Him necessarily calls me to the recognition of myself in the power of which--and this is the real act of the heart
of faith--I can only wish to be the man determined and stamped
by Him and set in His light" (IV, 1, 770). This reminds one of
Aquinas' teachings on the light of faith.[7] Through faith I become
parallel, a likeness of Jesus Christ, overcoming my pride and
fall, mortifying the old man, putting on Christ, in whom is my
confidence and vivificatio.

Sola Fide, Solus Christus

Sola fide is the echo of solus Christus for he alone is the one
in whom man is justified. Faith is an openness to the divine object, grasping the alien righteousness of Jesus Christ. Yet it
can only be humble and comforted despair insofar as it is a human act. The movement between God and man in Jesus Christ is
man's movement insofar as it has taken place for him.

> Everything depends on the fact that it is being in encounter
> with the living Jesus Christ, a being from and to this ob-
> ject. That is what is meant by Christian faith. That is the
> meaning of being, the act and experience in which man can
> believe in response to the Christian message. He knows
> and affirms and understands himself in Christian faith.

Not in the abstraction of his being for himself--he is not
for himself, but Jesus Christ is for him--but from and
to what he is in Jesus Christ. He is what he is insofar as
this One is for him. (IV, 1, 633)

The believer experiences a new feeling of freedom when he realizes that Jesus Christ is for him, that he is justified, his sins
forgiven, that he is a child of God, an heir of eternal life.

Faith is an imitation of Christ, an analogy to his attitude and
action, modeling itself on him, corresponding to him. As he
was emptied, humbled, obedient, poor, the believer must be
humble, obedient and poor--a human imitation of what God has
done for man in this One. "It cannot be denied that justifying faith
is, in fact, a concrete correspondence to the One in whom it
believes, and that if it is not, it is not justifying faith" (IV, 1,
636).

Conclusion

Karl Barth, as his Reformation predecessors, teaches a justification by faith alone, the faith that is a personal experience of
Jesus Christ. The "I-Thou" circle originating and completing itself in Christ is closed only in the faith-event, which constitutes
the Christian in the being and work of Jesus Christ. Certain that
Christ is for him, he orientates his life accordingly.

Reacting to liberal theology, Barth emphasizes the transcendent
God in Jesus Christ as the origin and object of faith, yet he does
not neglect the subjective, personal, and experiential side of faith.
Faith is a dialectic between the transcendent God and the humble
believer, initiated and completed by the all-encircling God in
Christ. The faith-event questing knowledge is Barth's foundation
stone of theology.

Barth has been called one of the greatest theologians of our
time. And although recent trends in secular theology seem to
have by-passed him for the more liberal ideas of the nineteenth
century, some would even see a Barthian influence here. Perhaps
his dialectical faith in the transcendent, giving hope for the future,
is not foreign to current thought in Christian eschatology.

2 RUDOLF BULTMANN (1884--); EXISTENTIAL SELF-UNDERSTANDING IN THE CHRIST EVENT

Bultmann's early works reflect Crisis Theology's attack on the liberals in the spirit of Karl Barth. However, he diverged from Barth especially after World War II when his demythologizing became the center of attention, as Barth's Crisis Theology had been after World War I.

Barth criticized Bultmann's application of Heideggerian existential analytics to scriptural hermeneutics, rejecting the idea that a philosophy can underlie exegesis as an absolute norm and thus weaken the sovereignty of God.[8] There is, however, a similarity between Bultmann and Barth, for both want to detach faith from history, both have identified man's act of faith with his existential self-giving, renouncing the objective guarantees of history. Although they have followed different paths, both started off opposing liberal theology.[9]

Bultmann's demythologizing is essential to his theology of faith. Actually insofar as it is an attempt to explain the gospels in contemporary terms, demythologizing goes back to the earliest days of Christianity. However, its more immediate roots can be found in the Enlightenment and the scriptural criticism of the eighteenth and nineteenth centuries. In a sense, Bultmann's demythologizing stands between literalism and liberalism, for, far from wishing to remove all mythology from scripture, rather he wishes to interpret it properly,[10] setting free the kerygma of Jesus Christ.

Bultmann describes mythology as "the use of imagery to express the other worldly in terms of this world and the divine in terms of human life, the other side in terms of this side."[11] The main problem is that this mythological language has been interpreted literally. Man must penetrate the mythology in order to understand the human existence hidden within. Then he must find contemporary terms to express it. For Bultmann these were the terms of existential philosophy. Thus demythologizing is "the use of non-mythological terms to express for the modern day the mythological understanding of human existence contained in the New Testament."[12] Bultmann's demythologizing is not ultra-liberal reductionism, ignoring elements in the New Testament which do not appeal to it,· nor is it merely Heidegger baptized, but rather it is the interpretation of the New Testament faith in terms of the understanding of human existence.[13]

For Bultmann demythologizing is parallel to Paul's and Luther's justification by faith and not by works, for it relieves man from all self-satisfying created securities, leaving him only his faith in God.

> Like the doctrine of justification it destroys every false security and every false demand for it on the part of man, whether he seeks it in his good works or in his ascertainable knowledge. The man who wishes to believe in God as his God must realize that he has nothing in his hand on which to base his faith. He is suspended in mid-air, and cannot demand a proof of the Word which addresses him. For the ground and object of faith are identical, security can be found only by abandoning all security, by being ready, as Luther put it, to plunge into the inner darkness.[14]

a "Faith as Venture" (1928)[15]

Faith is to venture something in faith and at the same time to venture faith itself. One must allow his concrete "now" to be determined by the proclamation and the faith which it engenders.

> If the proclamation of God's forgiving love is really valid for me, i.e., for me in my concrete life situation, then it is not at all understandable apart from that situation. And I am not to believe in general--also to believe alongside of or behind my other relationships--but rather am to believe here and now as one who has something to do (or to endure), and who is to do this thing in faith--who is to venture what he does in faith and venture faith in what he does. (56)

Unless this word qualifies my concrete present, I have not really believed, although I have heard the word. "Only when I understand myself and my situation in terms of the word, only when I see or venture to see my neighbor in the other person who encounters me, only then have I believed and do I believe now" (56). Our faith should not so much lie behind our works as something to be speculated or contemplated, but be in them.

The venture of faith is at the same time certain and uncertain, certain because of its divine object, uncertain because of my own weakness. Here Bultmann reminds one of Luther's dilemma, leading to the leap of faith.

Thus faith is a 'leap in the dark' because man would fain
find security by looking at himself and yet must precisely
let himself go in order to see the object of faith; and just
this is a 'leap in the dark' for the natural man. But this
does not mean any blind risk, any game of chance, any
random groping, but rather a knowing venture. For man
is not asked whether he will accept a theory about God that
may be false, but whether he is willing to obey God's will.
(57)

b "The Historicity of Man and Faith" (1930)[16]

Faith and Philosophy

The philosopher disregards whether something like faith or
unfaith exists. Since faith answers a contingent call here and
now to an individual, any explicit consideration of it by philosophy
would be just as absurd as a philosophical study of whether a
concrete marriage proposal should be accepted or not (93).

Theology does not destroy philosophy, but rather builds upon
it, allowing philosophy to refer it to the phenomenon itself and
allowing the phenomenon and man himself, whose structure philos-
phy seeks to explain, to teach it. Although faith may overcome
prior existence ontically, it does not destroy it. Faith, rather
than a quality that inheres in the believer, is a possibility of man
that must be constantly renewed, for man exists by constantly laying
hold of his possibilities (96).

Theology is dependent for clarification of its concepts on a pre-
theological understanding of man, often determined by a philosophical
tradition. For example, faith can be a holding of things as true,
trust, obedience, or a numinous experience, depending upon one's
philosophical orientation.

Revelation and Faith

How is revelation received by a man of faith in comparison with
a man of unfaith? The man of faith knows that revelation has encountered him,

that he really lives, that he is, in fact, graced, that he is
really forgiven and will always be so. And he knows this
in such a way that by faith in the revelation his concrete life
in work and in joy, in struggle and in pain is newly qualified.

127

He knows that through the event of revelation the events of his life become new--'new' in a sense that is valid only for the man of faith and visible only to him. That, indeed, only becomes visible in the now and thus always becomes visible anew. The only new thing that faith and faith alone is able to say about revelation is that it has become an event and becomes an event. (100)

This event clarifies man's profane existence as already graced. Philosophy can "understand" this in the formal sense, just as it can recognize that one's eyes are opened in an actual friendship. "But only the man of faith understands (in the ontic or existential sense) profane existence as graced" (101-02). In his faith the natural man is again discovered as a creature of God.

c "The Crisis of Belief" (1931)[17]

The Christ Event

How does Christian belief differ from other types of belief in God?

> Christian belief has its peculiar character in speaking of an event that gives it this right, in saying that it hears a Word which demands that it should recognize God as standing over against man. For Christianity belief in God is . . . belief in a definite Word proclaimed to the believer. The event is Jesus Christ, in whom, as the New Testament says, God has spoken, and whom the New Testament itself calls 'the Word.' That is, in what happened in and through Christ God has decisively manifested himself, and on this event a message is based and authenticated which confronts man as God's Word, not teaching him a new concept of God, but giving him the right to believe in God in whom he would fain believe. (11-12)

Christianity is characterized by and differs from other beliefs in God, in that Christianity is centered in the Christ-event, the Word of God in Jesus Christ. Belief in God can only arise as a response to God's Word, the Christ-event in the New Testament. This Word, passed on by the Church reassures the believer that God is and that God is his God (12).

Man can find God in his Word by a real and radical submission with confession of sin and forgiveness. This is the confession of guilt before God, guilt which can only be wiped out by a Word of forgiveness. The surrender of faith not only involves a negative recognition of human finiteness, but a positive recognition of the "Thou" as the criterion of my finiteness, especially in his un-bounding love (13).

Constant Crisis of Belief

If Christian belief in God, like any belief in God at all, is the silent and reverential submission to the power calling me into life and making me finite--if belief is the will to implement continually this submission in the 'moment' and in the recognition of the 'moment,' then the crisis in belief is a constant one; for this will always be implemented in a struggle with the self-will which refuses to recognize man's limitations. The summons must always be heard afresh. Belief in God, indeed, is never something we can have as a possession. On the contrary, it always implies a decision to be taken. (14-15)

Belief is not just the concern of a people or of an era, it is always my concern, not something I possess, but a matter of decision. Its crisis consists of the constant fight of self-will against the claims of the "moment" (15), which are the claims of the "Thou" and the demand of love. It is in the struggle of hate against love, which enters into every encounter with the "thou" which we would in selfishness disregard. Crises of belief due to the claims of natural and historical science can really be reduced to man's claim to and search for self-sufficiency to the neglect of the God-dependence of faith.

d "Grace and Freedom" (1948)[18]

Faith and Self-Recognition

Bultmann takes the standard Pauline and Reformation line of identifying justification by works with self-justification and boast-ing. The man seeking self-justification is merely displaying his need for recognition, seeing in his obedience to God an achieve-ment to be proud of, wanting to be recognized in the presence of God (170-71).

Faith is the attitude opposed to that urge for self-recognition
--the radical abandonment of self-glorification, of the desire
for recognition by one's own strength and achievement. It is
the knowledge that the recognition which makes him secure
for himself and in the presence of God can only be gifted.
Faith pronounces the saying 'What hast thou that thou didst
not receive? Now if thou didst receive it, why dost thou glory
as if thou hadst not received it?' (1 Cor 4:7) (171)

Faith Is Obedience

In faith-obedience man's pride and self-sufficiency are broken.
Obedience is not a strong self-control in order to accomplish a
task, but rather the abandonment of all power and full submission
to God, from whom all power comes. Rather than a general trust
that God will help me here and now, faith is a radical surrender
to God's will, completely unknown to me. It is man's decision
against himself and for God (175).

Freely Chosen Gift

It would seem that if faith is a gift predestined from all eternity,
it is no longer a free decision. On the other hand, faith can only be
faith insofar as it is a free decision. The paradoxical unity of freedom and grace in the gift of faith can be compared to an interpersonal relationship, where trusting self-surrender to the other is a
free decision.

And yet the person who trustingly surrenders himself knows
that he has his being entirely from the other party. He knows
that he does not bring about his friendship or his love as a
'work' by virtue of which he gains the friendship or love of
the other party, but that the other party in returning it is
just as free as he is in himself, and that he can only bestow
his friendship or his love as a gift. (178)

Loving friendship transforms me into a new being for my friend,
in overlooking my glaring weaknesses and defects and seeing in
me the man I would like to be, makes me such (179). Relations
between human friends reflect those between God and man, which
embrace man's whole human existence and completely renew him.
In the decision of faith, all other considerations are called
into question, leaving man free and open. Abandoning all security,

man realizes that his faith is not his own work, but a free gift of God.

e "Bultmann Replies to His Critics" (1948)[19]

Existential Self-understanding

Faith is genuine only when one understands himself to be a creature of God here and now in his own existential circumstances. "It can only be attained existentially by submitting to the power of God exercising pressure upon me here and now, and this too need not necessarily be raised to the level of consciousness" (198). But if we cannot speak of an act of God without speaking simultaneously of our own existence, does not this rob God of his objectivity? Is faith reduced to an experience of the soul? Faith for Bultmann is an encounter with God, but not an encounter which can be objectively measured, just as the mutual love of two lovers cannot be measured objectively.

Existential self-understanding should not be confused with the existentialist understanding of human being elaborated by philosophical analysis, for in the former one does not learn what existence means in the abstract, but rather he understands himself now in his concrete encounters. Although it need not be conscious, existential self-understanding permeates and controls imperceptibly all anxiety and firmness, all joy and fear. We find this even in a child in relation to his parents, in his trust, security, gratitude, reverence, and obedience. His disobedience is self-misunderstanding, although not completely so, since there appears a guilt of conscience (203).

Existential self-understanding is not only self-realization, but also an encounter with the other.

> By understanding myself in this encounter, I understand the other in such a way that the whole world appears in a new light, which means that it has in fact become an entirely different world. I acquire a new insight into and a new judgement of my own past and future in a new sense. I submit to new demands and acquire a new readiness for further encounters. Clearly such an understanding cannot be possessed as a timeless truth, for its validity depends upon its being constantly renewed, and upon an understanding of the imperative it involves. (203-04)

Just as in human love, there must be a permanent rapport with the subject of encounter, so the self-understanding of faith is kept pure only as a response to the repeated encounter with the Word of God in the Christ-event. This must be renewed every morning. "Granted this, however, I can know that I myself am renewed every morning by it, that I am one who allows myself to be renewed by it" (204). Far from being an abstract speculation or formula, faith is living and must constantly be renewed.

Conclusion

In Chapter II we studied Bultmann's Faith and his Theology of the New Testament, whereas in this chapter we have limited ourselves to his essays. Throughout all of his works the biblical faith is strong. Far from destroying faith, Bultmann's demythologizing sets the kerygma free to speak to me of God's decisive act in Christ,[20] although it sometimes runs the risk of undermining the historical foundations of the kerygma.

Faith for Bultmann is fundamentally dependence on God and not on self or on the world, for man is not justified by his own boastful works, but only by faith in God. Rather than a speculation or an abstract formula, faith is an existential relationship with the Word of God here and now in the Christ-event. It is "a readiness for the eternal to encounter us at any time in the present--at any time in the varying situations of our life . . . for surprisingly God can encounter us where we do not expect it."[21]

Misunderstanding himself as long as he seeks to be self-sufficient, man can only understand himself through his faith-encounter with God in Christ.

Faith is both a free decision and a gift of God and it is the former because it is the latter. Permeating man's whole life, as an existential faith it must constantly be renewed.

Bultmann has brought his keen existential insights to bear on the theology of faith, pointing out again that since the Bible was written in a more existential vein than a speculative one, perhaps existentialism is best suited for biblical interpretation.

3 PAUL TILLICH (1888-1965); ULTIMATE CONCERN,
   THE NEW BEING IN JESUS CHRIST

Considered as the foremost Protestant thinker of his time in America, Tillich was equally outstanding in both philosophy and theology. And, as Schelling whom he admired, he was keenly interested in the correlation or bordering of the two disciplines. Rather than destroying reason, faith aids man to reach ecstatically beyond himself, fulfilling his rationality to the utmost.[22] Thus Tillich always strove to keep a healthy balance between philosophy and theology. "As a theologian I have tried to remain a philosopher, and vice versa. It would have been easier to abandon the boundry and to choose one or the other. Inwardly this course was impossible for me. Fortunately, outward opportunities matched my inward inclinations."[23]

Tillich agreed with Barth that the essence of Christianity was the existential recognition of the transcendent God, the ultimate ground of the real. With Barth he rejected natural theology, since God can only be known through divine revelation. Yet God does reveal himself through nature and history so that man can find him at any time and any place where he faces his ultimate concern.[24] To the left of Neo-orthodoxy, Tillich settled on the boundry between liberalism and orthodoxy.

> Agreement with the Barthian paradox, the mystery of justification, does not mean agreement with Barthian supranaturalism; and agreement with the historical and critical achievement of liberal theology does not mean agreement with liberal dogmatics.[25]

Although Christian traditions are of great importance, they must be interpreted in the light of man's present situation. Attracted towards existentialism, Tillich found elements in Heidegger that reminded him of the Augustinian mysticism of German Pietism,[26] shades of which may be detected in Tillich's theology of faith.

a Dynamics of Faith (1956)

Ultimate Concern

Tillich defines faith briefly as the state of being ultimately concerned. Although man is concerned about many things such as food, clothing, housing, money, education, health--only the ultimate concern demands total surrender of the believer and promises total fulfillment. Expressed in Old Testament terms, ultimate concern is "You shall love the Lord, your God, with all your soul, and with all your might" (Dt 6:5). Thus one is ultimately concerned about Yahweh, and what he demands, threatens, or promises (3).

Personal Faith

Ultimate concern is an act of the total personality, with all
of man's faculties united in the act of faith. Participating in the
dynamics of the personal life, both conscious and unconscious,
faith is a free, centered, personal act. Faith is neither an act
of reason nor of the unconscious, rather it transcends both of
these elements. Involving the cognitive and affective parts, faith
unifies all elements in the centered self so that the whole man
believes (6).

Concern and Concerned

"Faith is a total and centered act of the personal self, the
act of unconditional, infinite and ultimate concern" (8). Since
faith is a relationship between the concern and the concerned,
it presupposes an element of infinity in man so that he can understand in an immediate-centered, personal act the meaning of the
ultimate, the unconditional, the absolute, the infinite. This awareness of the infinite to which he belongs, drives man towards faith,
as a passion for the infinite (9).

Ultimate concern unites fides qua and fides quae, the centered
personal act and the ultimate concern. In false or idolatrous faith,
finite realities are elevated to the rank of ultimacy, leading to
existential disappointment. Centering on the periphery, idolatrous
faith leads to a loss of center, to existential estrangement, and to
a disruption or disintegration of the personality.

Preliminary Ultimate Concern (The New Being)[27]

There is always a danger of making a penultimate concern
ultimate, that is, deifying it. "We maintain our preliminary concerns as if they were ultimate. And they keep us in their grasp if
we try to free ourselves from them. Every concern wants our
whole heart and our whole mind and our whole strength. Every concern tries to be our ultimate, our God" (157-58).

Since only one thing is necessary--to be ultimately, uncondition-
ally, infinitely concerned, as Mary was (Lk 10:38-42)--should we,
then, abandon all our finite concerns?

> If, in the power and passion of such an ultimate concern,
> we look at our finite concerns, at the Martha sphere of life,
> everything seems the same and yet everything is changed.

We are still concerned about all these things, but different-ly--the anxiety is gone! It still exists and tries to return. But its power is broken; it cannot destroy us any more. He who is grasped by the one thing that is needed has the many things under his feet. They concern him, but not ultimately, and when he loses them he does not lose the one thing that he needs and that cannot be taken from him. (159-60)

This reflects the age-old Christian tradition of ordaining all finite things to their ultimate, infinite end.

Doubting Faith

Faith is both certain and uncertain: certain because in it we experience the Holy; uncertain, because the infinite is received by finite man. Accepting this uncertainty with courage, ultimate concern is ultimate risk and ultimate valor. A necessary element in ultimate concern is the doubt of faith, an existential doubt aware of the element of insecurity in every existential truth, yet faced courageously in the act of faith. Doubt is not the negation of faith, rather existential doubt and faith are poles of the same reality, the state of ultimate concern (22). The certainty of the divine gift of faith, yet the uncertainty of the human believer are reminiscent of Luther's dilemma.

Faith and Community

Is dynamic, personal, doubting faith compatible with community faith? Only in the community of language can one actualize his faith. Yet how can faith be communal without suppressing the autonomy of man's spiritual life? If spiritual conformity is forced, risk and courage are removed from faith, for the static faith of creeds and councils does not admit doubt. Creeds, formulae, liturgy, and organization should point to the ultimate since the Church stands under God and his judgment. Since criticism and doubt are there, dynamic faith can be applied to the community. "Certainly, the life of the community of faith is a continuous risk, if faith itself is understood as a risk. But this is a character of dynamic faith, and the consequence of the Protestant principle" (29).

135

Life of Faith

In the life of faith there is a tension between the believer and his ultimate concern, for every act of faith presupposes a participation in that towards which it is directed. At the same time the believer is separated from the divine object which he desires to see. From participation comes the certitude of faith; from separation, the doubt. The state of being ultimately concerned implies a love, a desire of being united with the separated. This is the restless dynamism of Aquinas' theology of faith. Expressed in action, it is the actualization of the ultimate concern.

Integration of the Personality

> The ultimate concern gives depth, direction and unity to all other concerns, and, with them, to the whole personality. A personal life which has these qualities is integrated, and the power of the personality's integration is his faith. (105)

The New Being in Jesus Christ is the integrating center of the personal life of the believer, uniting all elements of man's life, body, soul; every fiber and desire takes part.

Faith is the centered movement of the whole personality towards something of ultimate meaning and significance. The body, too, is involved since it is a passionate act, including both conscious and unconscious participation. If a unifying center is absent, disintegration of the personality can begin. While the subjective side is the openness of the individual for the power of faith--how strong and passionate is his ultimate concern?--the objective side considers the degree to which faith has conquered idolatrous elements and is directed towards the really ultimate. Although idolatrous faith can heal for a time, it tends to break down and foster disintegration and estrangement, for something not ultimate is made the object of ultimate concern. Something peripheral is made the center (109).

b Systematic Theology, III (1963)[28]

Formal and Material Faith

The formal definition of faith, applicable to all religions is "the state of being grasped by that toward which self-transcendence

136

aspires, the ultimate in being and meaning" (130). Every one has some ultimate concern in which he has faith. But the real struggle in history is between faith in an ultimate reality and faith in preliminary realities claiming ultimacy. In pursuing his own ineffectual modes of self-salvation, man realizes his need for an ultimate concern, a New Being, a new reality replacing the old preliminaries which claimed to be ultimate, but which were not.

The material aspect of faith is "the state of being grasped by the Spiritual Presence and opened to the transcendent unity of the unambiguous life" (131), for example, Christian faith which is the "State of being grasped by the New Being as it is manifest in Jesus as the Christ" (131). Faith is not an act of cognitive affirmation or the acceptance of factual statements on authority, nor the will to believe, nor the fruit of an act of obedience, nor merely the emotions. Tillich agrees with the classical tradition that there is an assent in faith which is a cognitive acceptance of the truth, not true statements concerning finite things in time and space, but the truth about our relation with the ultimate concern and the symbols which express it (132).

The obedience of faith is the act of keeping ourselves open to the Spiritual Presence which has grasped us and opened us. The emotional element in faith is an oscillation between the anxiety of one's finite humanity and the courage which, overcoming the anxiety, takes unto itself the power of the transcendental unity of the unambiguous life (133). In faith man is grasped by the very power of being-itself, expressing itself in the courage to be. Tillich defines this courage as the self-affirmation of being in spite of non-being. Faith is the experience of the self-affirmation of this power. Even when man is in a state of radical and anxious doubt about the meaning of life, he can fall back on absolute faith, transcending the mystical and personal and giving him the courage to be.[29]

Faith cannot be reduced to mental functions, but it includes the intellect, will, and emotions within itself uniting them and subjecting them to the Spiritual Presence's transforming power. Man cannot reach the ultimate by the use of his own faculties, but the ultimate can grasp his faculties and raise them up beyond themselves in faith (133). In material faith man is opened up by the Spiritual Presence and receptive to the divine Spirit. Accepting this Presence despite the infinite gap between the divine and human spirit, he stands courageously in the Spiritual Presence. Expecting final participation in the transcendental unity of the unambiguous life, he hopes for the fulfilling creativity of the Divine Spirit, an eschatological anticipation. This reminds one of Aquinas' description of faith as the beginning, the guarantee, the title deed, and anticipated possession of eternal life.[30]

Conclusion

Tillich has illustrated well the ultimacy and the unambiguity of the object of faith. Moreover, he reflects the long tradition of the dissatisfaction of faith separated from its object. Since the whole personality must be integrated around the New Being in Jesus Christ, the center of ultimate concern, any placing of a finite or preliminary object as ultimate leads to disillusionment and dis-integration of personality. The penultimate must be ordered to the ultimate.

Tillich's belief-ful realism sees the eternal, the transcendent in the temporal, not through scientific analysis, but in the sympathetic intuition which is the fundament of the courage to be. Although Tillich explained well the interrelationship of faith and reason, the bordering of theology and philosophy, and the importance of theology as an integrating factor in psychology, sociology, politics, culture, and art, yet some would see a certain danger of ambiguity in his bordering.

4 DIETRICH BONHOEFFER (1909-1945);
    CONFORMED WITH CHRIST

Theologian, ecumenist, and martyr of the Confessing Church, Bonhoeffer was influenced by Harnack's historical honesty and Barth's dialectic. His theology of faith is strongly in the Reformation tradition: Christo-centric, personal, justifying, and vivifying. Released from self-preoccupied religion, the believer identifies himself with the day-to-day affairs of the world, for only by being truly a man in the world can he conform himself with the Incarnate Christ.

a Communion of Saints (1927)[31]

In his first work, his dissertation presented to the theological faculty of the University of Berlin, Bonhoeffer reflected the times in a brilliant sociological-theological explanation of the Church which Karl Barth has called a theological miracle.

I and Thou

Bonhoeffer, as Buber, relates the human "I-Thou" relationship with the divine Thou.

> The Thou of the other man is the divine Thou. So the way to the other man is also the way to the divine Thou, a way of recognition or rejection. In the "moment" the individual again and again becomes a person through the "other." (36)

In a sense, the other man presents us with the same problem of cognition as God does himself. As one first knows God's "I" in his self-revelation of love, so also with the other man. The Christian achieves his true nature only when God enters with him as "I." God in Christ enters into the Christian. In union with Christ, Christians seek union with each other in the communion of the saints.

Community of Spirit

The divine community of the Church is based on faith and love inspired by the Spirit.

> If Christ comes 'into' man through the Holy Spirit, then the church comes 'into' him, too. But the Holy Spirit moves man in such a way that in putting Christ into his heart, He (the Spirit) creates faith and love. The faith in Christ which the Spirit effects, however, involves faith in the church in which he reigns. But love, as the love or heart of Christ in man, is given to man as a new heart, as the will for good. Faith recognizes and receives God's lordship. Love makes the kingdom of God actual. (119)

It is love that makes concrete the moral, social relationship of the Church. One who lives in this fellowship is certain that he is loved, and by his faith in Christ is able to love in return. He now sees the other members of the Church as gifts of love. Hence "Thou" becomes to "I" no longer law, but gospel of love. The love of the other "Thou" frees me from my "I" so that I can love the other in Christ and reveal myself to him entirely. For Bonhoeffer, the Church is a communion of love encircled by the infinite love of Christ.

Belief in the Church

> We believe that God has made the actual empirical church,
> in which the Word and the sacraments are administered,
> into his community, that is, the body of Christ, that is,
> the presence of Christ in the world, and that according to
> the promise, God's Spirit becomes effective in it. We be-
> lieve in the church as the church of God and as the com-
> munion of saints, of those, that is, who are sanctified by
> God, but with the historical form of the empirical church.
> Thus we believe in the means of grace within the empirical
> church and hence in the holy congregation created by them.
> We believe in the church as una, for it is Christ existing
> as the Church and Christ is the one Lord over those who
> are all one in him; as sancta, since the Holy Spirit is at
> work in it, and as catholica, since as the church of God
> its call is to the whole world, and it is present wherever
> God's Word is preached in the world. (197)

The Church is not some far-away and unreachable ideal, but the
communion of saints, Christ living in community in the world
today.

b Act and Being (1931)[32]

In this second thesis, qualifying him as a teacher at Berlin,
Bonhoeffer tries to mediate between act and being, contingency
and givenness, the transcendentalism of Kant and the ontology of
Heidegger. Studying man's struggle for truth in the sphere of
autonomous self-understanding, he finds the solution of the problem of act and being in revelation and in the church, where act
and being meet, and where being is comprehended.

The Knowing of Revelation

The knowing of revelation is really believing. In revelation
God, as the Holy Spirit, understands himself. This is where he
is, rather than in man's conscious reflection on revelation.

> God is only in the act of my belief. In 'my' belief, the
> Holy Spirit is accrediting himself. This is no demonstrable
> matter of fact, but is merely 'existentially' true, i.e.,
> in the encounter with revelation, in the act of belief itself,

which for the rest remains an act psychic like the others. Accordingly my knowledge of God depends in the event on whether God has known me in Christ (1 Cor 13:12; Gal 4:9), whether he is effecting faith in Christ within me. (92-93)

Thus there is no approved method of acquiring knowledge of God, and man cannot on his own move into an existential situation from which he can address God.

Existential Knowing and Having

We cannot reduce God to any system, for the goal of cognition is to close the system, the "I" mastering the universe. Thus revelation is outside of the system, since God alone is master of the world. "From that it seems an inescapable conclusion that God can be known only in the act, i.e., existentially. Otherwise he would deliver himself into the system" (96).

Although faith is act, yet as being in the church of Christ, it encompasses all existence in Christ, as unbelief, being in Adam, includes the old way of existence. Belief is not only an act, but also a manner of being in Christ's church. Thus Paul speaks of "standing in faith."

In faith I "have" Christ, for he is my Lord, who has redeemed me.

> In faith there is no not-knowing, for there Christ is his own witness and confirmation. In faith, Christ is the creator of my new personal being and at the same time Lord, with reference to which (eis auton) the person is created. (41)

In my act of faith Christ creates within me, giving me the Holy Spirit. The Lord of my existence, he is the master of my faith. In faith I am assailed by Christ although I cannot ascertain exactly when and where, for this is known only to God and so I cannot determine it by my own reflection.

Faith and Faith-Wishfulness (Glaubigkeit)

Faith and 'faith-wishfulness' lie together in the same act. Every act of faith is 'wishful' insofar as it is a happening embedded in the psychic [sic] and there accessible to reflection. But faith properly so-called lies in the act's intention towards Christ, which is founded in the communion of Christ. . . . All praying, all searching for God in his Word, all

clinging to promise, all entreaty for his grace, all hoping
in sight of the cross, all this for reflection is 'religion,'
'faithwishfulness.' But in the communion of Christ, while
it is still the work of man, it is God-given faith, faith
willed by God, wherein by God's mercy he may really be
found. (175-76)

Bonhoeffer's criticism of "faith-wishfulness" and "religion" seem
to foreshadow his later doctrine of "religion-less" Christianity.

Dasein and Wiesein

It is only in faith in Jesus Christ that man's da and wie are
properly united, the former released from the oppression of the
latter which rediscovers itself in the divinely given da. Cries and
trials are answered in the quiet prayer of the child with the Father
in the Word.

Home is the communion of Christ, which is always 'future,'
the present 'in faith' because we are children of the future;
always act, because being; always being, because act. Here
in faith becoming reality, there in vision perfected, this is
the new creation of the new man of the future, who no longer
looks on himself, but only away from himself to the revelation of God, to Christ; the man who is born out of the
narrowness of the world into the breadth of heaven, who
becomes what he was or, it may be, never was: a creature
of God--a child. (183-84)

The "now" and "then" of faith illustrate an eschatology which
combines the da and the wie, man's existential situation and his
direction to Christ.

c Christ the Center (1933)[33]

Bonhoeffer in the Protestant tradition taught a Christo-centric
faith. Christ is present in the church today in relation to me. He
is pro me as the pioneer and head of all the brethren. He is for the
brethren, taking their place before God. Not only does he take the
place of the community, he is the community. Thus man is crucified, and judged in him. He is in the new humanity and it is in him;
so God acts graciously towards it in him. Jesus Christ, the God-man,
is in the church as he is pro me, as Word, sacrament, and community (48-49).

What does the pro me mean for faith. Rather than a belief in miracles or visible phenomena, it is faith that Jesus Christ is for me.

> There is only faith where a man so surrenders himself to the humiliated God-man as to stake his life on him, even when this seems against all sense. Faith is where the attempt to have security from something visible is rejected. In that case it is faith in God and not in the world. The only assurance that faith tolerates is the Word itself which comes to me through Christ. (114-15)

Whoever looks for proofs, remains unchanged. Only he who recognizes the Son through the scandal of the cross is a true believer, for seeing that Christ is for us, he is entirely renewed.

d The Cost of Discipleship (1937)[34]

Although Bonhoeffer's first two books (Communion of the Saints and Act and Being) are more theological treatises often based on the thought of others, in these next two (The Cost of Discipleship and Life Together) the real Bonhoeffer comes through. The Cost of Discipleship, which marked a turning point in his life from the professional theologian to a practical Christian, became immediately popular. Some, such as Karl Barth, think it is his greatest work.

Costly Grace

Bonhoeffer writes strongly against cheap self-justifying grace, the deadly enemy of the Church.

> Cheap grace is the preaching of forgiveness without requiring repentance, Baptism without church discipline, Communion without confession, absolution without personal confession. Cheap grace is grace without discipleship, grace without the cross, grace without Jesus Christ, living and incarnate.

> Costly grace is the treasure hidden in the field; for the sake of it a man will gladly go and sell all that he has. It is the pearl of great price for which the merchant will sell all his goods. It is the kingly rule of Christ, for whose

143

sake a man will pluck out the eye which causes him to stumble. It is the call of Jesus Christ at which the disciple leaves his nets and follows him. (47)

Costly grace calls us to follow Christ and its price is our lives. Costly because it condemns sin, it is grace because it justifies us and gives us life.

It is costly grace especially because it was bought with the life of Jesus Christ, the Son of God. What is so expensive for God cannot be cheap for men. Moreover, it is the greatest grace because God gave us his most precious gift, his own Son in the Incarnation.

Obedient Faith

As Paul, Luther, Barth, and Bultmann, Bonhoeffer too identifies faith with the costly obedience to the call of Christ.

> The idea of a situation in which faith is possible is only a way of stating the facts of a case in which the following two propositions hold good and are equally true: 'Only he who believes is obedient, and only he who is obedient believes.' . . . Since then we cannot adequately speak of obedience as the consequence of faith, and since we must never forget the indissoluble unity of the two, we must place the one proposition that only he who believes is obedient alongside the other, that only he who is obedient believes. In the one case faith is the condition of obedience, and in the other obedience is the condition of faith. In exactly the same way in which obedience is called the consequence of faith, it must be called the presupposition of faith. (69-70)

The obedience of faith is neither cheap nor easy. We shouldn't be surprised when we find our faith difficult, especially when we have been resisting and disobeying Jesus. Perhaps we have not yet surrendered some part of our lives, a sinful habit, an animosity or ambition. We wonder why the Spirit is reticent, why we have difficulty in prayer and why our requests go unanswered. Only upon renouncing sin can one recover faith. Only in receiving God's word, can he receive his grace. "How can you hope to enter into communion with him, when at some point in your life you are running away from him? The man who disobeys cannot believe, for only he who obeys can believe" (73). Experience has shown that

144

the disobedience of sin is at the root of most disbelief.

e Life Together (1939)[35]

In this account of his community experience at the seminary
of the Confessing Church at Finkenwalde, we see the strong
social dimension of Bonhoeffer's faith. Impressed by his visit to
monasteries in England, he was determined to bring some of
this community spirit to the Bruderhaus at Finkenwalde, which
proved to be a forerunner of some later Protestant communities
at Taizé, Imshausen, and Darmstadt.

Bonhoeffer found great joy in the physical presence of other
believers.

> The believer feels no shame, as though he were still living
> too much in the flesh, when he yearns for the physical
> presence of other Christians. . . Visitor and visited in
> loneliness recognize in each other the Christ who is present
> in the body. They receive and meet each other as one meets
> the Lord, in reverence, humility, and joy. They receive
> each other's benedictions as the benediction of the Lord,
> Jesus Christ. But if there is so much blessing and joy even
> in a single encounter of brother with brother, how inex-
> haustible are the riches that open up for those who by God's
> will are privileged to live the daily fellowship of life with
> other Christians? (9)

The Christian community is united by solid faith in brotherhood, rather than by mutual experience. We see faith as God's
greatest gift which he has given and wants to give to all. We are
happy, yet we must be willing to forego such experiences when
God at times does not grant them. So it is really faith, not experience, that binds together the Christian community.

f Ethics (1940-1943)[36]

Bonhoeffer never finished his work on ethics. Yet his insights
give us a valuable description of the man of faith, the ethical man,
conformed with Christ. With simplicity, wisdom, and faith, he is
responsible to both God and neighbor.

Experiential Faith

"Blessed are they who are persecuted for righteousness' sake, for theirs is the kingdom of heaven" (Mt 5:10) means that the poor and persecuted will experience God's loving kindness, costly grace. Jesus supports those who suffer for a just cause, even though it may not be exactly for the defense and confession of his holy name. So those persecuted for a just cause are led to Christ, who protects them (60). This is not just an abstraction, but a real experience that Bonhoeffer had undergone himself in prison. His persecution had brought him nearer to Christ.

Conformed with Christ

To be conformed with the Incarnate is to be a real man, to have the right to be the man one really is. No one need strain to be some one else, to be some impossible ideal, for only by being the real man that he is can he identify himself with the God-man, Jesus Christ.

As Paul, Bonhoeffer teaches a conformation with Jesus Christ which includes crucifixion and resurrection with him. "To be formed in the likeness of the Crucified--this means being a man sentenced by God. In his daily existence man carries with him God's sentence of death, the necessity of dying before God for the sake of sin" (82). Yet conformation with the crucified means conformation with the risen Lord and thus a new man before God. "In the midst of death he is in life, in the midst of sin he is righteous, in the midst of the old he is new" (82). Conformed with Christ, he lives because Christ lives. Although Christ bore the form of all men on the cross and in his resurrection, his longing to take form in all men is fulfilled only in a small band, his church, which is the living form of Christ among men (83).

Justification by Faith

The Reformation emphasized justification of the sinner by grace alone and also by faith alone. Man is not justified by love or by hope, but only by faith. "For indeed, faith alone sets life upon a new foundation, and it is this new foundation alone that justifies my being able to live before God" (121). Faith means finding and holding fast to the foundation which is the life, death, and resurrection of Jesus Christ. It means building my life on this foundation which is outside myself, an eternal foundation,

Jesus Christ. Captivated by him, I can no longer see anything else. Set free from my self-imprisonment, I see that Jesus alone is the foundation of my life. We are not justified through our own good works, but through the only one good work, the work of God in Jesus Christ.

Faith and the Ultimate

Reminiscent of Tillich, Bonhoeffer teaches the interdependence of ultimate and penultimate. Can man live by the ultimate alone, or rather does not faith become real in life, as the ultimate phase of a span of time or of many spans of time? "We are asking whether this faith is and ought to be realizable every day, at every hour, or whether here, too, the length of the penultimate must every time be traversed anew for the sake of the ultimate" (125).

Should the Christian deny the penultimate in pious self-deception, or take it so seriously as to incur guilt? Bonhoeffer sees two solutions to the problem of the penultimate and the ultimate in Christian life. The first is a radical solution, seeing only the ultimate and breaking off completely from the penultimate, with Christ as the enemy and the destroyer of the penultimate. In a compromise solution, the penultimate keeps its own right and is not threatened by the ultimate. The ultimate remains totally on the far side of the everyday, as the eternal justification of things in the world as they are.

The two solutions are extreme because they place penultimate and ultimate in a relationship of mutual exclusion.

> In the one case, penultimate is destroyed by the ultimate; and in the other case the ultimate is excluded from the domain of the penultimate . . . Thus creation and redemption, time and eternity confront one another in a conflict which cannot be resolved; the unity of God himself is sundered, and faith in God is broken apart. (128)

Christianity cannot be separated by itself from the world for this would destroy the world. On the other hand, man cannot exist of himself for this would exclude God. Only in the God-man can the solution be found, for in and through him the penultimate is preserved for the ultimate.

Christ alone brings us the ultimate in faith, and although the penultimate is swallowed up in the ultimate, it is still necessary.

147

Christian life is the dawning of the ultimate in me; it is
the life of Jesus Christ in me. But it is also always life
in the penultimate which awaits for the ultimate. . .
Ultimate and penultimate are closely allied. What must be
done, therefore, is to fortify the penultimate with a more
emphatic proclamation of the ultimate and also to protect
the ultimate by taking due care of the penultimate. (141-42)

Conclusion

In his Ethics and especially his Letters and Papers from Prison[37] we see evidence of Bonhoeffer's second conversion, a turning towards contemporaneity with the world and away from a
religion that is separated from the world, neatly folded in on itself, over-involved with the "rusty swords" of superficial intellectual speculations, and thus betraying the message of the suffering Christ in the world. Bonhoeffer is an example of man come
of age. Far from the self-reliant incurable optimist, he is rather
a mature adult who, accepting his responsibilities in the world,
refuses to escape into backward piety. As an adult Christian, he
is not afraid to partake of the suffering of Christ in the world.
Thus he wrote from prison:

This is what I meant by worldliness--taking life in one's
stride, with all its duties and problems, its successes and
failures, its experiences and helplessness. It is in such a
life that we throw ourselves utterly in the arms of God
and participate in his sufferings in the world and watch
with Christ in Gethsemane. This is faith, that is metanoia,
and that is what makes a man and a Christian (Jer 45).
How can success make us arrogant or failure lead us as-
tray, when we participate in the sufferings of God by living
in this world?[38]

The number of Bonhoeffer's followers is growing larger year
by year. Recently the radical theologians have brought attention
to his letters from prison. However, many have been attracted
also to his earlier works, dealing profoundly in ecclesiology,
ethics, Christology, and ecumenism. Bonhoeffer's faith is obedient, existential, Christo-centric, at the same time personal and
social. But it is also a worldly faith, contemporaneous with Christ
in the world and not bent in on itself. Both his vision and his profundity have made Bonhoeffer one of the great Protestant theologians
of the twentieth century.

5 CONCLUSION

In the last two chapters we have seen the personalist trend flowing through modern Protestant and Jewish theology of faith. We studied it first in Schleiermacher's consciousness of his absolute dependence on God, reflecting Pietism; in Kierkegaard's leap of faith, opposing Hegelian idealism and the impersonality of the established church; in Buber's "I-Thou" relationship; in Barth's experience of the Word of God in Christ; in Bultmann's existential self-understanding in the Christ-event; in Tillich's ultimate concern, integrating man's whole personality around Jesus Christ; and in the obedient and suffering faith of Bonhoeffer conformed with Christ in the world.

Kierkegaard gave the greatest impetus to modern personal existential faith. He and his followers drew a sharp distinction between the subjective and the objective, the real and the speculative. However, even the speculative faith of Aquinas is firmly grounded in the real, personal, experiential order. Nevertheless, existentialism has continually rebelled against the apparent abstractions of speculative philosophy. In many ways, the personal and existential approach to faith seems closer to the Gospels, for the Hebrews were not of a speculative mind. In fact, in some ways existentialism can trace its origins to the Hebrew thought of the Bible.

Notes

1 B. Willems, *Karl Barth; An Ecumenical Approach To His Theology* (Glen Rock, New Jersey: Paulist Press, 1965), pp. 26-31.

2 G. Wiegel, *A Survey of Protestant Theology in Our Day* (Westminster: Newman Press, 1953), pp. 29 ff.

3 Willems, *Karl Barth*, pp. 107-08.

4 E. Hoskyns, tr. (London: Oxford University Press, 1957).

5 Richmond, John Knox Press, 1960.

6 G. Bromiley & T. Torrance, eds. (Edinburgh: Clark, 1961). Parentheses include volume, part, and page.

7 See Chapter IV.

8 L. Malvez, *The Christian Message and Myth* (Westminster: Newman Press, 1958), p. 201.

9 Willems, *Karl Barth*, pp. 28-29.

10 E. Good, "The Meaning of Demythologizing," *The Theology*

of Rudolf Bultmann, C. Kegley, ed. (New York: Harper & Row Publishers, 1966), pp. 26-27.

11 "The New Testament and Mythology," Kerygma and Myth, H. Bartsch, ed., R. Fuller, tr. (New York: Harper & Row Publishers, 1960), p. 10, n. 2.

12 Good, "The Meaning of Demythologizing," pp. 27-28.

13 Ibid., pp. 28-29.

14 R. Bultmann, "Bultmann Replies to His Critics," Kerygma and Myth, p. 211.

15 Existence and Faith, S. Ogden, ed. (Cleveland: World Publishing Company, 1966), pp. 55-57.

16 Existence and Faith, pp. 92-110.

17 Essays, Philosophical and Theological, J. Grieg, tr. (London: SCM, 1955), pp. 1-21.

18 Essays Philosophical and Theological, pp. 168-81.

19 Kerygma and Myth, pp. 191-211.

20 J. Macquarrie, The Scope of Demythologizing (New York: Harper & Row Publishers, 1960), p. 13.

21 R. Bultmann, "The Idea of God and Modern Man," Translating Theology into the Modern Age (New York: Harper & Row Publishers, 1965), p. 94.

22 Dynamics of Faith (New York: Harper & Row Publishers, 1957), p. 76.

23 On the Boundry (New York: Charles Scribner's Sons, 1966), p. 58.

24 See G. Weigel, A Survey of Protestant Theology in Our Day, (Westminster, Md.: Newman Press, 1954), p. 40.

25 On the Boundry, p. 50.

26 Ibid., p. 57.

27 New York: Charles Scribner's Sons, 1955.

28 Chicago: University of Chicago Press, 1963.

29 The Courage to Be (New Haven: Yale University Press, 1952).

30 See Chapter IV.

31 New York: Harper & Row Publishers, 1963.

32 B. Noble, tr. (New York: Harper & Row Publishers, 1956).

33 J. Bowden, tr. (New York: Harper & Row Publishers, 1966).

34 R. Fuller, tr. (New York: Macmillan Company, 1965).

35 London: SCM, 1965.

36 E. Bethge, ed. (New York: Macmillan Company, 1965).

37 E. Bethge, ed., R. Fuller, tr. (New York: Macmillan Company, 1966).

38 Letters, July 21, 1944, p. 226.

CHAPTER IX

Personal faith

MARCEL TO CIRNE-LIMA

The existential, experiential, and personal faith so character-istic of much of Protestant theology from Luther on down through Kierkegaard, Barth, Bultmann, Tillich, Bonhoeffer, and others, may be seen in many current Roman Catholic authors who have come under the influence of the existential stream. We intend to look at three of these, namely, Gabriel Marcel, Jean Mouroux, and Carlos Cirne-Lima. Although they approach faith from dif-ferent angles, all stress the same "I-Thou" rapport between God and man.

1 GABRIEL MARCEL (1889--); CREATIVE FIDELITY

Gabriel Marcel, great French thinker, objecting to both the objective philosophy of positivism or linguistic analysis and the over-emphasis on the individual found in some existentialists, counters with a philosophy built on love, fidelity, availability, openness, communion, and intersubjectivity. Although he moves along existentialist lines, Marcel does not like to have the term applied to himself.[1]

Marcel has not only written brilliantly in philosophy and theology, but is an accomplished playwright as well. Since World War II he has criticized sharply modern social structures which have caused such "dis-ease" in man whereby he lost his sense of dignity and his individuality in functionalism.[2] Technomania or the deification of technology, Marcel feels, is at least partially responsible for this, for modern functionalism with its possession and "having" tends to make "Thou"s into "It"s. Restless in his present state, and uncomfortable with the temporal, man desires the eternal.[3]

Marcel's search for the truth and his conversion to Catholicism are clearly reflected in his theology of faith, especially in his quest for an "I-Thou" relationship with God, as seen in his Metaphysical Diary.[4] He takes a phenomenological approach to faith, studying the relationships between acts and object, rather than a noumenological approach of examining mental states. Uniquely combining being and having, man exists and acts in his own right, yet he needs others and so is not self-sufficient.[5]

a Being and Having, a Metaphysical Diary (1928-1933);
   Some Thoughts on Faith (1934)

I and Thou

Marcel first wrote on this theme as early as 1915, eight years before Buber's famous book. Here he elaborates:

> When I treat another as a Thou and no longer as a He, does this difference of treatment qualify me alone and my attitude to this other, or can I say that by my treatment of him as a Thou I pierce more deeply into him and apprehend his being or his essence more directly? . . . And the other, insofar as he is other, only exists for me insofar as I am open to him, insofar as he is a Thou. But I am only open to him insofar as I cease to form a circle with myself, inside which I somehow place the other, or rather his idea. For inside this circle the other becomes the idea of the other, and the idea of the other is no longer the other qua other, but the other qua related to me. And in this condition he is uprooted and taken to bits, or at least in the process of being taken to bits. (Nov. 11, 1932, pp. 106-07)

Here is the phenomenological and personal approach. When we allow persons to become mere ideas of persons within the small circles of our minds, they become "He"s and we lose our inter-subjective rapport with the Thou.

Transcendent Faith

Man's I-Thou rapport with his fellow man reflects his personal faith relationship with his Maker. However, due to his own weakness and God's transcendence, man is incapable of producing this I-Thou relationship of himself.

> As the soul approaches more nearly to faith, and becomes more conscious of the transcendence of her object, she perceives more and more clearly that she is utterly incapable of producing this faith, of spinning it out of her own substance. For she knows herself, she realizes more and more clearly her own weakness, impotence and instability; and thus she is led to a discovery. This faith of hers can only be an adherence, or, more exactly, a response . . . to an impalpable and silent invitation which fills her, or, to say it another way, which puts pressure upon her without constraining her. The pressure is not irresistible. If it were, faith would no longer be faith. Faith is only possible to a free creature, that is, a creature who has been given the mysterious and awful power of withholding himself. (207-08)

Faith couples God's transcendent invitation with man's free response.

Attestation

The realities of faith are transcendent, yet paradoxically they seem to need a humble witness, the believer, to attest to them. "There could surely be no better example of the incomprehensible, or perhaps rather supra-intelligible polarity which lies at the heart of faith" (211). Faith is unceasing attestation, witnessing especially in times of sorrow. The open growth of faith can be hindered by affluence and satisfaction which is closed in on itself and can pave the way to spiritual corruption.

The distinction between the open and the closed only takes on its full meaning when we are speaking of faith. Or, to go deeper still, when we are speaking of the free act of the soul, as she wills or refuses to acknowledge that higher principle which momently creates her and is the cause of her being, and as she makes herself penetrable or im-penetrable to that transcendent yet inward action without which she is nothing. (212)

In faith the Christian is open to Christ, the exact opposite of the closed, self-reliant, self-satisfied life of the unbeliever.

b Creative Fidelity (1940)[6]

Faith and Fidelity

"Faith became clear to me from the moment I thought directly about fidelity; while fidelity, on the other hand, was clarified beginning with a thou, with presence itself construed as a function of the thou" (149). Fidelity is the key to Marcel's theology of faith, for in it one takes responsibility for another, acknowledging him as one who has a lasting value. In promising our faithfulness to another, we recognize his very being, not just his life. He is a thou, not an it, a presence, not just an object of recognition.[7] It is the unconditionality of fidelity which links it with faith in God, for without an Absolute Being there can be no absolute commitments. It is in absence that fidelity is proved and above all in the absence, which some mistakenly consider absolute, death (152).

Creative Fidelity

When I commit myself, I grant in principle that the commit-ment will not be put into question. And it is clear that this active volition not to question something again, intervenes as an essential element in the determination of what in fact will be the case. It at once bars a certain number of possi-bilities. It bids one invent a certain modus vivendi, which I would otherwise be precluded from envisaging. Here there appears in a rudimentary form what I call creative fidelity. My behavior will be completely colored by this act embody-ing the decision that the commitment will not again be questioned. (162)

This creative commitment inspires my whole life. And, as faith operating through love, it must flower into works of charity.

But can this fidelity not be disappointed? The more my consciousness is centered on God and not on some created facsimile, the less probability of disappointment. And when disappointment does come, we can be sure that it is our fault, and not God's. Although the ground of our fidelity may sometimes seem precarious, it is unshakable, when it comes from the very depths of my own insufficiency reaching out to the eternal God. Marcel calls this the "last resort" when radical humility is polarized by the very transcendence of God, upon whom it calls (167).

Belief in a Thou. (toi)

Echoing an earlier theme, Marcel describes the Thou as a "reality, whether personal or supra-personal, which is able to be invoked, and which is as it were, situated beyond any judgment referring to an objective datum" (169). As soon as we represent this belief in our minds, it becomes belief in a him. Although the tendency is to make belief a type of knowing or a possession, it really is an openness to the reality recognized as a Thou, as assimilable to a Thou (171).

Faith is not a possession, rather it stems from being, it is the very ground of what I am. Yet it is not the same as existence since it is hidden much of the time. Incredulity is the equivalent of opacity, for insofar as one is not transparent, he does not believe, nor does he love. Credo ergo sum and the spark of this faith-existence is love (172).

c The Mystery of Being (1949-1950)[8]

Opinion-Conviction-Faith

Marcel reflects a popular medieval theme. Opinion concerns what one does not know, and so wavers between impression and affirmation, "seeming so" and "claiming that." An atheist may have an opinion "that God does not exist, for if he existed, he would not allow . . ." This conviction appears firm and unshakable, but without justification. Faith is a movement from the closed (opinion or conviction) to the open. Faith is believing in rather than believing that. It is opening credit to, or placing oneself at the disposal of some one, pledging oneself fundamentally, and affecting not only what he has, but what he is (II, 77).

This explanation of "belief in" goes back to Augustine.[9]

Belief has an existential index which is lacking in conviction, for convictions which do not pledge to anything force a self-enclosed existence. To believe is to follow.

> The metaphor of rallying may very profitably be used to fill out that of credit. If I believe in, I rally to; with that sort of interior gathering of oneself which the act of rallying implies. From this point of view one might say that the strongest belief, or more exactly the most living belief, is that which absorbs most fully all the powers of your being. (II, 78)

When I believe some one, I go to him, follow him, rally to his cause, in a complete and loving commitment.

Love and Faith

As the Fathers and theologians have always taught, love and faith are very closely interrelated. I believe those who are beloved to me.

> If I love him, I lay it down as an axiom that he can not deceive me. It is possible, of course, that I may be mistaken and that I may come to realize my mistake, but this will make no real difference to the fact that I have had faith in this being, and in a sense which transcends every possible supposition. This becomes infinitely more clear when it is a question of the transcendent Being, to whom I am compelled to open an absolute, that is to say unconditional, credit. And we should have no hesitation in saying that the more unconditional my faith is, the more genuine it will be. (II, 136-37)

True love and faith can never be deceived (Kierkegaard).

Conclusion

Although Gabriel Marcel has not written a systematic theology of faith, we can read some trends in his writings, namely, the popular "I-Thou" relationship with God, analogous to and reflected in human "I-Thou" fidelity. Creative fidelity is a firm commitment, an openness to, a rallying to, a belief in, that is a way of life. Faith is not so much a possession, as it is the very ground of our existence. And it is not just a relationship between myself and God, but involves others as well.

Pointing out the limits of modern philosophy and technology, without at the same time descending to romanticism or irrationality, Marcel has given a new impetus to concern for human dignity. In illustrating the eternal in the temporal and the great impact of faith, hope, and love in man's daily existence, Marcel has much to say to today's Christian secularists.

2 JEAN MOUROUX (1902--); THE EXPERIENCE OF FAITH

Canon Mouroux, Professor of Dogmatic Theology at Dijon, France, has the happy ability to combine traditional scholastic doctrines with the profound insights of the mystics and the latest developments of existential thought. His writings on religious experience and the theology of faith represent the most recent in personalist thought, yet are solidly grounded in Christian tradition.

a The Christian Experience (1952)[10]

Religious Experience

Religious experience is not just a pleasant feeling, emotion, or emperical event à la William James, but it is

> the act or group of acts--through which man becomes aware of himself in relation to God. It is, therefore, the most personal kind of experience that can take place, since it involves the meeting of the created person with the creative person, and by this very fact concerns the spirit in its total reality. And although it must be described according to the nature of the religious relationship, it must never be taken out of the personal context without which it could not exist. (15)

The whole man is involved, intellect, will and affections, in a religious commitment inspiring his whole life, and involving others as well. It is the experience of the sacred, the wholly Other, mystery, both transcendent and immanent. It is the presence of the transcendent God in man as the very cause of his being and the formal object of all his desires. From this arises man's deep, fundamental motion towards God (18).

The religious experience is an entrance into eternity, an awareness, a positing, a giving of self to God. It is "both a dialectical
return to self, and a propulsion towards God; a retirement within
oneself and a decentralization towards God. In the religious act
my center becomes God, and this is the essential paradox of religious experience" (19). God gives himself to me and I give myself
to God. When I posit God or some one transcendent, he really
posits me, for he takes me out of myself and delivers me to himself. And in the same act he is delivered over to me (22).

The religious experience is dynamic, self-giving, longing,
moving man towards God. The soul continually strives to close
the infinite distance between itself and God, desiring to see the
Unseen. Thus the experience is the seed of glory, as Aquinas
says, and the beginning of eternal life.

Experience within Faith

The very heart of the Christian experience is the soul's movement towards God, inclining towards God in its own acts directed
towards the end. "This polarization of the whole soul around God,
the first of all loves, is one of the normal signs of the experience"
(355). This strong inclination and polarization is seen in the dynamic faith of Christian tradition, striving restlessly to see the
Vision. In this movement of the soul in faith, it feels a need to be
with God in the midst of darkness and aridity. There is a spontaneous attraction towards God which is strong, humble, lived, loved
and which is for God despite temptations and hardships (356). This
religious experience is perceived by the soul as supernatural.
Rather than a confrontation, a recognition or deduction, it is a
direct grasp springing from spiritual affinity, a theocentric synthesis of man's powers (358).

Placing the Experience, Faith and Charity

"To go straight to the point, the Christian experience means
knowing through faith and hope that we love God, and the Christian
life means, quite simply, loving God" (363). The Christian life
adheres to God in faith, united to God in charity. Grasping God
through the veil of faith, it is aware of the possession of God, a
possession which is partial, obscure, embryonic, and subject
to change (364).

The norm of Christian experience is faith because faith is its
living principle, its vital medium. Yet the experience must be

guided by the teaching of the Church and the life within the Church. Each Christian experience has some things in common with other Christian experiences, but each is also unique, secret between the soul and God, a living relationship with Christ in the Church.

> The Christian experience, in fact, interiorizes the truths of faith, awakens desire and aspiration, sustains and nour- ishes faithfulness. It enables us to see, touch, and taste God. As it develops, it detaches man from himself and plunges him into God, and thus realizes the paradox of going deeper into oneself by centering oneself on God, going beyond oneself by building oneself up, going outside oneself by enriching oneself. (369)

The Christian experience is a faith and love encounter. We be- lieve in and love the personal God, and at the same time are con- scious of our personal relationship with him.

b I Believe (1959)[11]

Here Mouroux studies faith, synthesizing Aquinas with modern and ancient insights into a theology of personal faith.

Personal God (11)

The personal God is both the object and end of faith. Here Mouroux discusses the personal aspect of the famous three-fold credere of Augustine and his medieval commentators, namely, to believe God (credere Deum), to believe in God (credere in Deum), and to believe God (credere Deo).[12]

Credere Deum. Here God is not an abstract truth, but a per- sonal God, Creator and Redeemer, God the Father and Jesus Christ whom he sent, Son of God and Savior, the Spirit, living promise of the father and Christ's own gift--three Divine Persons, one personal God (13-14).

First Truth, the object of both faith and vision is not just spec- ulative truth, but rather the being who is Absolute Truth himself, Subsistent Truth, Personal Truth, God himself under the title or aspect of First Truth. So the material of faith--images, concepts, and articles--are not the ultimate object of faith, but lead us to him, the inchoate knowledge of faith tending towards the ultimate vision of First Truth in beatitude.

<u>Credere</u> <u>in</u> <u>Deum</u>. First Truth is also the end of all my desires
under the aspect of Supreme Good. Since First Truth designates
also the adorable Person, he is the proper end of the will in faith.
First Truth and Supreme Good are two aspects of the same divine
Person. Thus the truths of faith lead us to the beatifying God, personal God, truth and beatitude (17-19).

<u>Credere</u> <u>Deo</u>. This is belief in the testimony of God, bearing
witness to himself. Here the interior calling, illumination, and
inspiration of faith are involved. A person who is light and love
gives himself to one who is in need of light and love, the divine
interior instinct and the light of faith drawing man on to the eternal vision.

> The Interior Call and Grace of God Is
> Personal and Personalizing

The interior call of faith is personal because it is directed to
an individual soul in its own determined situation. It is personalizing since it makes the individual soul realize its own vocation.
God speaks to me through human lips, through the Word incarnate
and the Church, his Mystical Body, the Work of God coming to me
through the word of man (22-24).

The formal motive of faith is the testimony of God, First Truth,
through the voice of Christ and his Church. Christ tells us what he
learned from the Father, and the Apostles and the Church have
passed the Word down to us (25).

Faith is the response of the human person to this call of the
personal God. In this interpersonal meeting, the whole man is
involved with his will, intellect and spiritual feelings in one vital
act of a person who unites himself to another person (39-41).
Through faith the human person is drawn to the adorable Person
who is his beatitude.

In the act of faith, love must penetrate and direct knowledge,
for the whole person is apprehended in a spiritual contact and
communion in which love and knowledge are inseparable for both
are essential activities of a human person giving himself to God
(42-45).

Faith involves the self-revelation of one person to another and
this is always obscure to discursive reason. The discursive function of the intellect cannot accomplish the grasping of concrete
existence, cannot enter into the privacy of this spiritual person
who is unique and social, for the existence and the value of a person are obscure to the intellect. Here the act of faith takes place

in a sphere opaque and baffling to pure reason. Only love can penetrate it. Faith is essentially obscure because it is the revelation of a divine person through human testimony. Certainly a human being can reveal himself through his testimony, by signs that are homogeneous and adequate. But the divine Person revealing himself through human testimony is obscure. In a sense, human testimony is a barrier between God and man. With his clouded intellect man can only see with the eyes of faith which continually strive for the vision of the Unseen (49-52).

Faith is the act of communion with God, not an irrational impulse. The transition from unbelief to faith demands self-renunciation and brings about the integration of the personality around Christ. Is faith inferior? Actually pathological mythomania depersonalizes, but the act of faith personalizes, increasing the value of the spiritual being by the gift of self to God. Based on Christ's testimony, faith integrates the personality with Christ. The believer now no longer lives of himself, but Christ lives in him (60-65).

Mystical Plane and the Summit of Faith

Faith becomes more and more personal and personalizing with increasing domination by the Holy Spirit, through whom we become aware of Christian spirituality, free ourselves, possess ourselves, and give ourselves, to God through charity.

First in the stages of ascent is purification of the appetite, or rather unification and integration of the appetite, centered on Christ. In the ascendance of personalization of faith, the soul moves beyond the concepts of faith to the person of God, towards increasing union. Knowledge and presence of God bring into action the pure spiritual powers of intuition and communion. This communication with God simplifies and purifies the soul, making it more like God. This general knowledge is the experience of a person. In the average Christian the movement towards union and conceptual representation sustain each other, but the mystic in the night of the soul sees that the representative element in faith is inadequate. Gradually this element is discarded and transcended, while the spiritual movement is purified, fortified, divinized in the personal embrace of the Beloved (81-85).

Final Consummation of the Personal Character of Faith

Trinitarian indwelling is sometimes followed by awakening
and aspiration by the Son and Holy Spirit. The soul enters into
the Trinity of Persons, as the Persons enter into the soul. Mystical knowledge is most personal and personalizing, perfecting
and completing the person, in a transforming union with God. It
is the centrifugal experience of centrality towards God, advancing
into the profundity of God. The perfection of the person grows
along with his union with the divine Persons, the soul transformed
into pure, living relation to God, a perfect image of the subsistent
relations which are the divine Persons. In a word, the human person is made perfect by its communion with the divine Persons
through faith (86-89).

The Witness and Transmission of Faith

The transmission of faith is brought about by testimony, the
handing on of the Christian experience. Subjective testimony is
based on the Christian giving himself totally to God and to his
task, a personal pledge or engagement to the service of the Word
of God and the embodiment of this pledge in his life. The Christian
witness imitates Christ. "For this was I born and for this I came
into the World to bear witness to the truth" (John 18:37). His incarnation, his life among men, his redemptive death, all were
done in witness to the truth.

Paul is a slave of Christ, willing to give his life for the gospel
in testimony to the Gentiles. The faith is handed on by human
testimony in which the testimony of God shines forth. The Christian experiences power, life, and joy which Christ gives him
through faith shining forth in his life. This is an élan which reveals by act and thought a person wholly given to God, animated
by God. The Christian's self-surrender tends to evoke the same
in others who seek communion.

The Christian witness is a state of life. Confirmation is the
sacrament of witness, of Christian manhood and maturity of personality. In it the Spirit interiorizes in order to universalize.
The perfect member is a true witness in full Christian testimony
and full Christian personality. The Spirit makes the full Christian person by perfecting his faith and adapting him to his task
from within. If the Christian is docile, the Holy Spirit will make
him a perfect witness (90-96).

Complementary Aspects

Faith is constituted on personal relationships, but is also ecclesial. The eternal subsistent Word of God in Christ is pro - pagated by the Apostles and the Church. The Incarnate Word is encountered in the Eucharist (John 6:58). Personal faith in Christ is founded on the word of God transmitted by the Church, and ac - cepted through faith. The Christian faith is social, ecclesial, realized by entry into the Church and remaining in it. This faith, building up the Mystical Body, the incorporation in Christ, is certainly the experience of God and the seed of the Beatific Vision. But since we do not see we must be guided by the Church and live in the mystery of the sacramental body of Christ (99-108).

Conclusion

Mouroux successfully integrates traditional Thomistic teaching with the New Testament and more modern developments in the theology of personal faith. His synthesis reminds one of Aquinas who combined Augustinian traditions with the popular philosophy of Aristotle. Although Thomas did not teach a personal faith in the modern existential sense, nevertheless, Mouroux brings out well the experiential faith that underlies his abstract terminology.

3 CARLOS CIRNE -LIMA; INTUITIVE FAITH

Carlos Cirne-Lima, brilliant Brazilian student of Karl Rahner, has synthesized Maréchalian and Rahnerian thought with Scholastic traditions into a modern theology of personal, intuitive faith.

Influenced by Husserl, Heidegger, and existential thought in general, August Brunner and Hans Urs von Balthasar have taught the importance of the phenomonology of human consciousness for metaphysical reflection on man or on his world. They stress man's intuitive grasp of another in his concrete inconceptualizable unique - ness, his concrete awareness of the real prior to judgment by nature. Others, following Brunner and Rahner, have carried on

> the theory of intellectual awareness of the concrete prior
> by nature to the concept and judgment, the focus of all
> subsequent intellectual reflection and the objective evidence
> which must ground the truth of the judgments which explicate
> experience.[13]

This runs counter to Cajetan's interpretation of Thomas Aquinas for Cajetan had no intellectual intuition, but only sensible phantasm, and abstract universal form of the object which finds its expression in the concept. The intellect only has conjectural knowledge of the singular by a conversion to the phantasm from which the universal form has been abstracted.[14]

The primacy of intuition seems to offer distinct advantages in solving problems in Thomistic epistemology and rational psychology. It may help to overcome the over-abstract and impersonal aspects of Thomism in its encounter with modern existential thought. Some see in the intuition the bridge to close the gap between the subjective and the objective, practical and speculative, individual and universal.

Cirne-Lima's solution to the problem of the act of faith lies in the psychology of intuitive and personal knowledge, the pre-predicative encounter with a concrete personal being, which gives ground for the act of faith, and which is at the same time free and certain. Aware of another person in his concrete uniqueness, our intuition exceeds the concept in both breadth and depth. The personal knowledge of another from which faith proceeds

> is given in a new and deeper grasp of his concrete subjectivity, subsequent to the free decision in which I approve and accept as worthy of my trust and personal reality of this 'Thou' I encounter in reality and dialogue.[15]

Cirne-Lima has taken up the interpersonal "I-Thou" theme popularized by Martin Buber and so many modern existential thinkers. All reality is somehow communicated through the experience of other subjects to the knower. Thus, there is a personal sharing in the experience of others through the acceptance of their testimony in faith.

Science looks upon faith as uncertain, for science's abstract objective evidence, cannot transcend the material in order to reach the richness of human liberty and the unicity of history. Nor can it measure art or the human person. Therefore, the objective knowledge and concepts of scientific judgments cannot exhaust the range of human knowledge. Inobjective, personal knowledge can be grasped together with objective aspects of an experience which can be expressed in universal concepts. And it is through this personal knowledge that the human person becomes aware of the unique, "free, interior depths of the other person."[16]

Personal <u>Faith</u> (1959)[17]

Human Faith

Cirne-Lima, as so many others before him draws the analogy between human and divine faith, man's personal knowledge of his fellow man, and his personal knowledge of God. In Chapter Two, Cirne-Lima writes of a three-fold gradation of faith, namely, faith in a stranger, a mere acquaintance, and a friend (31). In each succeeding grade there is more of the personal, more love, more esteem, and so forth. In lesser types of faith we can accept a person with reservations, but in faith in a friend total acceptance is had. Here the total personality of a Thou is revealed to a friend and is wholly accepted by him.

> Faith between intimate friends is the culmination of inter-personal faith. It is an unconditional commitment to a Thou to whom we give our complete trust and whom we love from the bottom of our hearts. This faith includes a loving, self-forgetting, unreserved, approving 'Yes' spoken to the other. We have here an unconditional approbation given to the whole personality of a Thou. (40)

This is seen in husband-wife, father-son relationships, and also in any other rapport of a close personal friendship.

Faith is a personal attitude, not a concept, judgment, or syllogism. Belief is intuitive in nature, presenting the object complete with no separation of subject and predicate. However, although the act of faith is intuitional, it is not merely intuition.[18]

> The act of faith is not, as is the intuition, simply knowledge of an objectively given human Thou. It is in addition a free attitude toward this Thou adopted by our whole person. Or, to put it more exactly, the act of faith is the cognitive element of a free, fully personal attitude of one whole person toward another person in his historical concreteness. (52)

So it is the attitude of acceptance which makes the difference. Belief is not merely knowledge, but a personal acceptance of a Thou.

> The most proper and specific element of the act of faith, consequently, consists in the fact that the intuition of a Thou is the cognitive element of a total attitude of our

whole person toward this Thou. In this fact we find the distinction which exists between the act of faith and intuition and every other form of knowledge. (53)

The act of faith is a personal acceptance of a Thou, a personal "Yes" to a person and to all his propositions.

Intuition and Species Intelligibilis

Intuition signifies the intellectual view through which one sees the concrete object at the same time as both individual and universal, insofar as it is itself and also insofar as it points to a manifold of interrelationships. (93)

In the intuition, the universal shines through the individual, nonconceptual knowledge of totality. It is not a judgment or a syllogism. It is not discursive, but an individual insight, at the same time concrete and abstract (94).

If we assert that the species intellegibilis is an intuition, we are using this expression in the same sense that it possesses in common every day usage. By intuition then we understand that 'idea,' 'vision,' or 'insight,' that act, therefore, which without concept, judgment, or discursive reasoning, is the means of the knower's contact with a totality as such, a totality in which the universal shines through the medium of the concrete individual. (95)

This makes sense, for from our experience we know that we rarely consider an individual apart from his relations to other individuals. Thus the universal is seen reflected in the individual. The understanding, bringing this universal aspect into relief, conceives the concept. And from concepts arise judgments and syllogisms, and ultimately discursive thought passes beyond itself and ends in a single intuitive synthesis (97-107).

Personal Knowledge

Personal knowledge is not intuition or conceptual knowledge, for although these may concern persons, they do not involve the acceptance or the rejection of a Thou. Intuition and concept deal more with things, the "I-It" relationship, the "I" or "Ego" knowing the other as existent against the horizon of being.

> the Ego places itself and the other on the level of personal
> being, in the level of personal freedom, which includes both
> necessity as well as non-necessity. . . The decision of the
> Ego does not concern the essence or existence of a deter-
> mined object present to it here and now. The decision of
> the Ego concerns itself. I determine myself. In the decision
> the Ego relates itself to the Other and determines itself in
> relation to the Other. Through this self-determination of
> the Ego, which takes place in every decision, the Other
> becomes a partial element of the personal life of the Ego.
> For as the object of decision, it is a partial element of a
> personal attitude, and as such it becomes a partial element
> of the truly personal life of the Ego. (129)

This is personal knowledge, the knowledge of friendship, where
the "Thou" is absorbed, incorporated into the personal life of the
"I." This is no more clearly seen than in the deep personal union
of marriage.

How is personal knowledge related to intuition?

> If I am in the presence of a man and know him, I form an
> intuition of which he is the content. In this intuition every-
> thing that I know of him is presented in one total image,
> and so he is known intuitively as a person, yet this intuition
> of the other person remains an objective act of understand-
> ing. It is neither immediately free knowledge, nor is it
> personal knowledge in the proper sense. If I should make
> a decision, however, touching this person, and in my free
> decision I assume a personal attitude toward him, then all
> that was contained in my intuition becomes, through my
> free decision, personal knowledge. Personal knowledge (if
> we consider it superficially) is a medium through which
> no more is received than was already contained in the in-
> tuition prior to it. All that is added to the intuition by it is
> the incorporation of the Other into the personal sphere of
> the Ego. If this intuition of the other person becomes per-
> sonal knowledge, the Thou is incorporated into the personal
> life of the Ego and is known as such. (131)

Personal Knowledge is the cognitive element of this free attitude
of the whole person towards this Thou (131).

Personal Faith

Personal faith is "the cognitive moment of a free attitude in which the Ego determines itself in relation to a Thou insofar as it says Yes to a Thou" (132). And not only is the Thou accepted, but also his self-revelation.
What is the source of the certitude of this acceptance of faith?

a The intuition is the motive for the judgment's certitude.
b The intuition, however, has no motive; it is its own motive.
c Faith in an assertion has as its motive faith in a Thou. Faith in a Thou as a motive means the Thou who possesses knowledge and truthfully communicates it, insofar as he is a subject to whom we say 'Yes' in faith in a Thou.
d Faith in a Thou has no motive; it is self-motivated.
e The intuition is in no way the motive of belief. (162-63)

The source of the degree of certitude in faith in a Thou is then the content of which the intuition is the medium, or rather, to put it more accurately, it is the ontological perfection of the content, which in the case in point comes down to the ontological perfection or imperfection of an historical concrete Thou. (167)

Thus far we have considered Cirne-Lima's thought on personal knowledge and personal faith. Here the human is analogous to the divine.

The Personal Structure of Fides Divina

Here Cirne-Lima applies the results of his metaphysical inquiry into the a priori of faith to fides divina, "on the supposition that fides divina cannot be totally different from interpersonal faith" (194). In divine faith man encounters the personal God and Jesus Christ through his Church. At first this is a conglomeration of many acts of knowledge about Jesus Christ and his Church.

The individual acts of knowledge relate themselves to a single, large intuition. And in this single intuition I see the one single, holy God who speaks to me through Christ and through his Church. Every single element of knowledge is formed into the totality present in this one great intuition.

At this moment something new occurs. If perhaps up to this point I was still hesitant; if I still possessed no certitude by reason of my conceptual-discursive thought; if I did not know whether, after all, this was just an illusion; now all my uncertainty falls away. I know for sure that God speaks to me in Christ. This intuitive certitude is given to me all at once. (196-97)

Although this act reminds one of the judgment of credibility and credentity of scholastic philosophy, it is an intuition, not a concept or judgment.

This intuition contains not only an abstract credibility and the abstract credentitas corresponding to it, but more than that, an image of Christ and the Church around which all the content of revelation centers itself organically. They are the ex-pression of Christ. (197)

This intuition now becomes an act of faith, because it contains something personal; and because it is directed to the personal element in man, it demands a personal attitude, a decision coming from the total personality, the personal content of which it is the medium. If man now makes a free decision, if he takes a positive stand towards Christ, this intuition becomes the cognitive element of this attitude. The intuition itself is one of the constituents of this attitude. And, as we know, the cognitive moment of the free attitude of personal knowledge is a personal act of faith.

Thus, since I utter my personal 'Yes' to Christ in his concrete historical fulness, I say 'Yes' to everything belonging to that fulness, and so I assent to his assertions. I accept them as true. Fides divina is, therefore, my personal 'Yes' spoken to the person of Christ and to the God who reveals himself in him. It is a personal 'Yes' spoken to his teaching, or, to put it briefly, it is a personal 'Yes' spoken to Christ, who is present, who speaks and acts. (198)

This is the supernatural "I-Thou" rapport in which I say "yes" to my Thou, my personal friend and brother, Jesus Christ, but not, of course without Grace, who is Jesus Christ, the personification of God's graciousness towards sinful man.

169

Conclusion

We can see that Cirne-Lima developed the personal theme so reminiscent of biblical faith. Although the "I-Thou" relationship between God and man had been taught down through the ages by the Fathers, the mystics, the many Christian and Jewish theologians, modern emphasis on existentialism and phenomenology has brought "I-Thou" more into focus. In Cirne-Lima we find a synthesis of Rahner's Maréchalian metaphysics with the phenomenology of August Brunner based solidly on Christian tradition and illustrating the marvelous adaptability of Christian thought to zeitgeist philosophies.

4 CONCLUSION

We have seen here briefly three modern representatives of Roman Catholic theology of personal faith: Gabriel Marcel, and his creative fidelity; Jean Mouroux with his personal interpretation of Thomistic faith; and Carlos Cirne-Lima combining Rahnerian epistemology with traditional teaching into an intuitive faith. All three emphasize the personal "I-Thou" rapport of faith. Cirne-Lima's use of the intuition to explain faith may prove to be a key link between the subjectivity of the existentialists and the objectivity of scholastic philosophy.

At any rate, personal faith now seems to be common doctrine between Roman Catholics and the Separated Brethren and has already proved to be a solid ground for ecumenical discussions on the theology of faith.

Notes

1 S. Keen, Gabriel Marcel (Richmond: John Knox Press, 1967, p. 1.

2 See Man Against Mass Society (Chicago: Henry Regnery Company, 1962).

3 Keen, Gabriel Marcel, pp. 7-19.

4 In Being and Having (New York: Harper & Row Publishers, 1965), pp. 9-153.

5 See J. Collins' Introduction to Being and Having, vi-viii.

6 R. Rosthal, tr. (New York: Farrar, Straus & Giroux, Inc., 1964).

7 Keen, Gabriel Marcel, p. 36.

8 G. Fraser & R. Hague, tr. (Chicago: Henry Regnery Company, 1960).

9 See Chapter III.

10 G. Lamb, tr. (New York: Sheed & Ward, 1951).

11 M. Turner, tr. (New York: Sheed & Ward, 1959).

12 See Chapters III and IV.

13 G. McCool, "The Primacy of Intuition," Thought XXXVII (Spring, 1962), 58.

14 Ibid.

15 Ibid., p. 60.

16 Ibid., p. 63.

17 New York: Herder and Herder, Inc., 1965.

18 As McCool points out ("Primacy of Intuition," p. 66), there are two levels of intuition: "First is simple knowledge, devoid of any affective overtones. The second, conditioned by a free decision 'for' a person, leading to trust in him, is the truly personal knowledge which is faith."

CHAPTER X

Conclusion

In our discussion of the dimensions of faith, we have ranged from Israel's trust in Yahweh to modern existential interpretations of belief. Faith in supernatural spirits is almost universal throughout the world and gives the strongest evidence for their existence.

EMUNA

Although faith in spiritual beings was common among primitive peoples, we first find the "one God, one people, one faith" theme in the Old Testament, which is the story of the faith and the unfaithfulness of Israel to her one true God, Yahweh. This faith is personified in the great men of Israel such as Abraham and Moses. Moreover, the great realities of the Old Testament, namely, the Promise, the Covenant, the Kingdom, the Prophecies, were essentially faith relationships with Yahweh. Military defeats, exiles, and other hardships were looked upon as punishments for Israel's unfaithfulness.

Yahweh, the one true God, elected poor Israel to be his bride, his special people. The Hebrew emuna expresses the central fact that God is God and man is man. Man must be dependent on God and not on himself or on the world. Old Testament faith is the antithesis of self-deification or exaggerated humanism.

Israel believes in Yahweh, her personal God, because he is true to his promises. He is not false, as the pagan Gods are. The covenant is essentially a faith-agreement between Israel and Yahweh. If Israel is faithful, Yahweh will protect her; if not, he will not extend to her his merciful hesed.

In Hebrew faith, the whole man believes in an experiential, personal, yet corporate, relationship with Yahweh. The Hebrew, as Martin Buber says, [1] finds himself born into his long tradition of race memory of migrations and covenant and his faith is a persevering confidence in his guiding and covenanting Lord.

PISTIS

New Testament faith is a personal relationship to, dependence on and trust in Jesus Christ, the Son of God, the Revelation of the Father. The gospels are a story of the poor, rejected sinners, and the sick faithfully trusting in Christ, who rewards them with his miraculous graces.

Pistis in the New Testament can have all the connotations of emuna in the Old. It is the act whereby man separates himself from his self-reliance and dependence upon the world and turns toward God in Christ. We believe in Jesus Christ because he is true. New Testament faith is a personal, experiential relationship with our brother, Christ, whose inheritance we share. Moreover, it unites us in loving union with our fellow brothers in Christ.

For both Paul and John faith is a personal commitment to Christ. However, they stressed different antitheses: Paul, faith and the Law; John, faith and the world. But both insisted that faith is a full reliance on and dedication to Christ. John taught a personal faith-knowledge and vision and a close loving union with Christ, the Truth. Paul lives with Christ, and is crucified with him in order to share his victory. Both Paul and John taught the unity of the believers as brothers of Christ and brothers in Christ, living in a common bond of love.

For both Paul and John faith begins the new eschaton of eternal life. The old life of the Law and the world is left behind and the new life begins the loving union with Christ which will be fulfilled in the vision of beatitude.

173

THINKING WITH ASSENT

Faith and reason had been a favorite topic of the Fathers, especially as Christianity was adapting to the Hellenistic and Roman cultures. It was for Augustine to combine Neo-Platonism with Christian tradition into a theology of faith that was to be a major contribution to Christian thought.

Augustine had searched for the truth, first as a Manichaean, then as an Academic. However, it was only through faith that he was to find the Truth, Christ himself, the exemplar and cause of all truth. Augustine taught a close rapport between faith and reason. Only a reasoning man can believe, thus opening the road to understanding. Despite his firm assent, his mind still strives ceaselessly to see the Unseen, so that faith is "thinking with assent."

Augustine taught an affective faith, through which man's sick will is healed so that he can turn from the love of creatures to the love of God. Augustine's faith is an illuminating and purifying light, reflecting Neo-Platonism. Purified by the light of faith, man can see the eternal truths and recognize the Divine Light and see the world mirroring the divine ideas.

Augustine's theology of faith predominated medieval tracts until the popularity of Aristotle arose in the thirteenth century. But even in men influenced by Aristotle, such as Thomas Aquinas, we find a firm foundation of Augustinian thought.

THE BEGINNING OF ETERNAL LIFE

In the tract on faith of Thomas Aquinas we find the traditions of Augustine, but mixed with the epistemology of Aristotle, bringing a more intellectual slant in contrast to the affective faith of Augustine reflecting Neo-Platonism.

Thomas insisted on the basic eschatological drive of faith, as the beginning of eternal life. Moreover, he stressed the object of faith, First Truth, who determines and specifies the act and habit of faith. He it is who reveals himself to man and at the same time invites him to believe.

As Augustine, Thomas called the act of faith "thinking with assent," separating faith from all the other acts of man. In the act of faith the discursive thought restlessly strives for vision, yet it is simultaneous with firm assent. The intellect, commanded by the will--drawn on by the promised good--aided by the light of First Truth and the interior instinct to believe, assents to the unseen First Truth and at the same time strives earnestly to see him.

It is the virtue of charity which gives to faith its perfect drive for beatitude. Leading faith to its end, it directs its acts towards beatitude, rectifying the will and making of faith a perfect virtue.

Thomas successfully synthesized Augustine and Aristotle into an excellent contemporary theology of faith. He has been accused of depersonalizing faith. But in back of his abstract scholastic terminology lies a personal faith, for First Truth is really the personal God, inviting the individual man to believe in him.

With a more thorough knowledge of Thomas' theology of faith, we can understand better the Reformers who reacted against it and the Councils of Trent and Vatican I which are based strongly upon it.

THE EXPERIENCE OF GOD'S GRACIOUSNESS

By the time of the Reformation, medieval scholasticism was on the wane. Nominalism and Renaissance humanism placed the emphasis on the individual in contrast to the universal aspect of medieval philosophy.

Luther, a product of his times, firmly resisted the abstract medieval theology, especially that of an Aristotelian bent. Moreover, reflecting his scriptural research, he was strongly bible-centric, emphasizing a return to the Gospels, and teaching against practices adopted in the Church since gospel times.

Luther felt that the Church had become too human and worldly to the neglect of the divine. His strong Augustinian dualism prompted him to over-emphasize the corruption of man so that man could do nothing towards his own salvation. If everything is due to God, then man can do nothing. Justification is due to God's graciousness alone and is experienced through faith, freeing man from the slavery of works and giving him firm confidence in his own predestination. Opposed to the seemingly more intellectual faith of Aquinas, Luther distrusted any use of earthly reason in matters of faith, especially when the pagan Aristotle was involved.

Luther suffered from a painful dilemma: he was certain of God's saving graciousness in Christ, but equally uncertain due to his own sinful weakness. He was certain of his own justification, yet his sinfulness remained, although no longer imputed, but covered over by God's saving graciousness.

Luther's theology of faith set the pace for later Reformation thinkers, although many such as Melanchthon and Calvin sought for a greater participation of man in the process of salvation.

The Council of Trent, too, was interested in counter-balancing the "man can do nothing" theology of Luther with a strong "man can do something." Trent taught a mitigated dualism. Although the just man is still a sinner, nevertheless, his sin is removed by God's grace. Moreover, due to the merits of Christ, man can merit further graces by his works done in the justified state.

The Reformation forced the Church to rethink her theology and define more sharply her doctrines on the sacraments, justification, and so forth, and prompted her towards a badly needed internal renewal. A new trend in piety arose emphasizing man's part in salvation in cooperation with God.

REASONABLE FAITH

The Reformation's emphasis on faith over reason was to bring an eventual reaction in the form of the Enlightenment, deism, and rationalism. What began as an attempt to make faith reasonable, eventually led to natural religion and rationalism. Man was fast coming of age intellectually, politically, economically, scientifically. Besides the "isms" mentioned above, materialism, secularism, positivism, and empiricism steadily grew during the eighteenth and nineteenth centuries.

The Church answered the challenge with the First Vatican Council in which was taught a favorable balance between faith and reason. Both are necessary to each other so that neither has the right to exclusiveness. Although the mysteries of faith transcend man's natural reason, they do not contradict it. Reason is necessary to demonstrate the foundations of faith and to give analogous knowledge. Faith perfects reason and leads it on to supernatural mysteries.

In faith we humbly submit our intellects to the Uncreated Truth who reveals himself to us. We assent not because of any intrinsic evidence derived from philosophical demonstration, but because of the infallible authority of God revealing. Faith is reasonable, but not reasoned.

The liberal spirit of the eighteenth and nineteenth centuries is important for us today, for the radical theologians have again taken up the cry that man has come of age. This hubristic boast had been stilled during the past generation of wars and depression. But in the continuing prosperity following World War II, it was bound to reassert itself. So, once again man is self-reliant, mature, come-of-age, no longer needing the faith of immature weaklings. And once again the Church is girding herself to fight for faith.

PERSONAL FAITH

That faith is a personal relationship between man and God has been taught since Old Testament times. The individual Hebrew trusted in Yahweh within the corporate body of Israel. The Christian of New Testament times believed in Christ with a firm personal commitment. The Fathers taught personal faith. Although medieval theology tended more towards the speculative, yet the personal underlay it. Luther's faith was experiential opposing the abstract medieval treatises.

Personal faith has been taught by most modern Protestant theologians from Schleiermacher and Kierkegaard to Barth, Tillich, and Bonhoeffer. It is fundamentally the experiential faith of Luther, the "I-Thou" of the Gospels. It is the subjective over the objective, the experiential over the abstract, the existential over the essential, the phenomenological over the noumenological, the individual over the universal. This personal, experienced rapport with God in Christ has received a new impetus with modern existentialism which is popular not only in Protestant thought, but in Roman Catholic as well. The Church right now is going through a personalist movement which so often accompanies a return to the spirit of the Gospels. And this is as it should be for the spirit of the Gospels is nothing but the firm personal commitment to Jesus Christ.

FAITH AND RADICAL THEOLOGY

Recent years have seen a revival of the old liberal spirit reminiscent of rationalism. Modern radical theologians have centered upon the human, the secular, the immanent, and strongly de-emphasized the divine, the sacred, and the transcendent.

Man has come of age. He no longer needs the transcendent problem-solving God of more primitive times. The farmer with irrigation and chemical fertilizers has overcome the vagaries of nature. Medicine is conquering more diseases every day. Economics is making great progress in solving the problems of the business world. Science is pushing back the frontiers on all fronts from paleontology to astro-physics. Truly man is speedily coming of age and so would seem to need no longer the problem-solving God of old. Faith in such a God is but a sign of dependence, re-

177

liance, immaturity, and weakness. Of course, it was necessary
for primitive tribes who had no where else to turn except to their
gods. But modern man has reached adulthood; he is strong, mature, self-reliant.

Or is he? Clearly science has not solved all. For we still have
with us crime, war, hunger, drought, racism, injustice, insanity,
sickness, and death. Without descending into exaggerated dualism
we can say that evil will very likely always be a part of the world,
and certain problems, such as death, man will never solve. Therefore, even in the most euphoric hopes of the secular humanists man
will never come of age so that he will be completely independent of
outside forces beyond his control.

Here, of course, we are getting close to faith, for the very essence of biblical faith is a lack of self-reliance and dependence on
man and the world, and a firm confidence in the all transcendent
God of Truth. So that even though the faithless theme of Nietzsche
will keep recurring periodically, often as a reaction against the
over-religiosity of pietistic trends, nevertheless, it will never
succeed in convincing the average man that he has come of age,
that he is completely self-sufficient and self-reliant, especially
when he falls upon hard times. So that it will always be a part of
man to realize that God is God and man is man and that it is of
man's essence that he is of and to God.

FAITH AND THE DE-HELLENIZERS

Since Vatican II there has risen a de-Hellenizing trend in the
Church. In some ways it seems related to demythologizing, de-
Romanizing, and de-traditionalizing. Actually, the Church, in
general, and Protestantism, in particular, have gone through
periodic purifications, returns to the gospel, revivals, and so
forth. One has only to look at the Reformation, Puritanism,
and Pietism to see these trends in action.

However, after each new experiential wave settles down, the
second and third generations begin to slip back into dogmatism,
institutionalism, formalism, and so forth. No doubt our own wave
of personalism in the Church will end up with the same fate. Often
those who cry loudest for individualism, end up as rugged indivi-
dualists, quite insensitive to the personal rights of others.

The history of the Church from the beginning has been a struggle between heart and head, the personal and the institutional,
faith and reason, the practical and the speculative, the individual
and the universal. We see it today in the current existential,

phenomenological, personal trends made popular by Rahner, Schillebeeckx, Marcel, Mouroux, and so forth, which reflect earlier subjective experiential lines of Luther, Kierkegaard, Buber, and others. Existentialism is in, scholasticism is out; Rahner is in, Aquinas is out; personalism is in, institutionalism out. However, trends change and already there is a growing interest in medieval research. And so the cycle moves on.

It is no accident that most personalist trends accompany returns to the gospels, for the Hebrews were existentialists par excellence and the faith of the early Christians as described by Paul and John was a personal loving commitment to the living Christ, although not wholly without Hellenistic tones.

However, it was inevitable that sooner or later the head had to get into the act for man cannot resist the urge to speculate over his new found faith. Moreover, he had to adapt and synthesize his beliefs with the zeitgeist philosophies and culture of the time, first, Hellenism, then Romanism.

A question often asked by the De-Hellenizers is: did the Greek Fathers of the early councils mean to solidify their definitions for all time? Or rather were they primarily interested in settling urgent problems of their own era, such as, Arianism, Nestorianism, Monophysitism? Did they not realize that future generations might be forced to adapt to new philosophies just as they had mixed Hellenism with the Hebrew thought of the gospels?

These early creeds have always been the firm foundation stones of Christianity. But it is so easy for a creed to become a museum piece passed down carefully from one generation to the next, learned by rote, often without a clear knowledge of its true significance. Since these creeds are always couched in the language and culture of their times, in order to grasp their full meaning we must study them in their proper milieu. Moreover, it would prove fruitful to interpret them in the light of contemporary philosophies, without at the same time changing the essence of the dogmas.

This brings up an essential problem to Christianity, and all other religions as well, namely, the development of dogma. Can the explanations of the truths of revelation ever solidify so that they can never be changed or added to even though thousands of years later the old philosophia perennis has developed into a new one?

Of course, any living organism must adapt to its environment, for the inexorable law of nature is "adapt or die." Early Christianity saw this quickly in its first period of Hellenization. And it is to the marvelous credit of the Church and perhaps the greatest proof of her eternal living Spirit that she has, in general, adapted so well throughout the centuries, her latest and most glorious metamorphosis being that of Vatican II.

But is there not a danger of losing our long-standing traditions if we change at the slightest wind of every new culture or philosophy? This is a real danger for there have been some during the Reformation and others later who would all but do away with many of the ancient traditions of the Church. We hear phrases such as "the leap of faith, " "the leap out of history and back into the arms of Christ." This may sound appealing to some. However, any one who leaps out of history is leaping away from man's most essential mirror. Certainly one of the greatest problems in all theological controversies has been the ignorance on the part of one or both disputants of the history of the question. We must continually measure ourselves in the mirror of history and at the same time allow the Church to grow with the times.

One of the big fears in adaptation is that the very faith itself is changing. Thomas Aquinas treated well this recurring question of the changing formulations of faith (ST 2-2, q. 1, a 6-10). He followed tradition in declaring that the unity of the articles of faith is derived from the unity of their object, Jesus Christ, whereas their diversity comes from man's inability to see the divine object.

Man's faith does not terminate in the enunciable but in the res. He does not so much believe that Christ has risen as he believes in the Risen Christ. Recent attempts at the use of "transignification" in lieu of "transubstantiation" in order to explain the Eucharistic Presence come to mind. The Eucharistic Christ never changes. He is with us yesterday, today, and tomorrow. But weak human philosophical attempts to explain this miraculous presence will always change while faith continues to seek understanding.

In answer to the De-Hellenizers and others of similar mind, we might respond that a healthy balance is required in matters of faith, respecting the old, yet adapting to the new. We cannot and should not change our traditional creeds. But we should study carefully their milieu and seek to draw parallels in the current language of the people in order to make them more meaningful today. As Tillich has said so well, "One must stand between the archaic and contemporary terminologies to recapture, on the boundry, the original archetypal language."[2]

FINIS

We have seen some of the major dimensions of faith from the Old Testament to our own times whose existential personal faith resembles that of the early Hebrews and Christians. Whether we study the corporate faith of the Hebrews, the confidence of Paul and John, the inquiring assent of Augustine, the dynamic eschatological faith of Aquinas, the experiential faith of Luther, the reasonable faith of Vatican I, or the "I-Thou" rapport of modern existentialists we recognize a familiar theme running throughout.

All through the history of faith we have seen the struggle between the personal and the speculative. It is only natural for man to speculate on his personal belief, faith seeking understanding. Thus throughout the ages various philosophies have been applied to the mysteries of faith, with the lion's share going to the Greek thought of Plato and Aristotle, while more recent trends have moved more towards the existential and the phenomenological. But as reason has been applied to faith, the personal, experiential element has been minimized and sometimes lost. In reaction we see periodical revivals of the subjective element as in the Reformation, Puritanism, Pietism, and personalism. Currently the eschatological "then" is reacting to Existentialism's overemphasis on the "here and now." But the eschatology of men like Pannenberg and Moltmann, although firmly based on the theology of hope, cannot be independent of faith, for faith, as hope, possesses a dynamic and eschatological "now" and "then," a present openness to the future, as its very essence.

Today the Church is feeling a certain crisis of faith. Vatican II has opened the doors and windows to new developments of dogma. Some are disturbed at the new concepts of old articles of faith. Others are questioning the authoritarian structure of the Church. Certainly the Church has endured many crises of faith in the past, often following a general council. Strong proof of her divine origin lies in her ability to weather these storms over the millenia.

The theology of faith is one of the main topics of current ecumenical discussions. The renewed interest in personal faith in Roman Catholic circles gives high promise of a closer alliance with the more experiential faith so often seen in outstanding Protestant theologians such as Kierkegaard, Tillich and others. So the gap is closing between the personal and the impersonal, the subjective and the objective, the practical and the speculative, the existential and the eschatological, the individual and the corporate. New interest in eschatology links strongly with biblical faith as interpreted by the Fathers and Theologians. This author feels that on the common biblical foundation of the personal and eschatological faith commitment to Jesus Christ, the ecumenical movement will build a sound and unified structure. For faith, as Tradition has always taught, is the firm foundation of the whole spiritual edifice. The beginning of eternal life, it will truly be fulfilled in the eschaton.

Notes

1 Two Types of Faith, p. 10.
2 On the Boundry, p. 66.

Bibliography

I   Israel and Yahweh

The Holy Bible and Apocrypha. Revised Standard Edition.
    London: Thomas Nelson and Sons, Ltd., 1959.
Anchor Bible. Garden City, New York: Doubleday and Com-
    pany, Inc., 1964.
Old Testament. Confraternity Edition. New York: Guild Press,
    Inc., 1964.
The Jerusalem Bible. Garden City, New York: Doubleday and
    Company, Inc., 1966.

Bultmann, R. and A. Weiser. Key Words of the Bible. Vol. III,
    Faith. New York: Harper and Row Publishers, 1961. (from
    Kittel's Theologisches Wörterbuch zum Neuen Testament.)
Cahill, J. "Faith in the Old Testament," BT, (December, 1964),
    659-67.

Gelin, A. Key Concepts of the Old Testament. Glen Rock,
New Jersey: Paulist Press, 1963.
-----. The Poor of Yahweh. Collegeville: Liturgical Press,
1964.
Guillet, J. Themes of the Bible. Notre Dame, Indiana: Fides
Publishers, Inc., 1960. Pp. 32-40.
MacKenzie, R. A. F. Faith and History in the Old Testament.
New York: Macmillan Company, 1963.
McKenzie, J. The Two-Edged Sword. Garden City, New York:
Doubleday and Company, Inc., 1966.
-----. Dictionary of the Bible. Milwaukee: Bruce Publishing
Company, 1965. "Faith," pp. 267-71.
Robert, A., and A. Feuillet. Introduction to the Old Testament.
New York: Desclee, 1959.
Salm, L. Studies in Salvation History. Englewood-Cliffs, New
Jersey: Prentice-Hall, Inc., 1964.
Schnackenburg, R. "Glaube: die Aussagen der Schrift," LTK.
Freiburg: Herder and Herder, 1960. IV, 913-17.
Van Imschoot, P. "Faith," Encyclopedic Dictionary of the Bible.
L. Hartmann, tr. A. van den Born (ed.). New York: McGraw-
Hill Book Company, 1963. Pp. 744-50.

II Belief in Jesus Christ

Paul:

Ahern, B. The Epistles to the Galatians and to the Romans.
(NTRG, Vol. VII). Collegeville: Liturgical Press, 1960.
Amoit, F. Key Concepts of St. Paul. New York: Herder and
Herder, 1962.
Barrett, C. A Commentary on the Epistle to the Romans.
London: Black, 1962.
Benoit, P. "The Theologies of Paul and John," TD, XIII
(Summer, 1965), 135-41. (from NTS, IX [1963], 193-207).
Bultmann, R. Theology of the New Testament. New York:
Charles Scribner's Sons, 1955.
Bultmann, R. and A. Weiser. Key Words of the Bible. Vol. III,
Faith. New York: Harper and Row Publishers, 1961. (from
Kittel's Theologisches Wörterbuch zum Neuen Testament.)
Cerfaux, L. Christ in the Theology of St. Paul. New York:
Herder and Herder, 1959.
-----. The Church in the Theology of St. Paul. New York:
Herder and Herder., 1959.

Lyonnet, S. "St. Paul: Liberty and Law," TD, XI (Spring, 1963), 12-18. (from The Bridge. New York: Pantheon Books, Inc., 1961. IV, 229-51.)

McConnell, J. The Epistle to the Hebrews. (NTRG, Vol. XI). Collegeville: Liturgical Press, 1960.

McKenzie, J. Dictionary of the Bible. Milwaukee: Bruce Publishing Company, 1965. "Faith," pp. 267-71.

-----. The Power and the Wisdom. Milwaukee: Bruce Publishing Company, 1965.

Prat, F. The Theology of Saint Paul. New York: Benziger Brothers, Inc., 1926.

Ricciotti, G. Paul, the Apostle. Milwaukee: Bruce Publishing Company, 1952.

Robert, A., and A. Feuillet. Introduction to the New Testament. New York: Desclee, 1965.

Schnackenburg, R. "Glaube: die Aussagen der Schrift," LTK. Freiburg: Herder and Herder, 1960. IV, 913-17.

Taylor, G. "The Function of 'Pistis Christou' in Galatians," JBL, XXCV (March, 1966), 58-76.

Tresmontant, C. St. Paul. New York: Harper and Row Publishers, 1957.

Van Imschoot, P. "Faith," Encyclopedic Dictionary of the Bible. L. Hartmann, tr. A. van den Born (ed.). New York: McGraw-Hill Book Company, 1963. Pp. 744-50.

Wikenhauser, A. Pauline Mysticism. New York: Herder and Herder., 1960.

John:

Barrett, C. The Gospel According to St. John. London: SPCK, 1962.

Barrosse, T. "The Relationship of Love to Faith in St. John," TS, XVIII (December, 1957), 538-59.

Benoit, P. "The Theologies of Paul and John," TD, XIII (Summer, 1965), 135-41. (from NTS, IX [1963], 193-207.)

-----. "Pauline and Johannine Theology: A Contrast," CC, (Summer, 1965), 329-53.

Bonsirven, J. Theology of the New Testament. Westminster, Maryland: Newman Press, 1963.

Bouyer, L. The Fourth Gospel. Westminster, Maryland: Newman Press, 1964.

Brown, R. The Gospel of St. John. The Johannine Epistles. (NTRG, Vol XIII). Collegeville: Liturgical Press, 1960.

-----. New Testament Essays. Milwaukee: Bruce Publishing Company, 1965.

Bultmann, R. Theology of the New Testament. New York: Charles Scribner's Sons, 1955.

Bultmann, R. and A. Weiser. Key Words of the Bible. Vol. III, Faith. New York: Harper and Row Publishers, 1961. (from Kittel's Theologisches Wörterbuch zum Neuen Testament.)

Dodd, C. Interpretation of the Fourth Gospel. New York: Cambridge University Press, 1953.

Feuillet, A. Johannine Studies. Staten Island, New York: Alba House, 1964.

Lightfoot, R. St. John's Gospel, A Commentary. Oxford: Clarendon Press, 1956.

McKenzie, J. Dictionary of the Bible. Milwaukee: Bruce Publishing Company, 1965. "Faith," pp. 267-71.

-----. The Power and the Wisdom. Milwaukee: Bruce Publishing Company, 1965.

Robert, A. and A. Feuillet. Introduction to the New Testament. New York: Desclee, 1965.

Schnackenburg, R. "Glaube: die Aussagen der Schrift," LTK. Freiburg: Herder and Herder, 1960. IV, 913-17.

Van Imschoot, P. "Faith," Encyclopedic Dictionary of the Bible. L. Hartmann, tr. A. van den Born (ed.). New York: McGraw-Hill Book Company, 1963. Pp. 744-50.

Vawter, B. "The Biblical Idea of Faith," Worship, XXXIV, 443-50.

III Thinking with Assent

Patrologia Latina. J. Migne (ed.). 1844-1864. Vols. 32-47.

Corpus Scriptorum Ecclesiasticorum Latinorum. Vienna: Tempsky, 1866--. Vols. 12, 25, 28, 33, 34, 36, 40-44, 52, 53, 57-58, 60, 63, 74, 77, 80.

Corpus Christianorum. Series Latina. Turnai: Brepols, 1955--. Vols. 32, 33, 36, 38-40, 41, 47-48.

Oeuvres. Bibliotheque Augustinienne. Paris: Desclee de Brouwer, 1949--.

Biblioteca de Autores Cristianos. Madrid: La Editorial Catolica, 1944--. 10, 11, 21, 30, 39, 50, 53, 69, 79, 95, 99, 121, 139, 165, 168, 171-72, 187.

Ancient Christian Writers. Westminster, Maryland: Newman Press, 1946--. Vols. 2, 3, 5, 9, 12, 15, 22.

A Select Library of the Nicene and Post-Nicene Fathers of the Christian Church. Buffalo: Schaff, 1886-1888. Vols. 1-8.

Catholic University of America Patristic Series. Washington: Catholic University of America Press, 1922--. Vols. 8, 23, 72, 84, 85, 88-91.

The Fathers of the Church. New York: Cima Publishing Company, Inc., 1947--. Vols. 1-16.

The Library of Christian Classics. Philadelphia: Westminster Press, 1953--. Vols. 6-8.

Image Series. Garden City, New York: Doubleday & Company, Inc. Confessions, J. Ryan, tr., 1960; City of God, G. Walsh, et al., tr., 1962.

Altaner, B. Patrology. New York: Herder and Herder, Inc., 1961.

Bardy, G. Saint Augustin. Paris: Desclee de Brouwer, 1948.

Battenhouse, R., et al. A Companion to the Study of St. Augustine. New York: Oxford University Press, 1955.

Bourke, V. Augustine's Quest of Wisdom. Milwaukee: Bruce Publishing Company, 1945.

Brunhumer, A. "The Art of Augustine's Confessions," Thought, XXXVII (Spring, 1962), 109-28.

Campbell, J. and M. McGuire. The Confessions of St. Augustine. New York: Prentice-Hall, Inc., 1942.

Copleston, F. A History of Philosophy. Vol. I, Greece and Rome; Vol. II, Medieval Philosophy, Pt. 1, "Augustine to Bonaventure." Garden City, New York: Doubleday and Company, Inc., 1960, 1962.

Cushman, R. "Faith and Reason in the Thought of Augustine," Church History. New York: AMS Press Inc., 1950. XIX, 271-94.

D'Arcy, M., et al. St. Augustine. Cleveland: Meridian Books, World Publishing Company, 1960.

Du Roy, O. L'intelligence de la foi en la Trinité selon Saint Augustin. Paris: Études Augustiniennes, 1966.

Gilson, E. Christian Philosophy of St. Augustine. New York: Random House, Inc., 1960.

Holte, R. Béatitude et Sagesse, Saint Augustin et le problème de la fin de l'homme dans la philosophie ancienne. Paris: Études Augustiniennes, 1962.

Lohrer, M. Der Glaubensbegriff des hl. Augustinus in seinen ersten Schriften bis zu den Confessiones. Eisiedeln: Benziger Brother, Inc., 1955.

-----. "Glaube und Heilsgeschicte in De Trinitate Augustins,"
FZPT, IV (1957), 385-419.

Marrou, H. St. Augustine. New York: Harper & Row Publishers.

Mourant, J. Introduction to the Philosophy of St. Augustine:
Selected Readings and Commentaries. University Park,
Pennsylvania: Pennsylvania University Press, 1964.

Oates, W. Basic Writings of St. Augustine. New York: Random
House, Inc., 1948.

O'Brien, E. The Essential Plotinus. Toronto: New American
Library of Canada, Ltd., 1964.

O'Meara, J. The Young Augustine: The Growth of St. Augustine's
Mind Up to His Conversion. Ontario: Longmans Canada, Ltd.,
1954.

Pope, H. St. Augustine of Hippo. Garden City, New York: Doubleday and Company, Inc., 1961.

Portalie, E. A Guide to the Thought of St. Augustine. R. Bastian,
tr. Chicago: Henry Regnery Company, 1960.

Pryzwara, E. An Augustine Synthesis. New York: Harper & Row
Publishers, 1958.

Rouet de Journel, M. J. Enchiridion Patristicum. Barcelona:
Herder and Herder, 1959.

Turnbull, G. (ed.). The Essence of Plotinus. S. MacKenna,
tr. New York: Oxford University Press, 1934.

Van der Meek, J. Augustine the Bishop, Religion and Society at
the Dawn of the Middle Ages. New York: Harper and Row
Publishers, 1965.

Wolfson, H. The Philosophy of the Church Fathers. Cambridge,
Massachusetts: Harvard University Press, 1956.

IV The Beginning of Eternal Life

Opera. Leonine Ed. Rome: Ex Typographia Polyglotta, 1883-
1948.

Scriptum super Sententiis, III. Paris: Lethielleux, 1882-1948.

De Veritate, Quaestiones Disputatae. Turin: Marietti, 1949.

Summa Contra Gentiles. 4 vols. Turin: Editio Leonina Manualis,
1946; Paris: Lethielleux, 1951-1961.

Opuscula Theologica. R. Spiazzi and M. Calterra (eds.). 2 vols
Turin: Marietti, 1954.

Summa Theologiae. 3 vols. Turin: Marietti, 1952.

Truth (De Veritate). R. Mulligan, et al. 3 vols. Chicago: Henry
Regnery Company, 1952-1954. Especially Vol. 2, q. 14.

On the Truth of the Catholic Faith (Summa Contra Gentiles).
A. Pegis, et al., tr. 5 vols. Garden City, New York:
Doubleday and Company, Inc., 1955-1956.

Basic Writings of St. Thomas Aquinas. A. Pegis (ed.). 2 vols.
New York: Random House, Inc., 1945. Especially Vol. II,
2-2, q. 1-14.

Summa Theologica. Translated by the Fathers of the English
Dominican Province. 3 vols. New York: Benziger Brothers,
Inc., 1947.

Summa Theologiae. Latin text, English translation, introduction, notes by Blackfriars. New York: McGraw-Hill
Book Company, 1964--.

Alfaro, J. "The Supernaturality of Faith in St. Thomas," TD,
XIV (Summer, 1966), 111-16. (from "Supernaturalitas
fidei iuxta S. Thomam," Greg., XLIV [1963], 501-42,
731-88.)

Aubert, R. Le problème de l'acte de foi. Louvain: Warny,
1958.

Bernard, R. Saint Thomas d'Aquin, Somme Théologique, La
Foi. Paris: Desclee, 1950. 2-2, q. 1-7.

Betzendorf, W. Glauben u Wissen bieden grossen Denkern des
Mittelalters. Gotha, 1931.

Burke, V. Aquinas' Search for Wisdom. Milwaukee: Bruce
Publishing Company, 1965.

Chenu, M. La foi dans l'intelligence. Paris: Cerf, 1964.

-----. Toward Understanding St. Thomas. Chicago: Henry
Regnery Company, 1964.

Copleston, F. A History of Philosophy. Vol. II, Medieval
Philosophy. Garden City, New York: Doubleday and Company, Inc., 1962.

Deferrari, R., et al. A Lexicon of St. Thomas Aquinas.
Washington: Catholic University of America Press, 1948.

DeGhellinck. Le mouvement théologique du XIIe siècle.
Paris: Desclee de Brouwer, 1948.

Denifle, H., and F. Ehrle (eds.). Archiv fur Literatur und
Kirchengeschicte des Mittelalters. 7 vols. Berlin: Weid-
mannsche, 1885.

Dunas, A. Connaissance de la foi. Paris: Cerf, 1963.

Duroux, B. La psychologie de la foi chez St. Thomas
D'Aquin. Tournai: Desclee, 1963.

Englhardt, G. Die Entwicklung der dogmatischen Glauben-
psychologie in der mittelalterlichen Scholastik. BGPTM,

b. 30. Munster: Aschendorff, 1933.

Gilson, E. The Spirit of Medieval Philosophy. A. Downes, tr. New York: Charles Scribner's Sons, 1940.

-----. History of Christian Philosophy in the Middle Ages. New York: Random House, Inc., 1954.

-----. The Christian Philosophy of Saint Thomas Aquinas. L. Shook, tr. New York: Random House, Inc., 1956.

Grabmann, M. Thomas Aquinas, His Personality and Thought. V. Michel, tr. New York: Longmans, Green & Company, 1928.

Guerard des Lauriers, M. Dimensions de la foi. 2 vols. Paris: Cerf, 1952.

Heitz, T. Essai historique sur les rapports entre la philosophie et la foi de Béranger de Tours à saint Thomas d'Aquin. Paris: Lecoffre, 1909.

Jansen, F. "La psychologie de la foi dans la théologie du XIIIe siècle." NRT, LVI (1934), 604-15.

Lang, A. "Die Gliederung und die Reichsweite des Glaubens nach Thomas v. Aquin und den Thomisten," DTF, XXI (1943), 79 ff.

Lang, H. Die Lehre des Heil. Thomas von Aquin von der Gewissheit des ubernaturlichen Glaubens. Augsburg: Filser, 1929.

Maritain, J. St. Thomas Aquinas. J. Evans and P. O'Reilly, trs. Cleveland: Meridian Books, World Publishing Company, 1958.

Mohler, J. The Beginning of Eternal Life, The Dynamic Faith of Thomas Aquinas. New York: Philosophical Library, Inc., 1968.

Parent, J. "La notion de dogme au XIIIe siècle," ER, Ottawa (1932), pp. 141-63.

Pieper, J. Scholasticism. London: Faber and Faber, Ltd., 1960.

-----. Guide to Thomas Aquinas. Toronto: Mentor Books, New American Library of Canada, Ltd., 1964.

-----. The Silence of Thomas Aquinas. J. Murry and D. O'Connor, trs. Chicago: Henry Regnery Company, 1965.

Van Steenberghen, F. Philosophie des Mittelalters. Bern, 1950.

V Justification by Grace through Faith

Luther and Calvin:

Corpus Reformatorum. C. Bretschneider and H. Bindseil (eds.).
Halle, 1834-1860.

D. Martin Luthers Werke, Kristische Gesamtausgabe. Weimar,
1883-1903.

Luther's Works. J. Pelikan and H. Lehmann (eds.). Philadelphia:
Muhlenberg and Fortress; St. Louis, Concordia Publishing
House.

Martin Luther, Selections from His Writings. J. Dillenberger
(ed.). Garden City, New York: Doubleday and Company, Inc.,
1961.

Luther: Lectures on Romans. W. Pauck, tr. and ed. Philadelphia:
Westminster Press, 1961. (LCC, XV.)

A Compend of Luther's Theology. H. Kerr, (ed.). Philadelphia:
Westminster Press, 1943.

Joannis Calvini, Opera Quae Supersunt Omnia. J. Baum, et al.
(eds.). Brunsvigal, 1863-1900.

Calvin: Institutes of the Christian Religion. F. Lewis, tr.
J. McNeill (ed.). Philadelphia: Westminster Press, 1960.
(LCC, XX and XXI).

A Compend of the Institutes of the Christian Religion by John
Calvin. H. Kerr (ed.). Philadelphia: Westminster Press,
1964.

Bainton, R. The Age of Reformation. Princeton, New Jersey:
D. Van Nostrand Company, Inc., 1956.

-----. Here I Stand. Cleveland: Mentor Books, World Publishing
Company, 1960.

-----. The Reformation of the Sixteenth Century. Boston:
Beacon Press, 1965.

Bovis, A., et al. "Foi," DSP, V, 529-630.

Bring, R. Das Verhaltnis v Glaube u Werken in der Luth.
Theologie. Munich, 1955.

Copleston, F. A History of Philosophy. Vol. III, Late Medieval
and Renaissance Philosophy. Garden City, New York: Doubleday and Company, Inc., 1963.

Daniel-Rops, H. The Protestant Reformation. 2 vols. Garden
City, New York: Doubleday and Company, Inc., 1963.

Dillenberger, J., and C. Welch. Protestant Christianity. New
York: Charles Scribner's Sons, 1954.

Dowey, E. The Knowledge of God in Calvin's Theology. New
York: Columbia University Press, 1952.

Farner, O. Zwingli the Reformer. New York: Philosophical
Library, Inc., 1952.
Fosdick, H. Great Voices of the Reformation, An Anthology.
New York: Random House, Inc., 1952.
Gerrish, B. Grace and Reason. Oxford: Clarendon Press,
1962.
Grimm, H. The Era of the Reformation. New York: Macmillan
Company, 1954.
Hacker, P. Das Ich im Glauben bei Martin Luther. Graz:
Styria, 1966.
Harent, S. "Foi," DTC, VI, 55-514.
Hughes, P. A Popular History of the Reformation. Garden
City, New York: Doubleday and Company, Inc., 1960.
Lindsay, T. A History of the Reformation. 2 vols. New York:
Charles Scribner's Sons, 1916-1917.
Lortz, J. Die Reformation in Deutschland. Freiburg: Herder
and Herder, 1948.
McShane, E. "Martin Luther," Thought, XLIV (Spring, 1966),
104-16.
Niesel, W. Die Theologie Calvins. Munich, 1957.
Pannenberg, W. "Im Prot. Glaubenverstandnis," LTK, IV,
925-28.
Pauck, W. The Heritage of the Reformation. Glencoe, Illinois:
Free Press, 1950.
Pfurtner, S. Luther and Aquinas on Salvation. New York:
Sheed and Ward, 1964.
Richter, F. Martin Luther and Ignatius Loyola, Spokesmen
for Two Worlds of Belief. L. Zwinger, tr. Westminster,
Maryland: Newman Press, 1960.
Sykes, N. The Crisis of the Reformation. London: Centenary
Press, 1946.

Trent:

Sacrorum Conciliorum Nova et Amplissima Collectio. J.
Mansi (ed.). Paris-Leipzig, 1901-1927. Vol. XXXIII.
Canones et Decreta Concilii Tridentini. A. Richter (ed.).
Leipzig, 1853.
Concilium Tridentinum. Freiburg: Societas Goerresiana,
1901--.
Canons and Decrees of the Council of Trent. (Original text
and English translation). H. Schroeder, tr. St. Louis:
Herder Book Company, 1950.

Enchiridion Symbolorum. H. Denzinger and A. Schönmetzer
(eds.). Barcelona: Herder and Herder, 1963.
The Church Teaches. J. Clarkson, et al. (eds.). St. Louis:
Herder Book Company, 1955.

Bovis, A., et al. "Foi," DSP, V, 529-630.
Cristiani, L. L'église a l'époque du Concile de Trente. 1948.
Daniel-Rops, H. The Catholic Reformation. 2 vols. Garden
City, New York: Doubleday and Company, Inc., 1964.
Harent, S. "Foi," DTC, VI, 55-514.
Hefele, J., and H. LeClercq. Histoire des conciles. 1930-
1938. Vols. IX-X.
Hughes, P. Church in Crisis. Garden City, New York: Double-
day and Company, Inc., 1961.
Richard, P. Le concile de Trente. 1930-1931.

VI Reasonable Faith

Enlightenment:

Berlin, I. (ed.). The Age of Enlightenment; Eighteenth Century
Philosophers. New York: New American Library, Inc.,
1963.
Bredvold, L. The Brave New World of the Enlightenment. Ann
Arbor: University of Michigan Press, 1961.
Cassirer, E. The Philosophy of the Enlightenment. C. Koelln
and J. Pettegrove, trs. Boston: Beacon Press, 1955.
Copleston, F. A History of Philosophy. Vol. IV, Modern Philos-
ophy: Descartes to Leibnitz; Vol. V, The British Philosophers;
Vol. VI, The French Enlightenment to Kant. Garden City,
New York: Doubleday and Company, Inc., 1963-1964.
Cragg, G. Reason and Authority in the Eighteenth Century.
Cambridge, England, 1964.
Fellows, O. and N. Torrey (eds.). The Age of Enlightenment,
An Anthology of Eighteenth Century Literature. New York:
F. S. Crofts and Company, 1942.

Rationalism:

Benn, A. The History of English Rationalism in the Nineteenth
Century. New York: Russell and Russell Publishers, 1962.
Heimann, E. Reason and Faith in Modern Society. Middletown,
Connecticut: Wesleyan University Press, 1961.

Knox, R. Broadcast Minds. London: Sheed and Ward, 1932.
Lecky, W. History of the Rise and Influence of the Spirit of
   Rationalism in Europe. New York: Appleton and Company,
   1872.
Lunn, A. Flight from Reason. New York: Dial Press, 1931.
The Rationalists. J. Veitch, et al., trs. Garden City, New
   York: Doubleday and Company, Inc., 1961.

Kant:

Critique of Pure Reason. F. Muller, tr. New York: Macmillan
   Company, 1957.
The Doctrine of Virtue, Part 2 of Metaphysic of Morals. M.
   Gregor, tr. New York: Harper and Row Publishers, 1964.
Critique of Practical Reason. T. Abbott, tr. London: Longmans,
   Ltd., 1898.
First Introduction to the Critique of Judgement. J. Haden, tr.
   Indianapolis: Bobbs-Merrill Company, Inc., 1965.
Critique of Judgement. J. Bernard, tr. London, 1931.
Religion Within the Bounds of Reason Alone. T. Greene and
   H. Hudson, tr. New York: Harper and Row Publishers,
   1960.
An Immanuel Kant Reader. R. Blakely, tr. and ed. New York:
   Harper and Row Publishers, 1960.
Kant Selections. T. Greene (ed.). New York: Charles Scribner's
   Sons, 1957.

Ardley, G. Aquinas and Kant. London: Longmans, Ltd., 1950.
Copleston, F. A History of Philosophy. Vol. VI, Modern
   Philosophy, Pt. 2, Kant. Garden City, New York: Double-
   day and Company, Inc., 1964.

Vatican I:

Sacrorum Conciliorum Nova et Amplissima Collectio. J. Mansi
   (ed.). Paris-Leipzig, 1901-1927. Vols. XLIX-LIII.
Collectio Lacensis Conciliorum Recentium. 5 vols. Freiburg,
   1870-1890.
Enchiridion Symbolorum. H. Denzinger and A. Schönmetzer
   (eds.). Barcelona: Herder and Herder, 1963.
The Church Teaches. J. Clarkson, et al. (eds.). St. Louis:
   Herder Book Company, 1955.

Aubert, R. Le problème de l'acte de foi. Louvain: Warny, 1958.

Butler, C. Vatican I. Westminster, Maryland: Newman Press, 1962.

Granderath, T. Geschicte des Vatikanischen Konzils. 3 vols. 1903-1906.

Harent, S. "Foi," DTC, VI, 55-514.

Hennesey, J. First Council of the Vatican, The American Experience. New York: Herder and Herder, 1963.

Hughes, P. The Church in Crisis. Garden City, New York: Hanover House Books, Doubleday and Company, Inc., 1961.

Stolz, A. "Was definiert das Vatikanische Konzil uber den Glaubensweifel?" TQ, CXI (1930), 499-560.

Trutsch, J. "Glaubensfall," LTK. Freiburg: Herder and Herder, 1957-1965, IV, 931-34.

Vacant, A. Études sur les constitutions du concile du Vatican. Paris, 1895.

VII I and Thou

Schleiermacher:

Religion, Speeches to Its Cultured Despisers. J. Oman, tr. New York: Harper and Row Publishers, 1958.

Schleiermacher's Soliloquies. H. Freiss, tr. La Salle, Illinois: Open Court Publishing Company, 1957.

The Christian Faith. H. Mackintosh and J. Stewart (eds.). 2 vols. New York: Harper and Row Publishers, 1963.

Brandt, T. The Philosophy of Schleiermacher; Development of His Theory of Scientific and Religious Knowledge. New York: Harper and Row Publishers, 1941.

Gerdes, H. Das Christusbild Sören Kierkegaards, verglichen mit der Christologie Hegels und Schleiermachers. Dusseldorf: Diederichs, 1960.

Mackintosh, H. Two Types of Modern Theology; Schleiermacher to Barth. New York: Charles Scribner's Sons, 1937.

Niebuhr, R. Schleiermacher on Christ and Religion. New York: Charles Scribner's Sons, 1964.

Kierkegaard:

The Journals of Soren Kierkegaard. A. Dru, tr. New York:
  Oxford University Press, 1951.
Edifying Discourses. D. and L. Swenson, trs. 2 vols.
  Minneapolis: Augsburg Publishing House, 1962.
Either-Or. W. Lowrie, tr. 2 vols. Garden City, New York:
  Doubleday and Company, Inc., 1959.
Fear and Trembling. W. Lowrie, tr. Princeton, New Jersey:
  Princeton University Press, 1946.
Philosophical Fragments. D. Swenson, tr. Princeton, New
  Jersey: Princeton University Press, 1958.
Concept of Dread. W. Lowrie, tr. Princeton, New Jersey:
  Princeton University Press, 1946.
Stages on the Way of Life. W. Lowrie, tr. Princeton, New
  Jersey: Princeton University Press, 1940.
Kierkegaard's Concluding Unscientific Postscript. D. Swenson
  and W. Lowrie, trs. Princeton, New Jersey: Princeton Uni-
  versity Press, 1941.
Purity of Heart Is to Will One Thing. D. Steere, tr. New York:
  Harper and Row Publishers, 1956.
Works of Love. H. and E. Hong, trs. New York: Harper and
  Row Publishers, 1962.
Sickness Unto Death. W. Lowrie, tr. Princeton, New Jersey:
  Princeton University Press, 1946.
The Last Years, Journals, 1853-1855. R. Smith, tr. and ed.
  London: Collins, 1965.
Kierkegaard's Attack Upon Christendom. W. Lowrie, tr.
  Princeton, New Jersey: Princeton University Press, 1952.

Diem, H. Kierkegaard's Dialectic of Existence. H. Knight, tr.
  Edinburgh: Oliver and Boyd, 1959.
Dupre, L. "La dialectique de l'acte de foi chez S. Kierkegaard, "
  D. Phl., XII (1956), 418-55.
-----. Kierkegaard as Theologian. New York: Sheed and Ward,
  1963.
Gerdes, H. Das Christusbild Sören Kierkegaards, verglicken
  mit der Christologie Hegels und Schleiermachers. Dusseldorf:
  Diederichs, 1960.
Johnson, H., and N. Thulstrup (eds.). A Kierkegaard Critique.
  New York: Harper and Row Publishers, 1962.
Lowrie, W. Kierkegaard. 2 vols. New York: Harper and Row
  Publishers, 1962.

Pelikan, J. From Luther to Kierkegaard. St. Louis: Concordia
Publishing House, 1950.

Buber:

I and Thou. R. Smith, tr. New York: Charles Scribner's Sons,
1958.
The Prophetic Faith. New York: Harper and Row Publishers,
1960.
Between Man and Man. R. Smith, tr. New York: Mac-
millan Company, 1948.
Pointing the Way. New York: Harper and Row Publishers, 1967.
Two Types of Faith. N. Goldhawk, tr. New York: Harper
and Row Publishers, 1961.
Eclipse of God. New York: Harper and Row Publishers, 1957.
The Writings of Martin Buber. W. Herberg (ed.). Cleveland:
Meridian Books, World Publishing Company, 1965.

Agus, J. Modern Philosophies of Judaism. New York: Behrman's
Jewish Book House, 1941.
Balthasar, H. von. Martin Buber and Christianity. A. Dru, tr.
New York: Macmillan Company, 1961.
Diamond, M. Martin Buber, Jewish Existentialist. New York:
Oxford University Press, 1960.
Friedman, M. Martin Buber; The Life of Dialogue. New York:
Harper and Row Publishers, 1960.
Kohn, H. Martin Buber, sein Werk und seine Zeit. Hegner:
Hellerau, 1930.
Smith, R. Martin Buber. Richmond: John Knox Press, 1967.

VIII Christ Alone

Barth:

The Epistle to the Romans. E. Hoskyns, tr. London: Oxford
University Press, 1957.
The Word of God and the Word of Man. D. Horton, tr. New
York: Harper and Row Publishers, 1957.
Anselm: Fides Quaerens Intellectum. Richmond: John Knox
Press, 1960.
The Knowledge of God and the Service of God According to the
Teaching of the Reformation. J. Haire and I. Henderson,
trs. London: Hodder and Stoughton, 1955.

Church Dogmatics. G. Thomson, tr. Edinburgh: Clark, 1960.
Church Dogmatics, A Selection. H. Gollwitzer (ed.). G.
  Bromiley, tr. New York: Harper and Row Publishers, 1962.
Dogmatics in Outline. New York: Harper and Row Publishers,
  1959.
How I Changed My Mind. Introduction by J. Godsey. Richmond:
  John Knox Press, 1966.
Evangelical Theology: An Introduction. G. Foley, tr. London:
  Collins, 1965.

Berkouwer, G. The Triumph of Grace in the Theology of Karl
  Barth. Grand Rapids: William B. Eerdmans Publishing
  Company, 1956.
Hamer, K. Karl Barth. Westminster, Maryland: Newman
  Press, 1962.
Hartwell, H. The Theology of Karl Barth. Philadelphia:
  Westminster Press, 1964.
Kung, H. Justification, the Doctrine of Karl Barth and a
  Catholic Reflection. T. Collins, et al., trs. Camden,
  New Jersey: Thomas Nelson and Sons, 1964.
Matczak, S. Karl Barth on God. New York: St. Paul Publi-
  cations, 1962.
Niebuhr, R. "An Answer to Karl Barth," Christian Century,
  LXVI (February 23, 1949), 234 ff.
Pauck, W. Karl Barth. New York: Harper and Row Publishers,
  1931.
Voeckel, R. The Concept of Faith in the Theology of Karl Barth,
  A Critique of the Barthian Theology. New York: Union Theolo-
  gical Seminary, 1962.
Weber, O. Karl Barth's Church Dogmatics. Philadelphia:
  Westminster Press, 1953.
Willems, B. Karl Barth, an Ecumenical Approach to his
  Theology. M. van Velzen, tr. Glen Rock, New Jersey:
  Paulist Press, 1965.

Bultmann:

Existence and Faith, Shorter Writings of Rudolf Bultmann. S.
  Ogden, tr. Cleveland: World Publishing Company, 1966.
Essays, Philosophical and Theological. London: Library of
  Philosophy and Theology, 1955.
Jesus and the Word. L. Smith and E. Lantero, trs. New York:
  Charles Scribner's Sons, 1958.

198

"New Testament and Mythology," Kerygma and Myth. H.
    Bartsch (ed.). R. Fuller, tr. New York: Harper & Row
    Publishers, 1960. Pp. 1-44.
Jesus Christ and Mythology. London: SCM, 1960.
Theology of the New Testament. 2 vols. New York: Charles
    Scribner's Sons, 1955.
Primitive Christianity in Its Contemporary Setting. R. Fuller,
    tr. Cleveland: World Publishing Company, 1965.
----- and K. Jaspers. Myth and Christianity. New York:
    Noonday Press, 1958.
The Presence of Eternity, History and Eschatology. New York:
    Harper and Row Publishers, 1962.
"The Idea of God and Modern Man," Translating Theology into
    the Modern Age. R. Funk, et al. (eds.). New York: Harper
    and Row Publishers, 1965.

Gogarten, F. Demythologizing and History. London: SCM,
    1955.
Henderson, I. Myth in the New Testament. Chicago: Henry
    Regnery Company, 1952.
-----. Rudolf Bultmann. Richmond: John Knox Press, 1966.
Kegley, C. (ed.). The Theology of Rudolf Bultmann. New
    York: Harper and Row Publishers, 1966.
Macquarrie, J. An Existentialist Theology, A Comparison
    Between Heidegger and Bultmann. New York: Harper and
    Row Publishers, 1965.
-----. The Scope of Demythologizing. New York: Harper
    and Row Publishers, 1966.
Malvez, L. The Christian Message and Myth, the Theology of
    Rudolf Bultmann. Westminster, Maryland: Newman Press,
    1958.
Miegge, G. Gospel and Myth in the Thought of Rudolf Bultmann.
    Richmond: John Knox Press, 1960.
Ogden, S. Christ Without Myth, A Study Based on the Theology
    of Rudolf Bultmann. New York: Harper and Row Publishers,
    1961.
Wolf, H. Kierkegaard and Bultmann; A Quest for the Historical
    Jesus. Minneapolis: Augsburg Publishing House, 1965.

Tillich:

The Religious Situation. Cleveland: Meridian Books, World
    Publishing Company, 1956.

On the Boundry. New York: Charles Scribner's Sons, 1966.
Shaking Foundations. New York: Charles Scribner's Sons,
   1948.
The Courage To Be. New Haven: Yale University Press, 1952.
Love, Power, and Justice. New York: Oxford University Press,
   1960.
The New Being. New York: Charles Scribner's Sons, 1955.
Dynamics of Faith. New York: Harper and Row Publishers,
   1958.
Systematic Theology. Chicago: University of Chicago Press,
   1963.
The Eternal Now. New York: Charles Scribner's Sons, 1962.

Adams, J. Paul Tillich's Philosophy of Culture, Science, and
   Religion. New York: Harper and Row Publishers, 1965.
Armbruster, C. The Vision of Paul Tillich. New York: Sheed
   and Ward, 1967.
Brown, D. (ed.). Ultimate Concern; Tillich in Dialogue.
   London: SCM, 1965.
Kegley, C. and R. Bretall, (eds.). Theology of Paul Tillich.
   New York: Macmillan Company, 1952.
Leibrecht, W. (ed.). Religion and Culture; Essays in Honor
   of Paul Tillich. London, 1959.
McKelway, A. Systematic Theology of Paul Tillich, A Review
   and Analysis. Richmond: John Knox Press, 1964.
Martin, B. The Existential Theology of Paul Tillich. New
   Haven: College and University Press, 1964.
O'Meara, T., and C. Weisser. Paul Tillich in Catholic
   Thought. Dubuque: Priory Press, 1964.
Schick, T. "Reason and Knowledge in the Epistemology of
   Paul Tillich," Thomist, XXX (January, 1966), 66-79.
Smith, R. "Paul Tillich's Concept of Faith," CW, (December,
   1964), pp. 162-71.
Thomas, J. Paul Tillich. Richmond: John Knox Press, 1966.
Weigel, G. "Contemporaneous Protestantism and Paul Tillich,"
   TS, XI (1950), 177-202.

Bonhoeffer:

The Communion of Saints. New York: Harper and Row Publishers, 1963.
Act and Being. New York: Harper and Row Publishers, 1930.

Christ, The Center. J. Bowden, tr. New York: Harper and
Row Publishers, 1966.

No Rusty Swords, Letters, Lectures, Notes 1928-1936. E.
Robertson, tr. New York: Harper and Row Publishers,
1965. Vol. I.

Temptation. K. Downham, tr. New York: Macmillan Company,
1956.

The Cost of Discipleship. R. Fuller, tr. New York: Macmillan
Company, 1965.

Life Together. London: SCM, 1965.

Ethics. N. Smith, tr. E. Bethge (ed.). New York: Macmillan
Company, 1965.

Letters and Papers from Prison. R. Fuller, tr. E. Bethge (ed.).
New York: Macmillan Company, 1966.

Bethge, E. Dietrich Bonhoeffer.

Cox, A. "Beyond Bonhoeffer," Commonweal, XXCII (September,
17, 1965), 653 57.

Godsey, J. The Theology of Dietrich Bonhoeffer. Philadelphia:
Westminster Press, 1960.

Green, C. "Bonhoeffer's Concept of Religion," TD, XIII (Spring,
1965), 47-51.

Hardwick, E. "The Place of Bonhoeffer," HJ, V (July, 1964),
297-99.

Levi, A. "Bonhoeffer and Delp: Papers from Prison," Month,
XXXI (July, 1964), 328-36.

Marty, M. The Place of Bonhoeffer, Problems and Possibilities
in His Thought. New York: Associated Press, 1962.

Robertson, E. Dietrich Bonhoeffer. Richmond: John Knox
Press, 1966.

IX   Personal Faith

Marcel:

Being and Having. New York: Harper and Row Publishers,
1965.

Creative Fidelity. R. Rosthal, tr. New York: Farrar,
Straus and Giraux, Inc., 1964.

Homo Viator, Introduction to a Metaphysic of Hope. E.
Crauford, tr. Chicago: Henry Regnery Company, 1951.

The Philosophy of Existentialism. M. Harari, tr. New York:
Citadel Press, 1964.

The Mystery of Being. G. Fraser and R. Hague, tr. Chicago: Henry Regnery Company, 1960.

Man Against Mass Society. Chicago: Henry Regnery Company, 1962.

The Existential Background of Human Dignity. London: Oxford University Press, 1965.

Keen, S. Gabriel Marcel. Richmond: John Knox Press, 1967.

Miceli, V. Ascent to Being, Gabriel Marcel's Philosophy of Communion. New York: Desclee, 1966.

Mouroux:

The Meaning of Man. Garden City, New York: Doubleday and Company, Inc., 1961.

The Christian Experience: An Introduction to Theology. New York: Sheed and Ward, 1954.

I Believe, The Personal Structure of Faith. New York: Sheed and Ward, 1959.

From Baptism to the Act of Faith. Boston: Allyn and Bacon, Inc., 1964.

The Mystery of Time: A Theological Inquiry. New York: Desclee, 1964.

Cirne-Lima:

Personal Faith. New York: Herder and Herder, 1965.

Balthasar, H. von. Wahrheit, ein Jersuch. Einsiedeln/Zurich: Benziger Brothers, Inc., 1947.

Brunner, A. Erkenntnistheroie. Cologne: Bachem, 1948.

-----. Glaube und Erkenntnis. Munich: Kosel-Verlag, 1951.

McCool, G. "Recent Trends in German Scholasticism, Brunner and Lotz," IPQ, I (December, 1961), 668-82.

-----. "The Primacy of Intuition," Thought, XXXVII (Spring, 1962), 57-73.

Rahner, K. Geist in Welt. Munich: Kosel, 1957.

INDEX OF SUBJECTS

Absurd. See Faith and the Absurd
Academy, 45, 53, 174
Acceptance, 165
Act and Being, 140ff.
Adoption, Divine, 17ff., 21, 26, 28
Aeterni Patris, 90
Agapē, 39
Alētheia, 33, 35
Amen, 7 ff., 65
Anticipated Possession, 59f., 66, 77
Anxiety, 101, 135, 137
Appetite for the Promised Good, 64
Arianism, 179
Atheism, 90
Attestation, 153
Authority of God, 46, 88, 91, 92

Baptism, 71, 80
Beatitude, Beatific Vision, 41, 46, 47, 48, 51, 52, 58ff., 62, 63f., 65, 66, 159f., 163, 174f.
Being, Absolute, 154
Being and Having, 152f.
Belief, Christian, 97, 128f., 137
  Crisis of, 128ff.
  -ful Realism, 138
  in the Church, 140
  in God, 27f., 49f., 53, 63f., 68, 73, 119, 155f., 159f.
  in Jesus Christ. See Jesus Christ
  that, 22, 112, 118, 155, 180
  Three-fold, 49f., 54, 69, 73, 159f.
  Two-fold, 88f.
Boasting, 24, 73, 117f., 129, 132, 176
Boundry, 133
Brotherhood, 21, 26, 145

Charity. See also Faith, Affective;

Faith and Charity
Form of the Virtues, 64
Christ-event, 128f., 132, 149
Christo-centric, 138, 142ff.
Church, 79ff., 92, 97, 138ff., 163, 168f., 175, 176
Classical Formula of Faith, 58f.
Collegia Pietatis, 95, 97
Commitment, 26, 40, 41, 99, 154, 173
Communion, 97, 152, 161
  of the Saints, 138ff.
Community of Faith, 121f., 135, 145
  of Spirit, 139
Confession, 11, 22, 26, 116, 123, 129, 143, 146
Confidence, 11, 24, 26, 73, 82, 112
Conformed with Christ, 138ff., 146, 149
Conversion, 11, 111, 117, 152
  of Augustine, 44f., 46, 49, 52
  of Paul, 14, 39
Conviction, 58, 78, 88, 101, 116
Courage to Be, 137, 138
Covenant, 1, 2, 3, 4, 11, 17ff., 40, 111, 173
  See also Testament (diathēkē)
Creation, 86, 90f.
Credibility, 88
Creeds, 135, 179, 180
Crisis Theology, 94, 115, 125

Dasein, 58
  and Wiesein, 142

203

Death of God, 89
Decision, 121, 129, 130, 132, 167, 169
Dei Filius, 90ff.
Deism, 86, 176
De-Hellenizing, x, 178ff.
Demythologizing, 125f., 132, 178
Dependence on God, 8, 40, 95ff., 132, 173, 177f. See also Poverty; Reliance on God, Anawim
Depersonalizing, 64, 65, 98, 161, 175. See also I-It Relationship
De-Romanizing, x, 178
Desecularization, 29
Despair, Comforted, 101, 123
Dialectic, 116, 118, 124, 138, 158
Dis-ease, 152
Discipleship, 143f.
Dogmatism, 178
Doubt, 63, 75, 88f., 91, 135, 136, 137
Dualism, 28ff., 85, 116
    Luther's, 76, 82, 85, 175

Election, 1
Emuna, 7, 8, 10, 110ff., 172f.
Empiricism, 89, 97
Enlightenment, 85f., 88, 95, 125, 176
Enunciable, 180
Eschatology, 11, 23, 25f., 26, 31, 41, 51f., 57ff., 59, 62, 77, 92, 137f., 142, 173, 174, 181, 182
Eternal Life, 30, 78
    Beginning of, 54, 57ff., 63, 66, 77, 80, 91, 119, 158, 174, 182
Ethics, 145ff.
Eucharist, 11, 71, 180
Evidence (Elenchos), 58, 59

Evolution, 86
Existentialism, 94, 107, 108, 115, 125, 132, 151f., 157, 170, 177, 178f., 181
Existential Self-understanding, 125, 131f., 149
Experience, 87f., 89, 108
    Christian, 95ff., 157ff.
    Religious, 157ff.

Faith
    and the Absurd, 100, 103, 104
    Act of, 60, 61, 62f., 122f.
    Affective, 11, 30f., 48ff., 53, 54, 63f., 66, 95ff., 119, 151f., 156, 174
    Articles of, 61, 76, 180, 181
    Assent of, 11, 62f., 65, 66, 91, 99
    Certitude of, 62, 73, 74f., 88, 91, 97, 105, 126, 135, 136, 168f., 175
    and Charity, 63f., 158f., 175. See also Faith, Affective; Love
    Circle of, 121, 122, 124
    Community of. See Community of Faith
    Crisis of, 128f., 181
    Decision. See Decision
    Definition of, 58ff., 80f., 91, 105, 116, 136f. See also Eternal Life, Beginning of; Thomas' Formula of Faith
    Difficult, 103, 143f.
    Dissatisfied, 62f., 101, 138. See also Faith Seeks Knowledge; Knowledge, Imperfect
    Divine, 168f. See also Belief

204

in God
and Doubt. See Doubt
Dynamic, 19f., 26, 57ff., 66,
   73, 135, 136, 158, 174f.
Ecclesial, 64f., 122, 138f., 145,
   163. See also Community of
   Faith; Church
Encounter, 131f.
Eschatological. See Eschatology
Event, 122, 128f.
Existential, x, 57, 58, 62, 88,
   102, 124, 131f., 181
Experiential, 6ff., 26, 33f.,
   40f., 65, 72, 81, 88, 94ff.,
   124, 141, 146, 151, 173, 177,
   181
and Fidelity, 154. See also
   Fidelity, Creative
Formal and Material, 136f.
Formal Motive of, 60f., 160
Formed, 63f., 77
Formless, 64, 77
Foundation of the Spiritual Edi-
   fice, 51f., 53, 58, 64, 182
Free. See Freedom
Grades of, 19, 20, 165
Habit of, 59, 60, 61, 62, 63f.
Hellenistic, x, 33f., 110ff.,
   178f.
and History, 125, 129, 133,
   137, 180
Human, 108f., 130, 152f., 154,
   164, 165f. See also Faith and
   Fidelity; Faith, Personal;
   Fidelity, Creative; Husband-
   Wife Relationship; I-Thou;
   Yada
Idolatrous, 134, 136
Intellectual, 54, 57, 60, 66, 80f.,
   92, 102, 174, 175
Israel's, Hebrew, 6ff., 65, 109,
   110ff., 172f., 181
Justifying. See Justification

Knowledge, 22, 31ff., 88,
   119f., 123
and Law, 14ff., 16f., 26,
   41, 52f., 73f., 173.
   See also Faith and Works
Leap of, 98, 99, 101, 103,
   104, 111, 115, 117, 126,
   127, 149, 180
Light of, 50f., 52, 53f.,
   58, 61f., 123, 174
Living, 19ff., 26, 57f.,
   81, 123
and Love. See Faith, Affective; Faith and Charity
and Miracles, 12f., 86,
   89, 91, 98, 143
New Testament, 10ff., 40f.,
   110ff., 173
Obedient, 5, 11, 19, 22, 24,
   26, 37, 109, 112, 116,
   121, 122, 123, 124, 129f.,
   131, 137, 144f., 149
Object of, 60ff., 105, 120f.,
   123, 174. See also Truth,
   First
Obscurity of. See Faith, Dis-
   satisfied; Faith Seeks
   Knowledge; Knowledge,
   Imperfect
Old Testament, 1ff., 110ff.,
   172f.
Personal, x, 6ff., 9, 10,
   20f., 26, 33f., 36ff., 40f.,
   57, 64ff., 69, 72, 88, 93,
   94, 95ff., 102, 107ff.,
   121f., 131f., 134, 139,
   149, 151ff., 159ff., 173,
   177, 181, 182
Preambles of, 93, 169
and Proof, 89, 92f., 101,
   104f., 119, 143
and Reason, 45ff., 53, 54,
   75ff., 82, 85ff., 91f.,

Illumination, Divine, 50f., 53f.,
    61f., 123. See also Faith,
    Light of
Imago Dei, 50f., 119
Imitation of Christ, 20f., 124, 162
Immortality, 88
Indifferentism, 90
Individualism, 178
Indwelling, 162
Inheritance, 16, 17ff., 26
Institutionalism, 178f.
Intellect, 49, 62f., 65, 157, 174.
    See also Faith, Intellectual
    Speculative, 60
Interior Instinct, 61, 66, 92, 160,
    174
Intersubjectivity, 66, 102, 152f.,
    160, 165, 168
Intuition, 87, 138, 161, 163ff.,
    170
Inwardness, 49, 50, 99, 105, 122,
    158
I-Thou Relationship, x, 52, 57,
    94ff., 107ff., 124, 129, 139,
    149, 151ff., 154, 155, 156,
    164, 166f., 168, 169, 170,
    177, 181. See also Faith,
    Personal; Yada

Justification (dikaiosunē), 15, 16,
    17ff., 52f., 71ff., 74, 76,
    77, 82, 129f. See also Right-
    eousness
    by Grace through Faith, 16ff.,
    52f., 71ff., 78f., 80, 81f.,
    95, 117f., 123f., 126, 138,
    146f.
    Preparation for, 80, 82

Kerygma, 19, 21f., 26, 98, 125,
    132
Kingdom, 2f., 76, 172
    of God, 76, 111, 139

Knowing and Having, Exis-
    tential, 141
Knowledge. See Gnosis
    A-priori, 87
    Experiential, 6f., 33f.,
    87f., 89. See also
    Yada
    Faith. See Faith, Know-
    ledge; Faith Seeks
    Knowledge
    of Father and Son, 32, 34f.
    Greek, 6, 33f.
    Hebrew, 6f., 33f.
    Imperfect, 63, 65, 161
    Inchoative, 58f.
    Living, 123
    Personal, 6f., 20f., 33ff.,
    132, 164, 166f. See
    also I-Thou; Yada
    Speculative, 81

Law, 2, 14ff., 26
    External, 15f., 26
    and Faith. See Faith and Law
    Interior, 15f., 26
    Moral, 88
    Slavery of, 16f., 18
Liberalism, 115f., 124, 125,
    133
Life and Death, 30, 31
Light and Dark, 28f., 30, 50f.
    See also Dualism
Literalism, 125
Living in Christ, 20f.
Love, 15f., 20, 30f., 37ff.,
    41, 48ff., 80, 109,
    130, 136, 139, 151,
    156, 158f., 160. See
    also Faith, Affective;
    Faith and Charity
    Believes all, 106f., 156

Manichaeism, 45, 53, 174

Trent, 79ff., 82, 175, 176
Trust, 17ff., 24, 72, 74, 75, 80,
   81, 111, 116, 130, 131. See
   also Pistis
Trustfulness, 19
Truth, 35, 36, 41, 45, 46, 47, 49,
   50, 51, 53, 54, 65
   First, 36, 54, 57, 60ff., 63,
   65, 66, 91, 159, 160, 174f.
Truths, Eternal, 50, 54

Ultimate and Penultimate, 147f.
Ultimate Concern, 57, 132ff., 149
   Preliminary, 134f., 136
Unambiguous Life, 137f.
Unbelief, Unfaithfulness, 2, 8, 72,
   80, 121, 141, 172
Understanding, 63. See also Faith
   Seeks Knowledge and Under-
   standing
Union of Father and Son, 34f., 36ff.
   With Christ, 21, 34f., 36ff., 39,
   40f.
Universals, 70, 103, 164, 166, 175,
   177, 178

Vatican I, 90ff., 175, 176,
   181
Vatican II, 178, 180, 181
Virtues Related to Faith, 22ff.

Will, 48f., 63, 65, 73, 157,
   174. See also Faith, Af-
   fective; Faith and Charity
   Command of, 63
   Primacy of, 48f.
   Rectification of, 63f., 175
Wisdom, 45f.
Works. See Faith and Works;
   Faith and Law
   of Law, 15f., 52f., 71, 73f.
   of Love, 15f., 39
World. See Faith and the World;
   Desecularization, Secular-
   ization
Worldliness, 148

Yada, 6f., 20, 26, 33f., 37
Yes to Christ, 121, 169
   to God, 41, 169
   to Man, 41, 211
   to a Thou, 166, 168

INDEX OF PERSONS